XERXES™

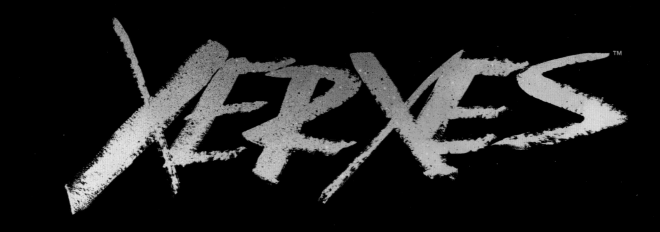

STORY & ART
FRANK MILLER

COLORS
ALEX SINCLAIR

THE FALL OF THE HOUSE OF DARIUS AND THE RISE OF ALEXANDER

Dark Horse Books

PRESIDENT & PUBLISHER
MIKE RICHARDSON

EDITOR
FREDDYE MILLER

ASSISTANT EDITORS
JUDY KHUU
KEVIN BURKHALTER
JENNY BLENK

DESIGNER
LIN HUANG

DIGITAL ART TECHNICIAN
CHRIS HORN

LOGO DESIGN
STEVE MILLER

Front cover and chapter break art by Frank Miller, with colors by Alex Sinclair.

Special thanks to Flint Dille, Terri Dille, Robert Rodriguez, Richard Miller, Ariane Thomas, Dan Didio, Silenn Thomas, Paula Andrade, Andy Kubert, Bill Sienkiewicz, and Walter Simonson.

DarkHorse.com

First edition: March 2019
ISBN 978-1-50670-882-9
Digital ISBN 978-1-50670-905-5

10 9 8 7 6 5 4 3 2 1
Printed in China

Published by Dark Horse Books
A division of Dark Horse Comics LLC
10956 SE Main Street
Milwaukie, OR 97222

This volume collects the Dark Horse comic book series *Xerxes: The Fall of the House of Darius and the Rise of Alexander* #1–#5, originally published April–August 2018.

Neil Hankerson, Executive Vice President • Tom Weddle, Chief Financial Officer • Randy Stradley, Vice President of Publishing • Nick McWhorter, Chief Business Development Officer • Dale LaFountain, Chief Information Officer • Matt Parkinson, Vice President of Marketing • Cara Niece, Vice President of Production and Scheduling • Mark Bernardi, Vice President of Book Trade and Digital Sales • Ken Lizzi, General Counsel • Dave Marshall, Editor in Chief • Davey Estrada, Editorial Director • Chris Warner, Senior Books Editor • Cary Grazzini, Director of Specialty Projects • Lia Ribacchi, Art Director • Vanessa Todd-Holmes, Director of Print Purchasing • Matt Dryer, Director of Digital Art and Prepress • Michael Gombos, Senior Director of Licensed Publications • Kari Yadro, Director of Custom Programs • Kari Torson, Director of International Licensing

To find a comics shop in your area, visit comicshoplocator.com

Library of Congress Cataloging-in-Publication Data

Names: Miller, Frank, 1957- author, artist. | Sinclair, Alex, colourist.
Title: Xerxes : the fall of the House of Darius and the rise of Alexander / story and art, Frank Miller ; colors, Alex Sinclair.
Description: First edition. | Milwaukie, OR : Dark Horse Books, February 2019.
Identifiers: LCCN 2018042779 | ISBN 9781506708829
Subjects: LCSH: Xerxes I, King of Persia, 519 B.C.-465 B.C. or 464 B.C.--Comic books, strips, etc. | Darius I, King of Persia, 548 B.C.-485 B.C.--Comic books, strips, etc. | Alexander, the Great, 356 B.C.-323 B.C.--Comic books, strips, etc. | Graphic novels.
Classification: LCC PN6727.M55 X47 2019 | DDC 741.5/973--dc23
LC record available at https://lccn.loc.gov/2018042779

CHAPTER ONE

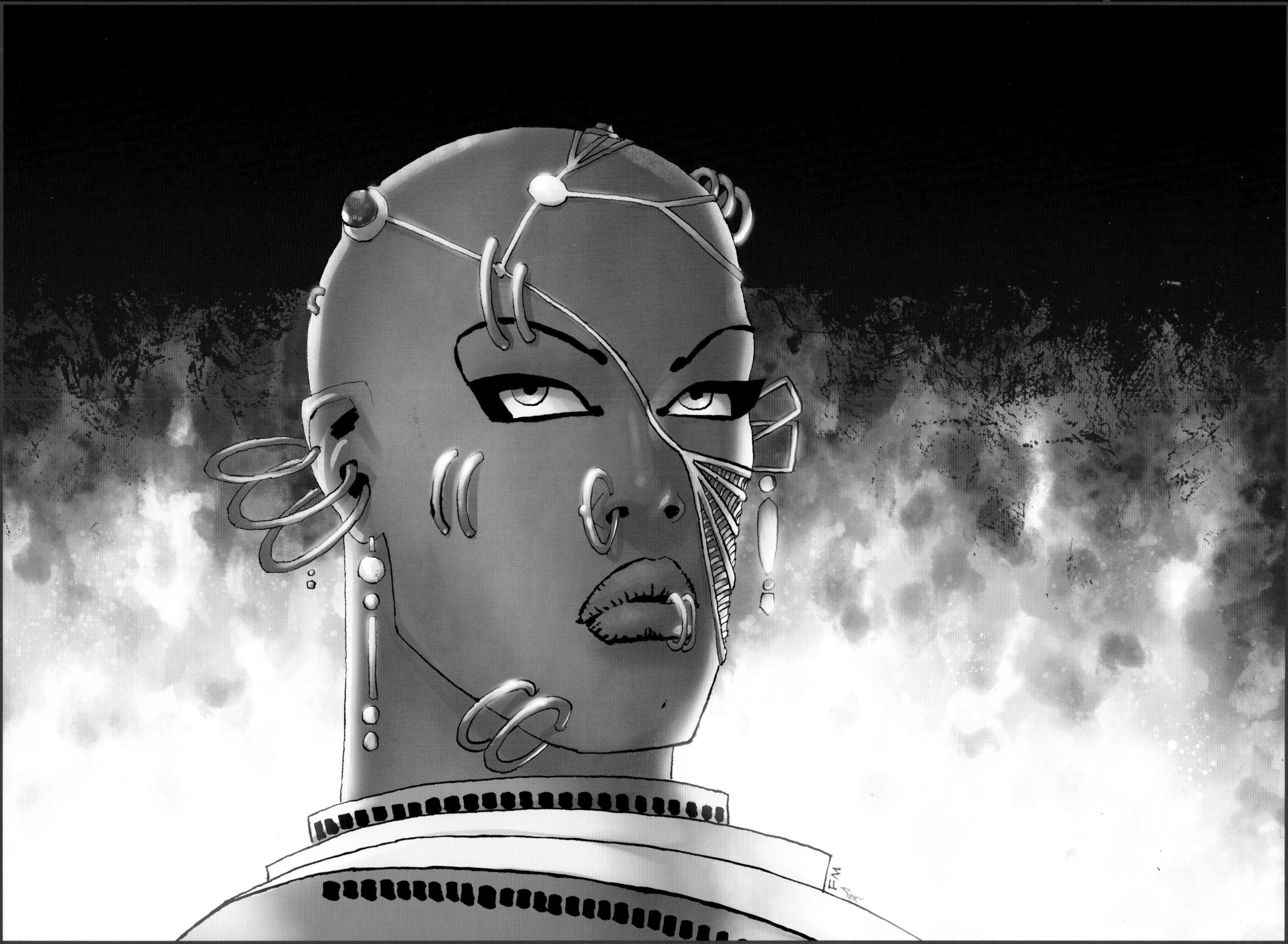

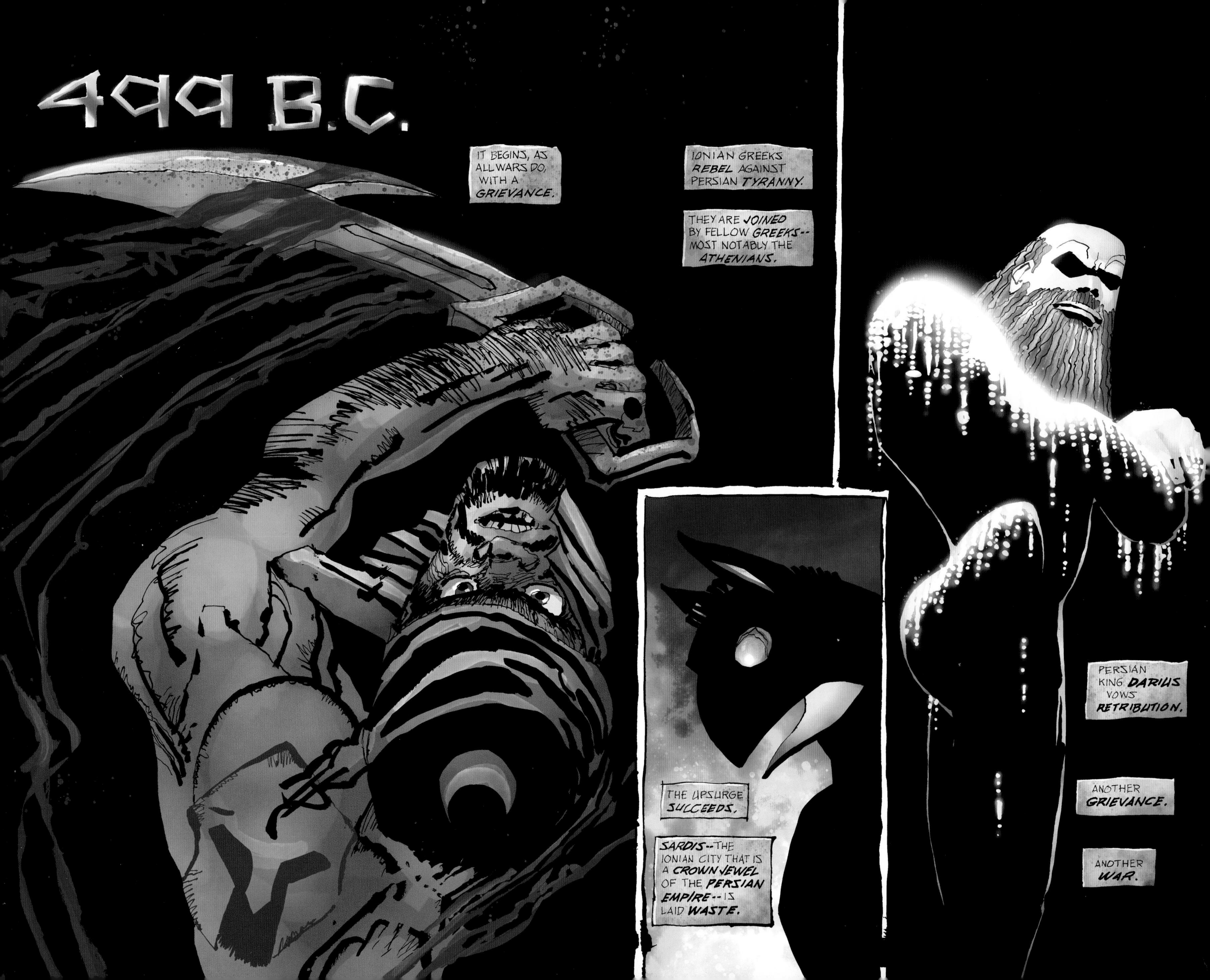
499 B.C.
IT BEGINS, AS ALL WARS DO, WITH A GRIEVANCE.
IONIAN GREEKS REBEL AGAINST PERSIAN TYRANNY.
THEY ARE JOINED BY FELLOW GREEKS-- MOST NOTABLY THE ATHENIANS.
THE UPSURGE SUCCEEDS.
SARDIS--THE IONIAN CITY THAT IS A CROWN JEWEL OF THE PERSIAN EMPIRE--IS LAID WASTE.
PERSIAN KING DARIUS VOWS RETRIBUTION.
ANOTHER GRIEVANCE.
ANOTHER WAR.

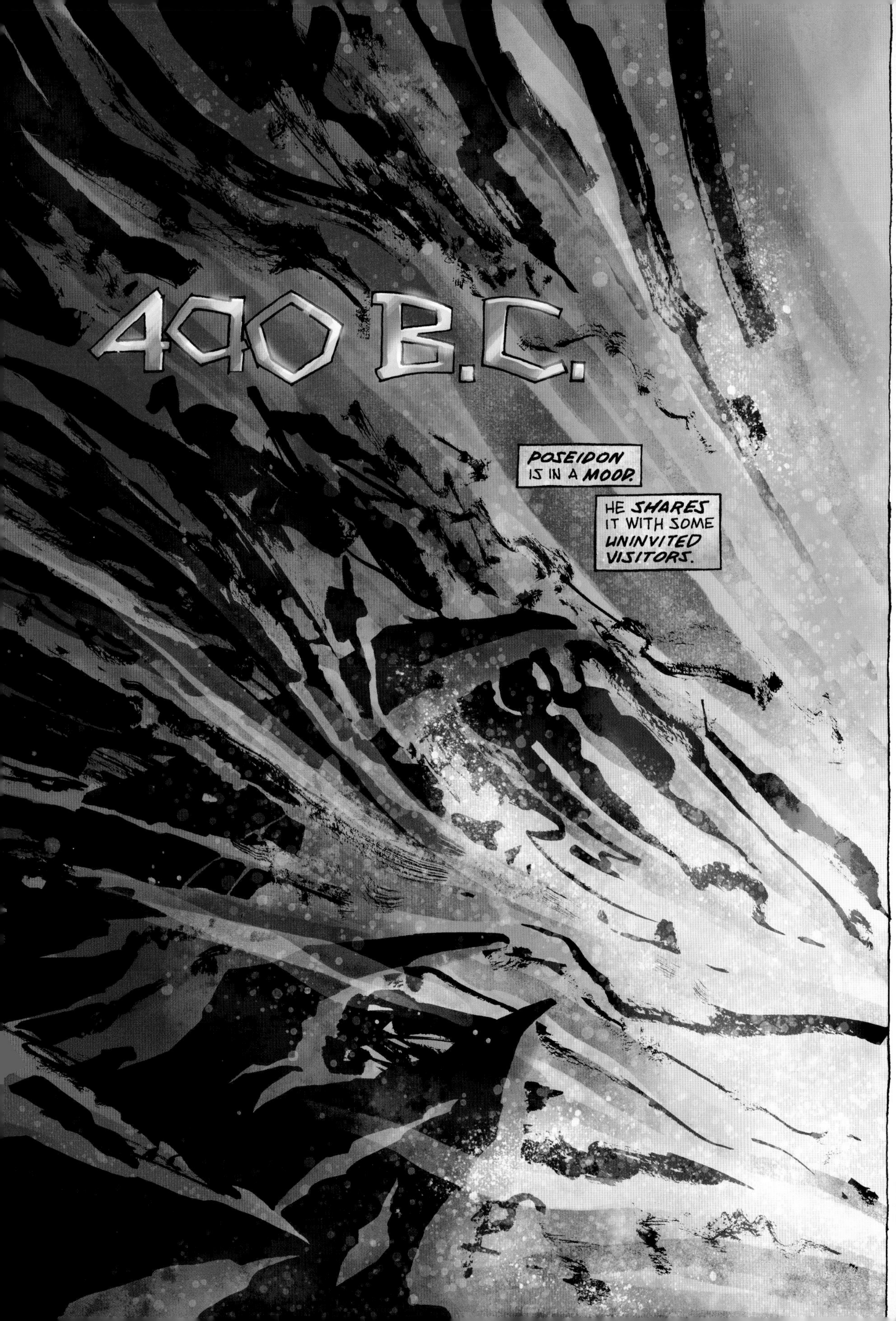

440 B.C.
POSEIDON IS IN A MOOD.
HE SHARES IT WITH SOME UNINVITED VISITORS.

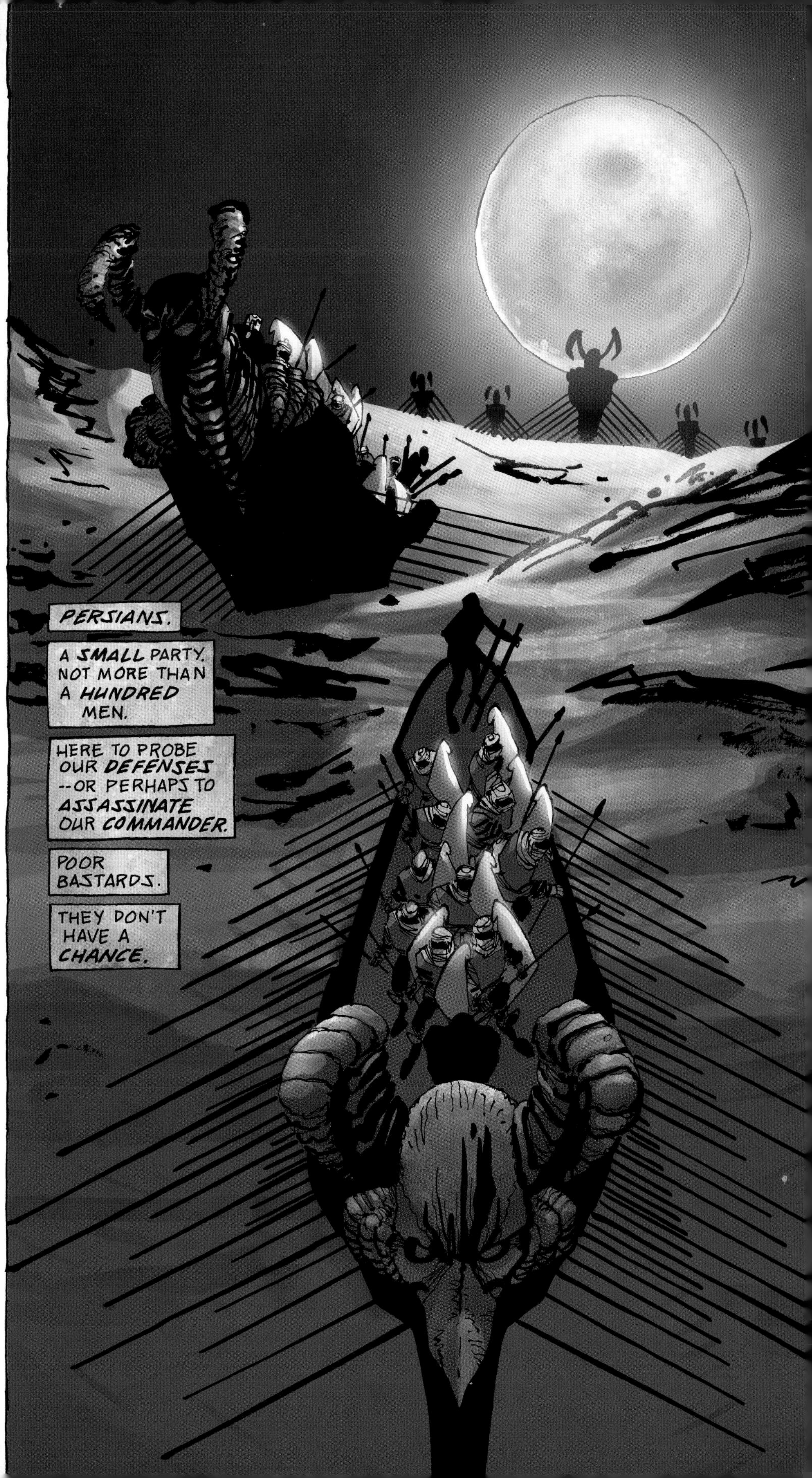

PERSIANS.
A SMALL PARTY. NOT MORE THAN A HUNDRED MEN.
HERE TO PROBE OUR DEFENSES --OR PERHAPS TO ASSASSINATE OUR COMMANDER.
POOR BASTARDS.
THEY DON'T HAVE A CHANCE.

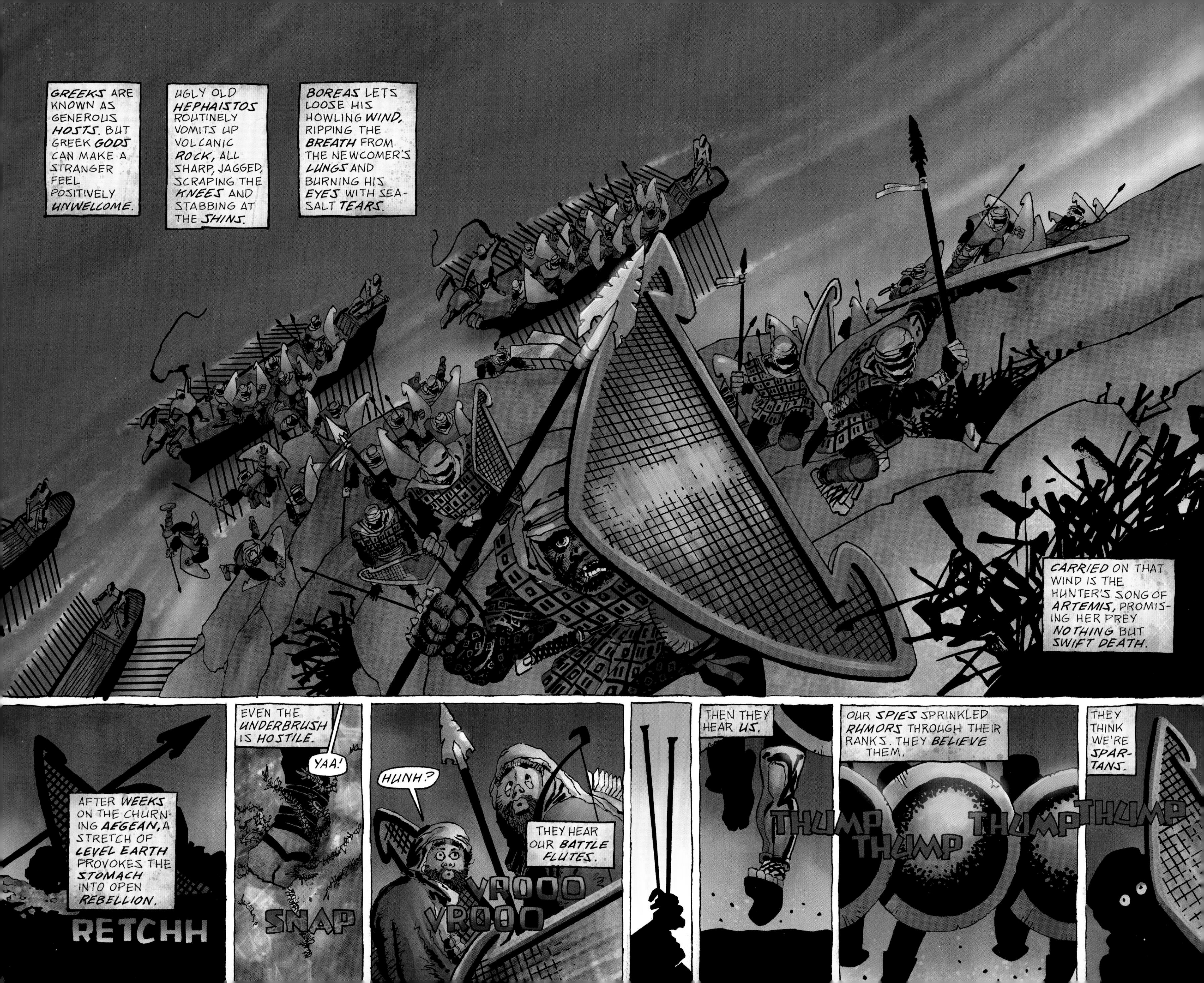
GREEKS ARE KNOWN AS GENEROUS HOSTS. BUT GREEK GODS CAN MAKE A STRANGER FEEL POSITIVELY UNWELCOME.
UGLY OLD HEPHAISTOS ROUTINELY VOMITS UP VOLCANIC ROCK, ALL SHARP, JAGGED, SCRAPING THE KNEES AND STABBING AT THE SHINS.
BOREAS LETS LOOSE HIS HOWLING WIND, RIPPING THE BREATH FROM THE NEWCOMER'S LUNGS AND BURNING HIS EYES WITH SEA-SALT TEARS.
CARRIED ON THAT WIND IS THE HUNTER'S SONG OF ARTEMIS, PROMISING HER PREY NOTHING BUT SWIFT DEATH.
AFTER WEEKS ON THE CHURNING AEGEAN, A STRETCH OF LEVEL EARTH PROVOKES THE STOMACH INTO OPEN REBELLION.
RETCHH
EVEN THE UNDERBRUSH IS HOSTILE.
YAA!
SNAP
HUNH?
THEY HEAR OUR BATTLE FLUTES.
VROOO
VROOO
THEN THEY HEAR US.
THUMP
THUMP
THUMP
THUMP
OUR SPIES SPRINKLED RUMORS THROUGH THEIR RANKS. THEY BELIEVE THEM.
THEY THINK WE'RE SPARTANS.

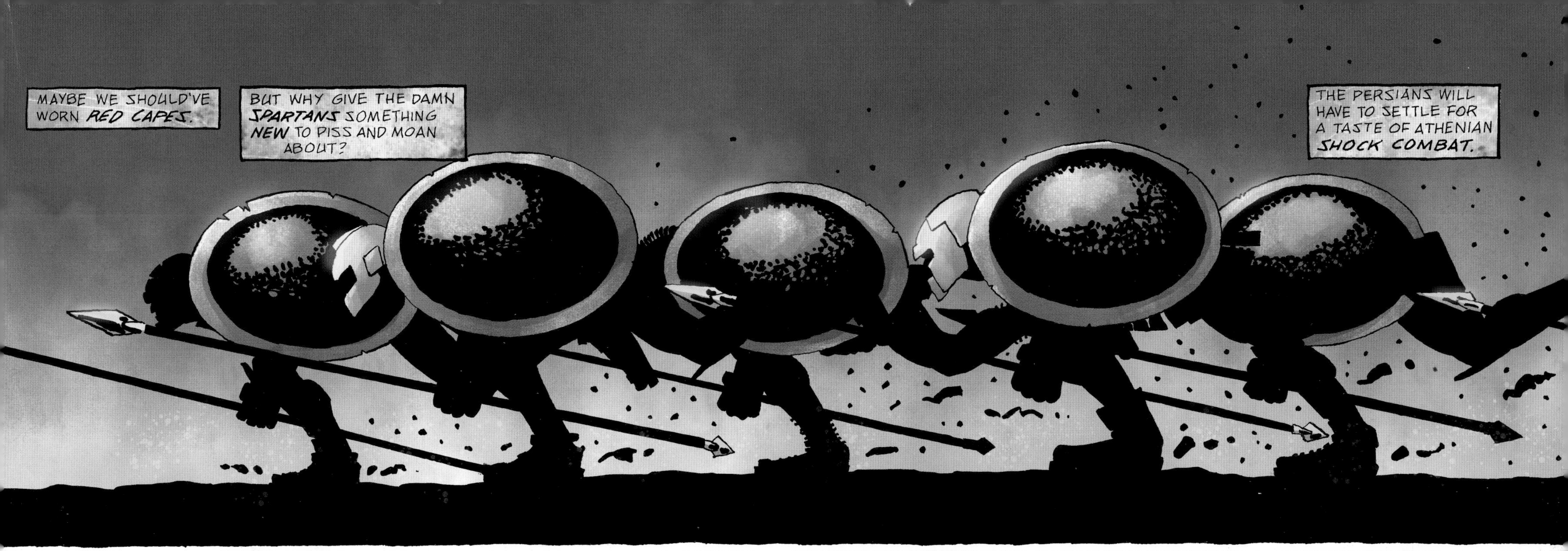
MAYBE WE SHOULD'VE WORN RED CAPES.
BUT WHY GIVE THE DAMN SPARTANS SOMETHING NEW TO PISS AND MOAN ABOUT?
THE PERSIANS WILL HAVE TO SETTLE FOR A TASTE OF ATHENIAN SHOCK COMBAT.

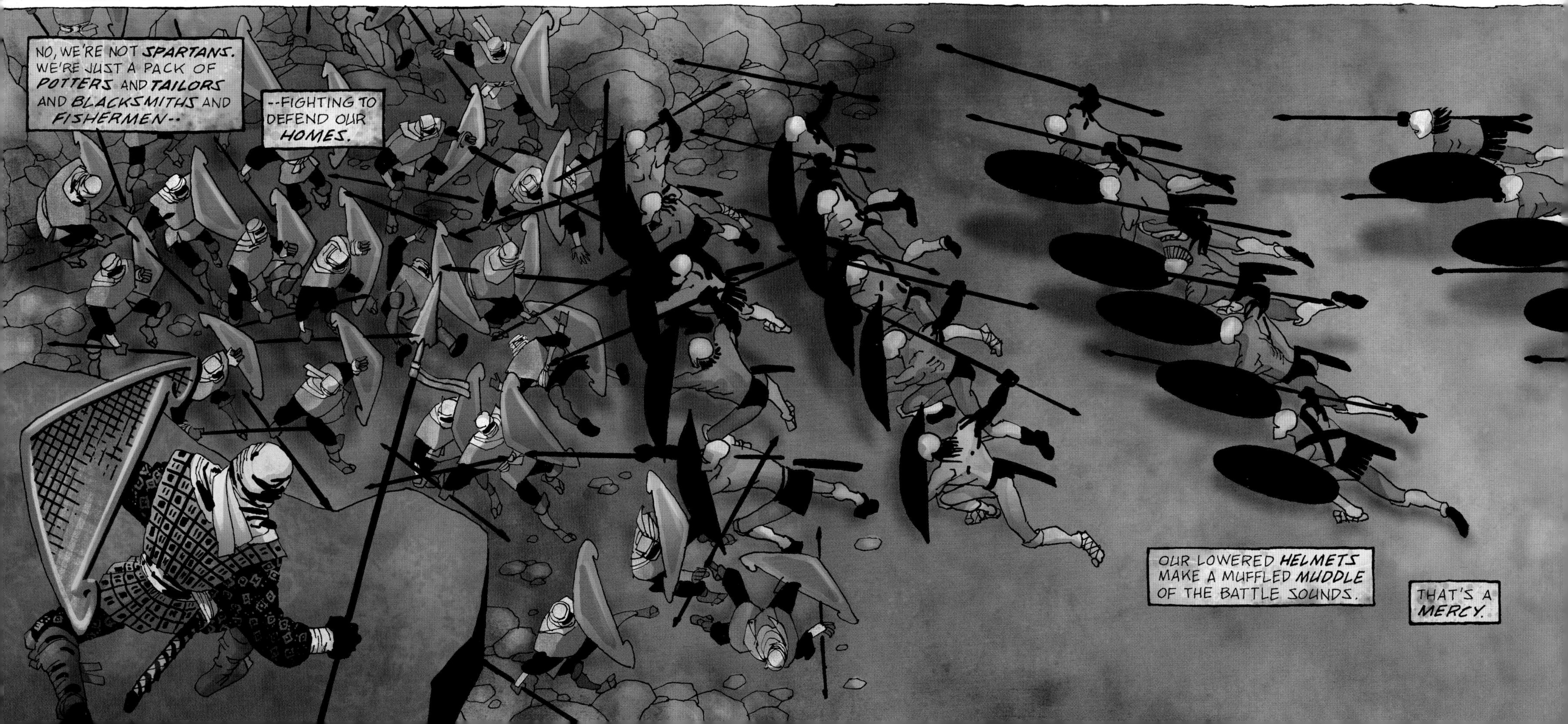
NO, WE'RE NOT SPARTANS. WE'RE JUST A PACK OF POTTERS AND TAILORS AND BLACKSMITHS AND FISHERMEN--
--FIGHTING TO DEFEND OUR HOMES.
OUR LOWERED HELMETS MAKE A MUFFLED MUDDLE OF THE BATTLE SOUNDS.
THAT'S A MERCY.

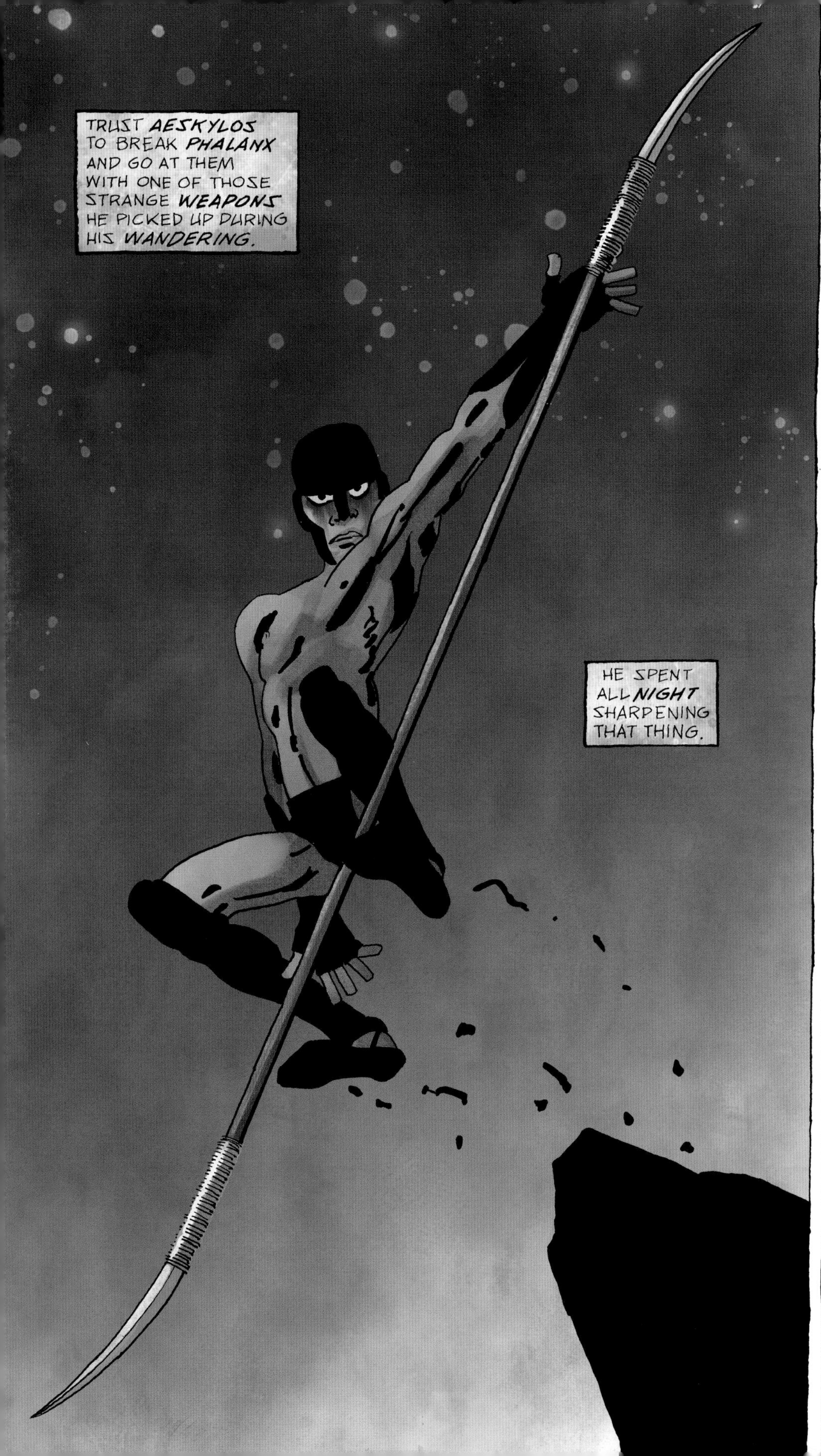
TRUST AESKYLOS TO BREAK PHALANX AND GO AT THEM WITH ONE OF THOSE STRANGE WEAPONS HE PICKED UP DURING HIS WANDERING.
HE SPENT ALL NIGHT SHARPENING THAT THING.

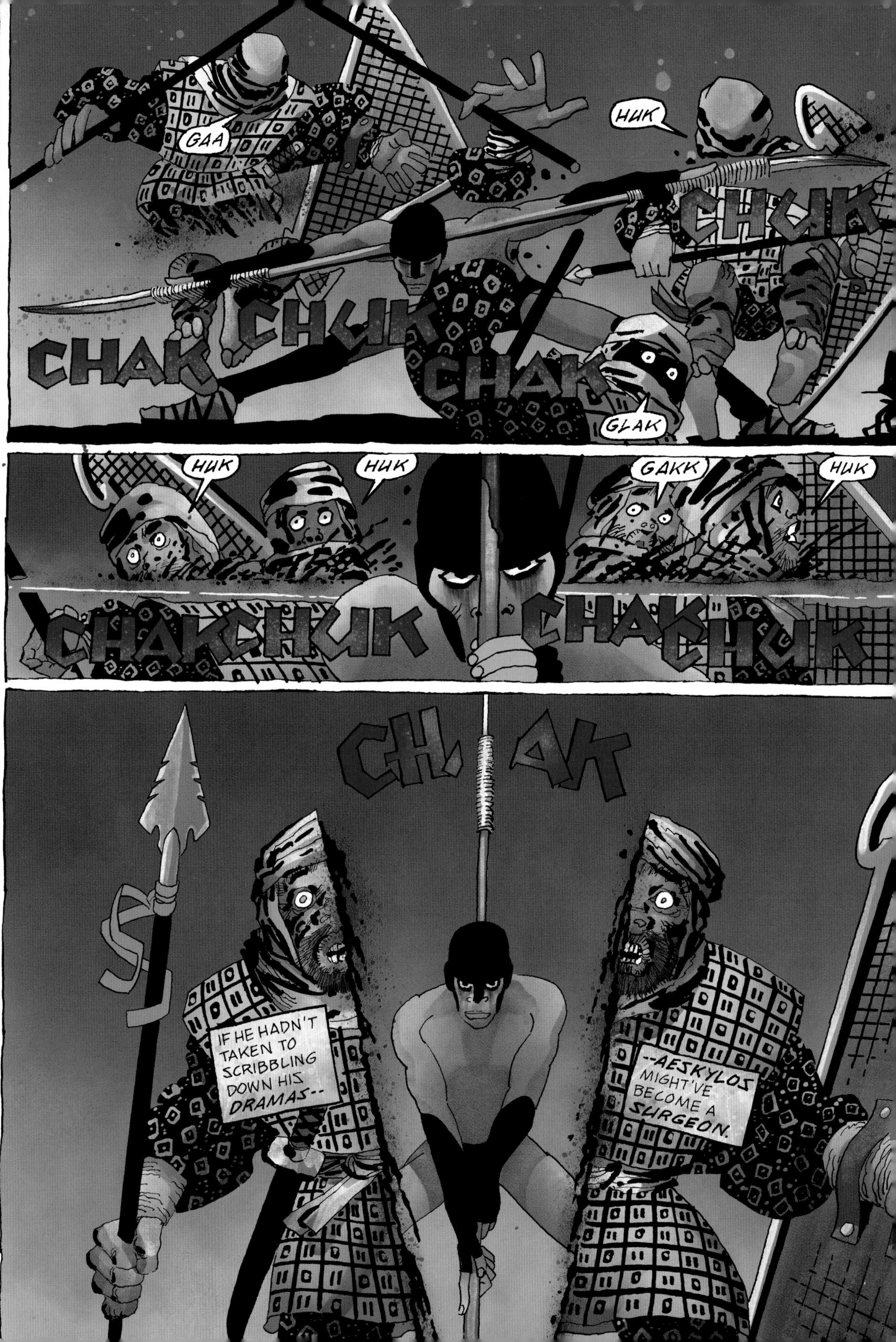
GAA
HUK
CHUK
CHAK
CHUK
CHAK
GLAK
HUK
HUK
GAKK
HUK
CHAKCHUK
CHAKCHUK
CH AK
IF HE HADN'T TAKEN TO SCRIBBLING DOWN HIS DRAMAS--
--AESKYLOS MIGHT'VE BECOME A SURGEON.

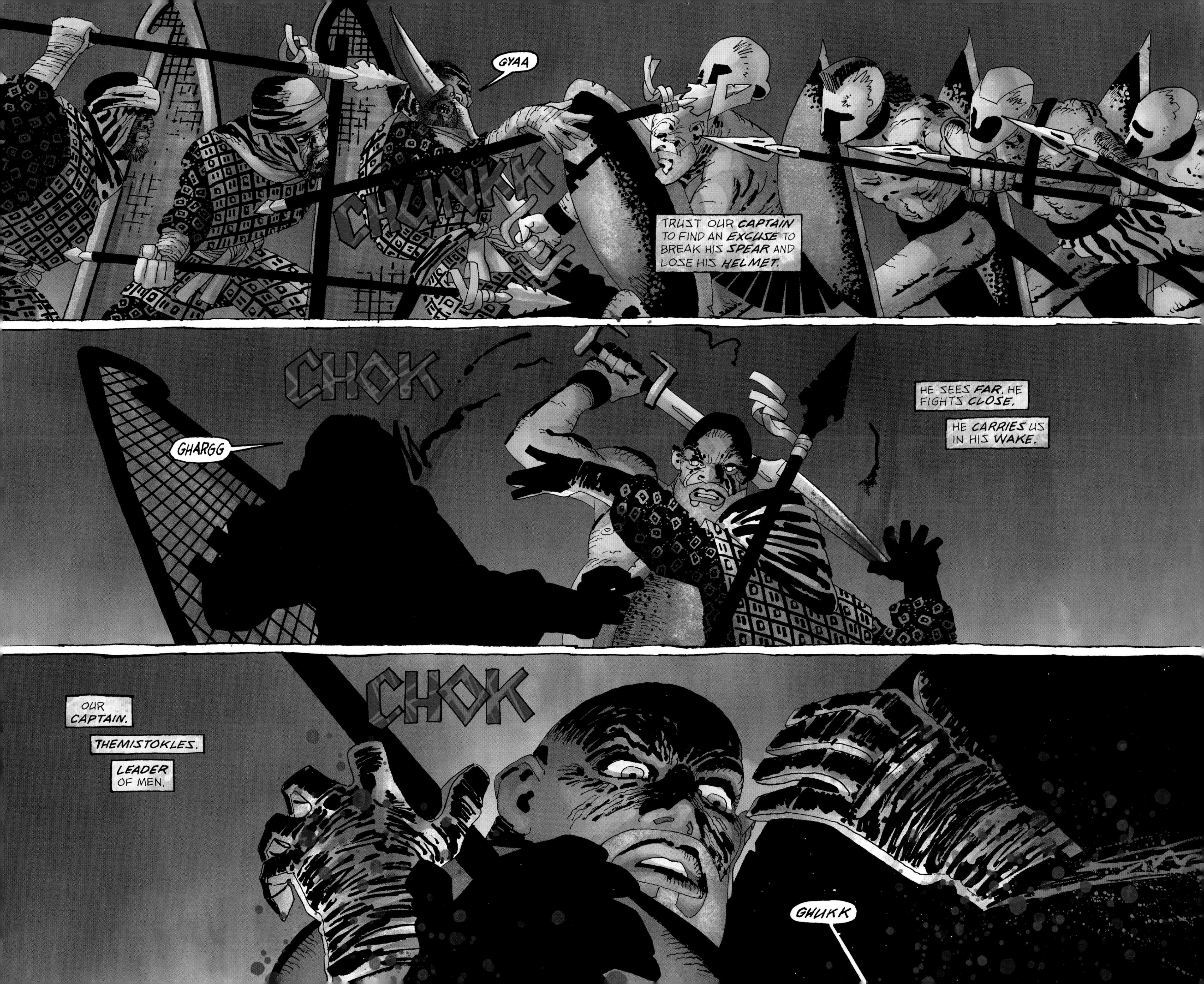
GYAA
CHUNKK
TRUST OUR CAPTAIN TO FIND AN EXCUSE TO BREAK HIS SPEAR AND LOSE HIS HELMET.
CHOK
GHARGG
HE SEES FAR, HE FIGHTS CLOSE.
HE CARRIES US IN HIS WAKE.
CHOK
OUR CAPTAIN.
THEMISTOKLES.
LEADER OF MEN.
GHUKK

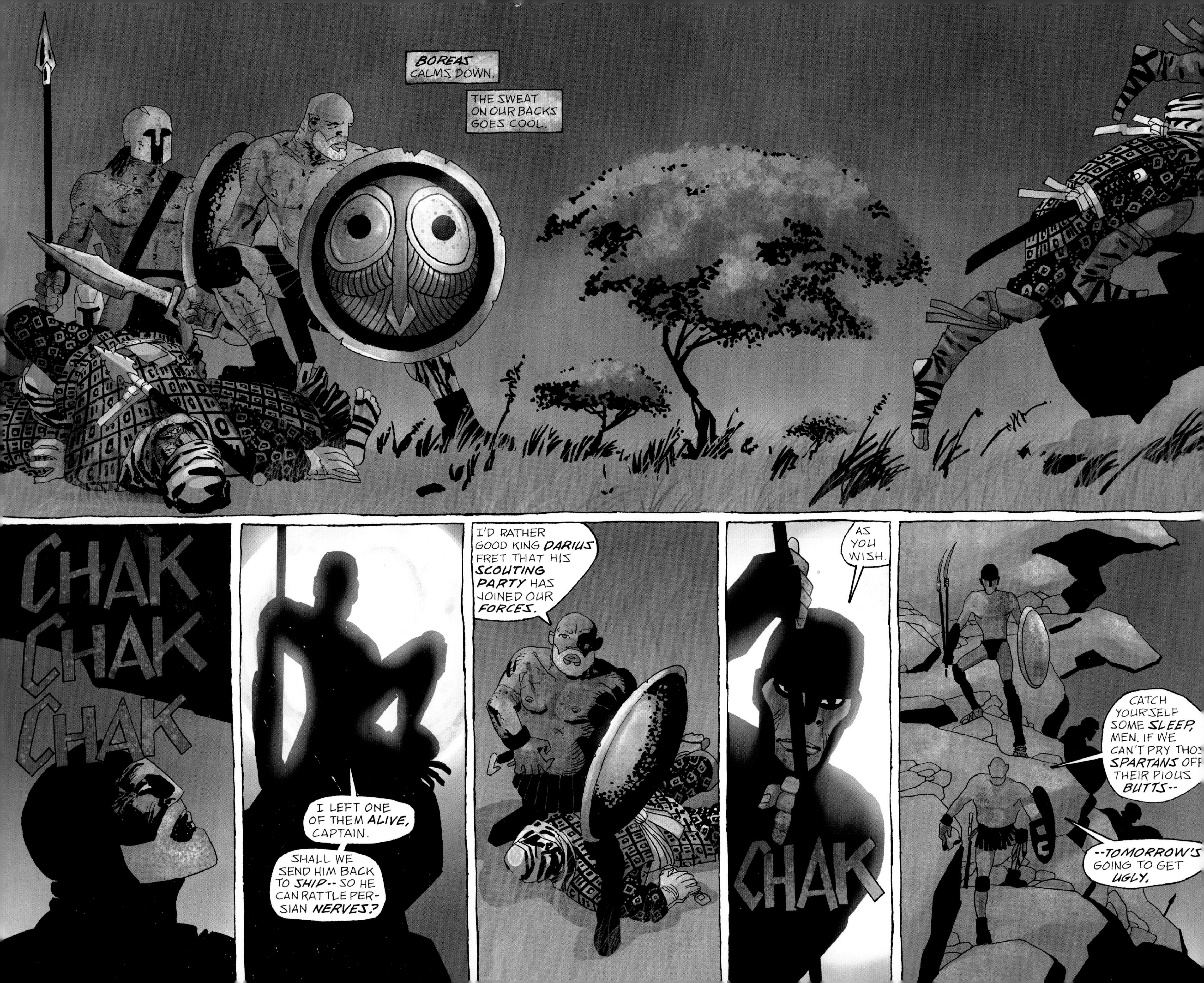
BOREAS CALMS DOWN.
THE SWEAT ON OUR BACKS GOES COOL.
CHAK CHAK CHAK
I LEFT ONE OF THEM ALIVE, CAPTAIN.
SHALL WE SEND HIM BACK TO SHIP-- SO HE CAN RATTLE PERSIAN NERVES?
I'D RATHER GOOD KING DARIUS FRET THAT HIS SCOUTING PARTY HAS JOINED OUR FORCES.
AS YOU WISH.
CHAK
CATCH YOURSELF SOME SLEEP, MEN. IF WE CAN'T PRY THOSE SPARTANS OFF THEIR PIOUS BUTTS--
--TOMORROW'S GOING TO GET UGLY.

HONOR THE CARNEIA!

OUR *DAY RUNNER* BRINGS WORD FROM *SPARTA*.

OUR BRAVE *ALLIES* ARE CELEBRATING *ANOTHER* OF THEIR CONFOUNDED HOLI-

DAYS--THIS ONE A A FESTIVAL OF *FERTILITY*. RUMOR HAS IT THIS IS THEIR ONLY *CHANCE* TO SHARE *BUNKS* WITH THEIR *WIVES*.

SMALL WONDER THEY'RE SO *FIERCE*.

COMMANDING GENERAL *MILTIADES* SHOWS OFF HIS *HORSE*. IT'S A PUREBRED *STALLION*, OF COURSE.

DARIUS HAS BEGUN TO *WITHDRAW* HIS *NAVY* FROM THIS SHORE. TAKE NO *COMFORT*. HIS SHIPS SURELY SAIL TO WAR ON *ATHENS* HERSELF--AND HE LEAVES FOR US A *MIGHTY* ARMY.

THE *SPARTANS* ARE *USELESS* TO US. WE WILL BE EASY TO *SURROUND*--OUR *DEFEAT* IS *CERTAIN*--UNLESS WE *SHATTER* THE RULES OF THE PHALANX.

THE *PHALANX* IS AN IMPENETRABLE *JUGGERNAUT*--*EIGHT MEN DEEP. UNSTOPPABLE*.

NO MAN HAS EVER CHANGED THE *PHALANX*.

NO MAN-- UNTIL *MILTIADES*.

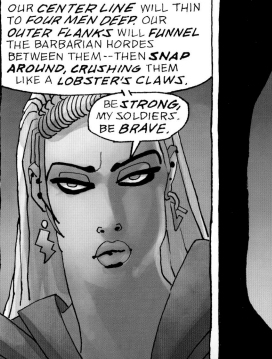

OUR *CENTER LINE* WILL THIN TO *FOUR MEN DEEP*. OUR *OUTER FLANKS* WILL *FUNNEL* THE BARBARIAN HORDES BETWEEN THEM--THEN *SNAP AROUND, CRUSHING* THEM LIKE A *LOBSTER'S CLAWS*.

BE *STRONG*, MY SOLDIERS. BE *BRAVE*.

FOP.

HE REALLY GETS YOUR *GOAT*, DOESN'T HE?

 HE'S A *FOP*.

 HE'S *BRILLIANT*.

YEAH. HE'S *BRILLIANT*.

OUR IONIAN *SPIES* REPORT.

THE *PERSIANS* ARE ON THE *MOVE*.

WE SAY OUR *PRAYERS*.

WE GRAB OUR *GEAR*.

DAWN BREAKS.

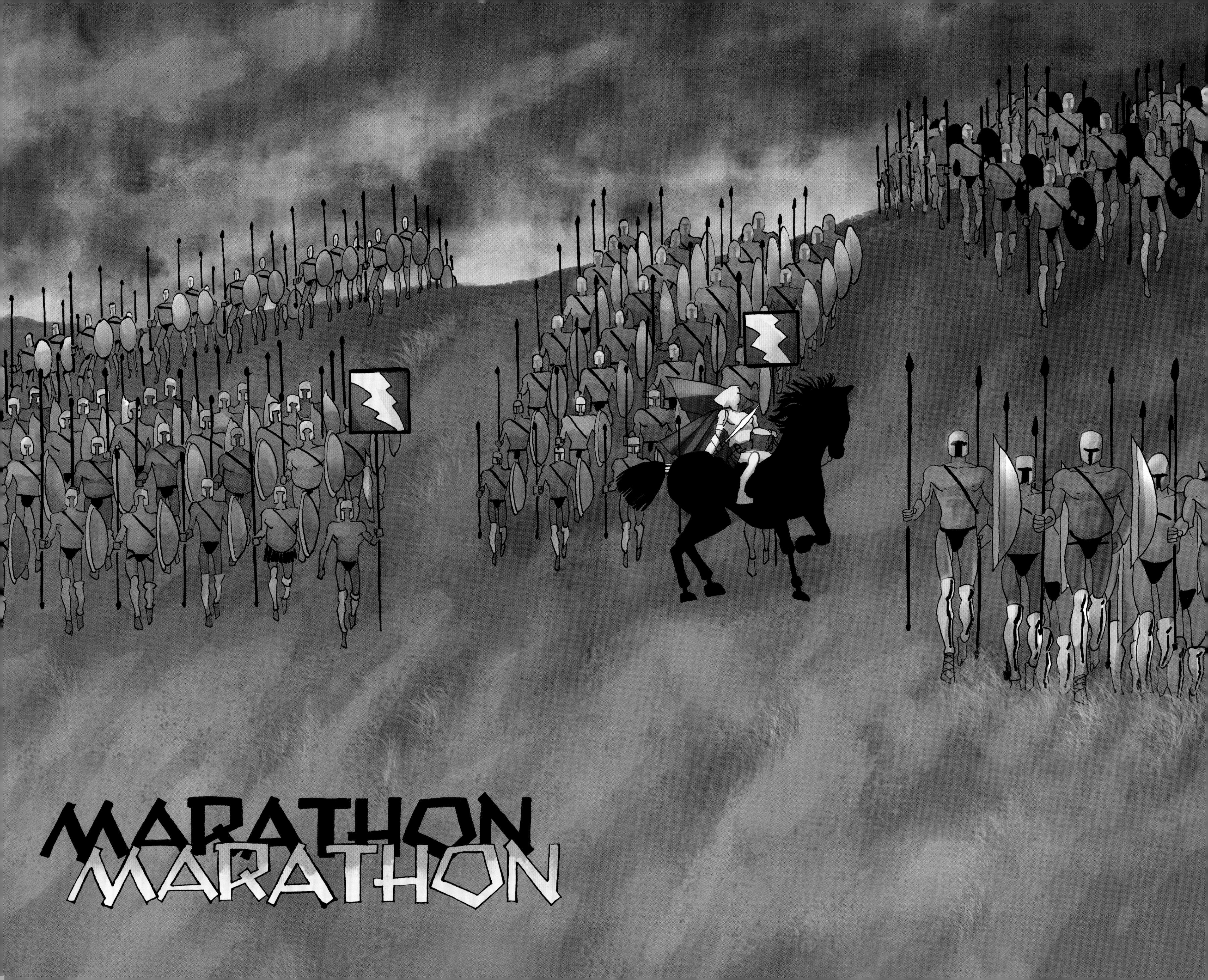
MARATHON
MARATHON

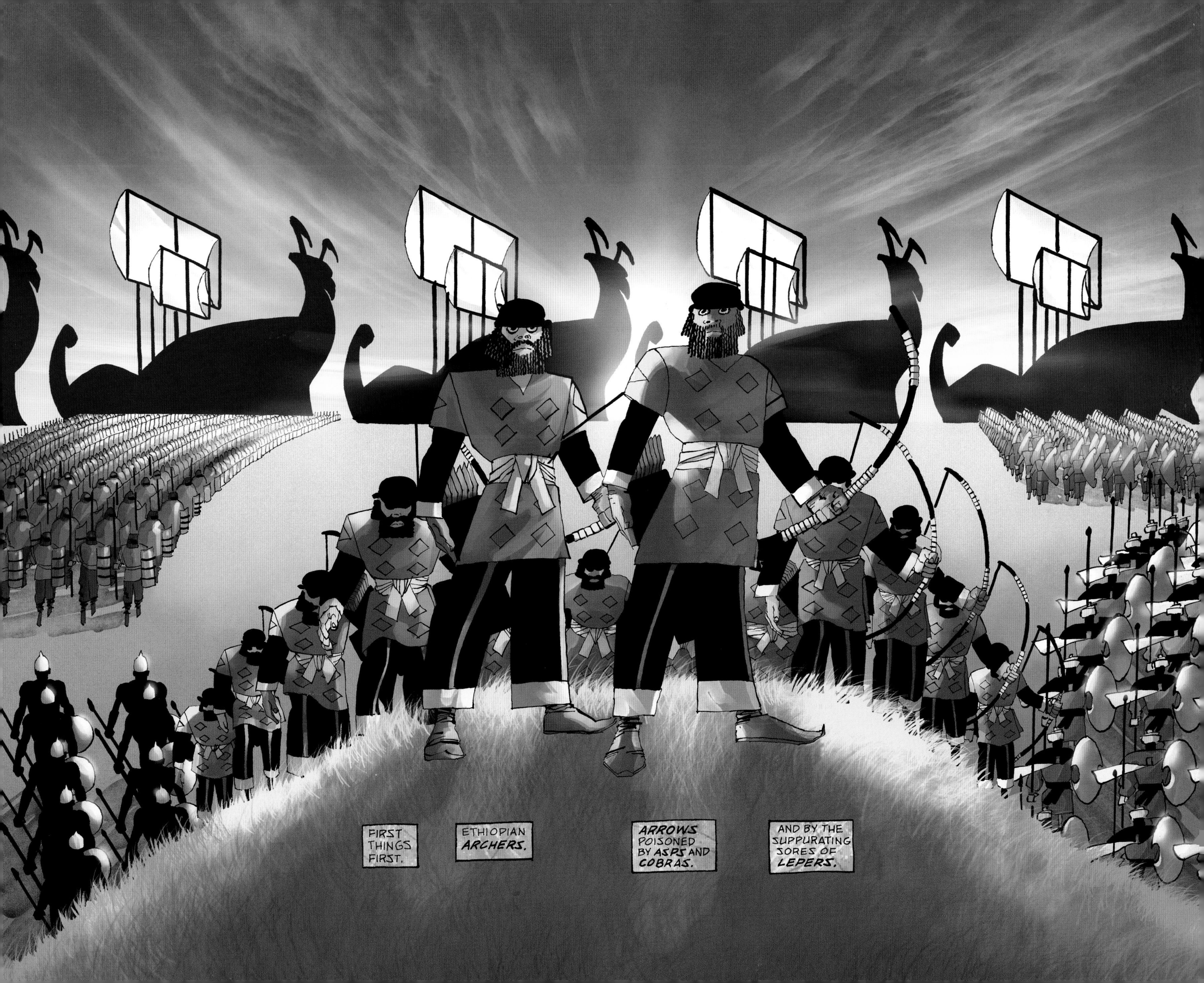
FIRST THINGS FIRST.
ETHIOPIAN ARCHERS.
ARROWS POISONED BY ASPS AND COBRAS.
AND BY THE SUPPURATING SORES OF LEPERS.

POSEIDON SLEEPS.

SMOOTH SAILING FOR THE PERSIANS.

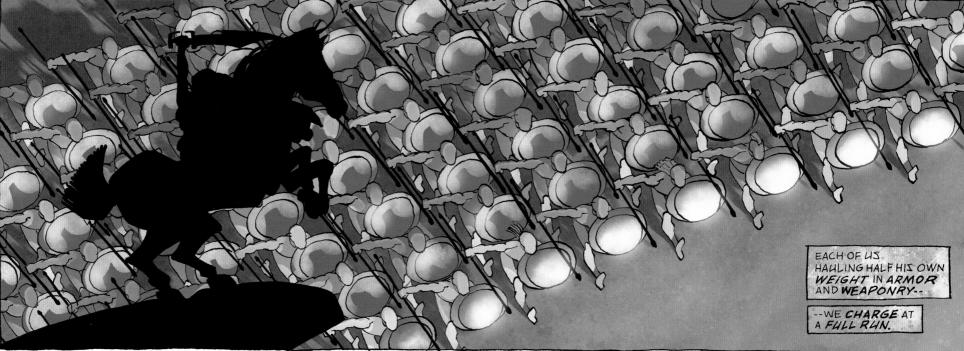

THERE WILL BE NO *SECOND CHARGE.* WE WILL *RUSH* THE ENEMY AND *CUT HIM DOWN* WHERE HE *STANDS.* WE WILL *TRAMPLE* HIM. WE WILL *ANNIHI-LATE* HIM--OR WE WILL *DIE!*

EACH OF US HAULING HALF HIS OWN *WEIGHT* IN ARMOR AND *WEAPONRY*--

--WE *CHARGE* AT A *FULL RUN.*

THIS IS GOING TO BE *GREAT!*

YOUR HELMET, CAPTAIN, PLEASE PUT IT ON.

FIVE HUNDRED STRANDS OF *CATGUT* PULL TIGHT, COMPLAINING.

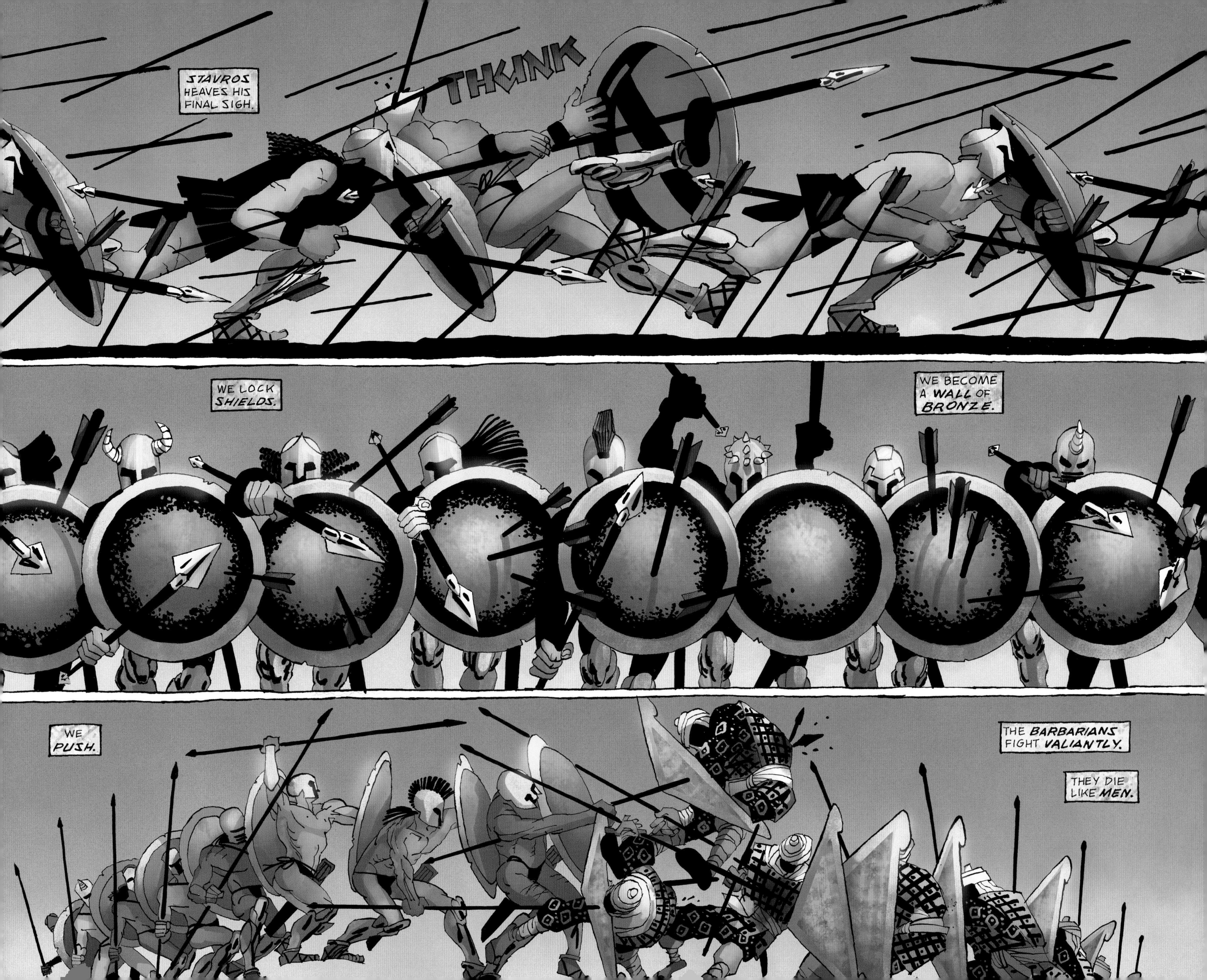
STAVROS HEAVES HIS FINAL SIGH.
THUNK
WE LOCK SHIELDS.
WE BECOME A WALL OF BRONZE.
WE PUSH.
THE BARBARIANS FIGHT VALIANTLY.
THEY DIE LIKE MEN.

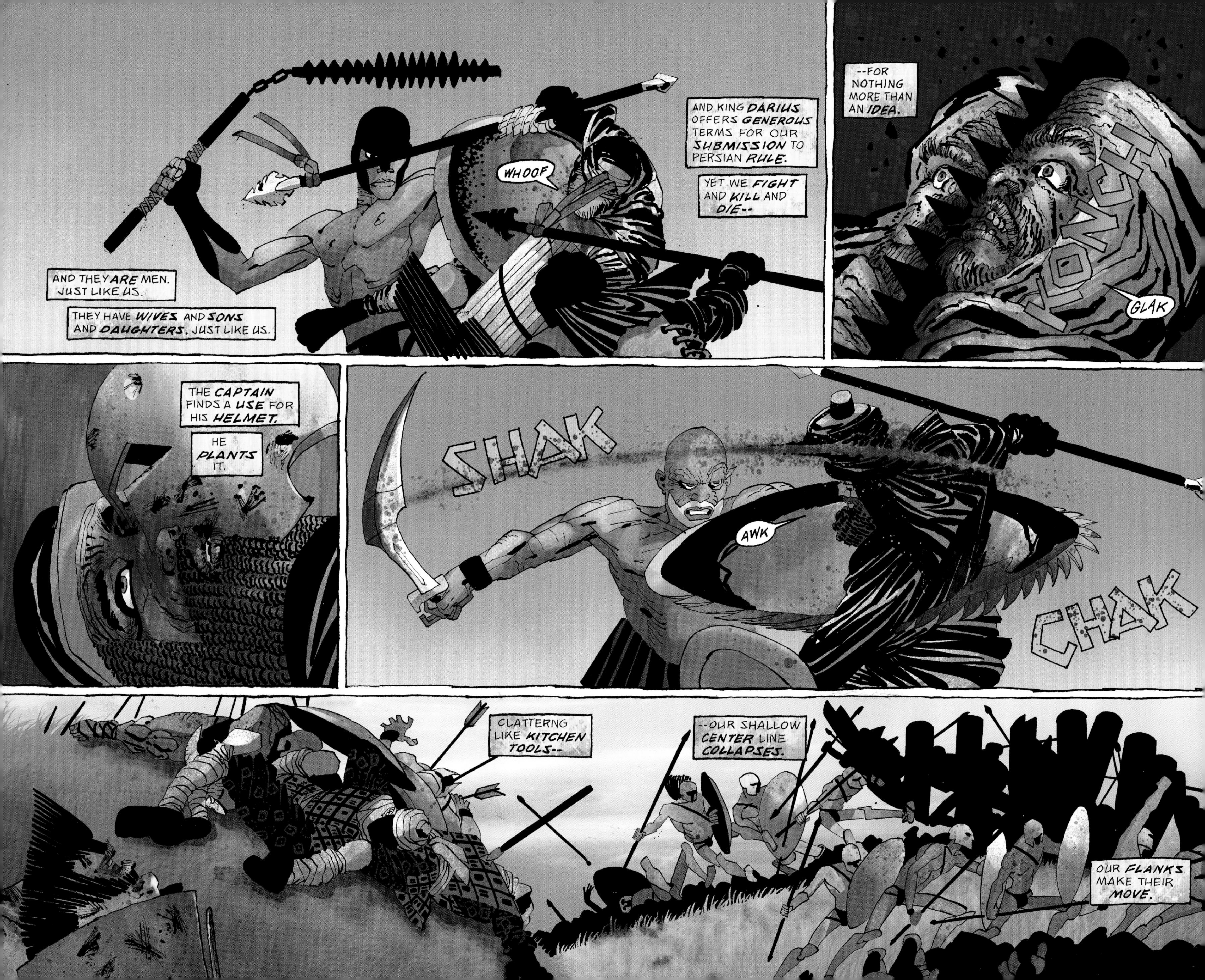
AND THEY ARE MEN. JUST LIKE US.
THEY HAVE WIVES AND SONS AND DAUGHTERS. JUST LIKE US.
WHOOF
AND KING DARIUS OFFERS GENEROUS TERMS FOR OUR SUBMISSION TO PERSIAN RULE.
YET WE FIGHT AND KILL AND DIE--
--FOR NOTHING MORE THAN AN IDEA.
YONCH
GLAK
THE CAPTAIN FINDS A USE FOR HIS HELMET.
HE PLANTS IT.
SHAK
AWK
CHAK
CLATTERNG LIKE KITCHEN TOOLS--
--OUR SHALLOW CENTER LINE COLLAPSES.
OUR FLANKS MAKE THEIR MOVE.

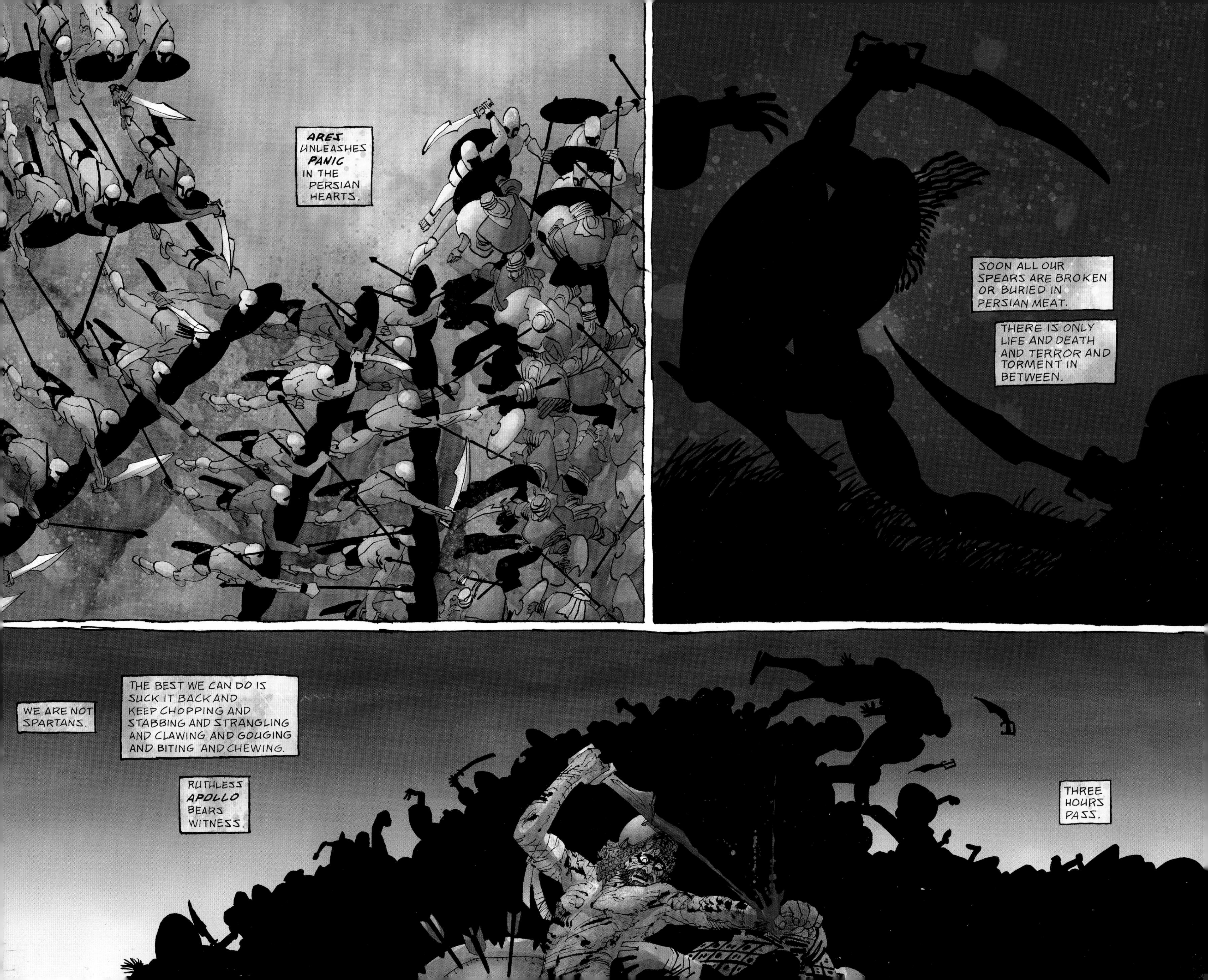
ARES UNLEASHES PANIC IN THE PERSIAN HEARTS.
SOON ALL OUR SPEARS ARE BROKEN OR BURIED IN PERSIAN MEAT.
THERE IS ONLY LIFE AND DEATH AND TERROR AND TORMENT IN BETWEEN.
WE ARE NOT SPARTANS.
THE BEST WE CAN DO IS SUCK IT BACK AND KEEP CHOPPING AND STABBING AND STRANGLING AND CLAWING AND GOUGING AND BITING AND CHEWING.
RUTHLESS APOLLO BEARS WITNESS.
THREE HOURS PASS.

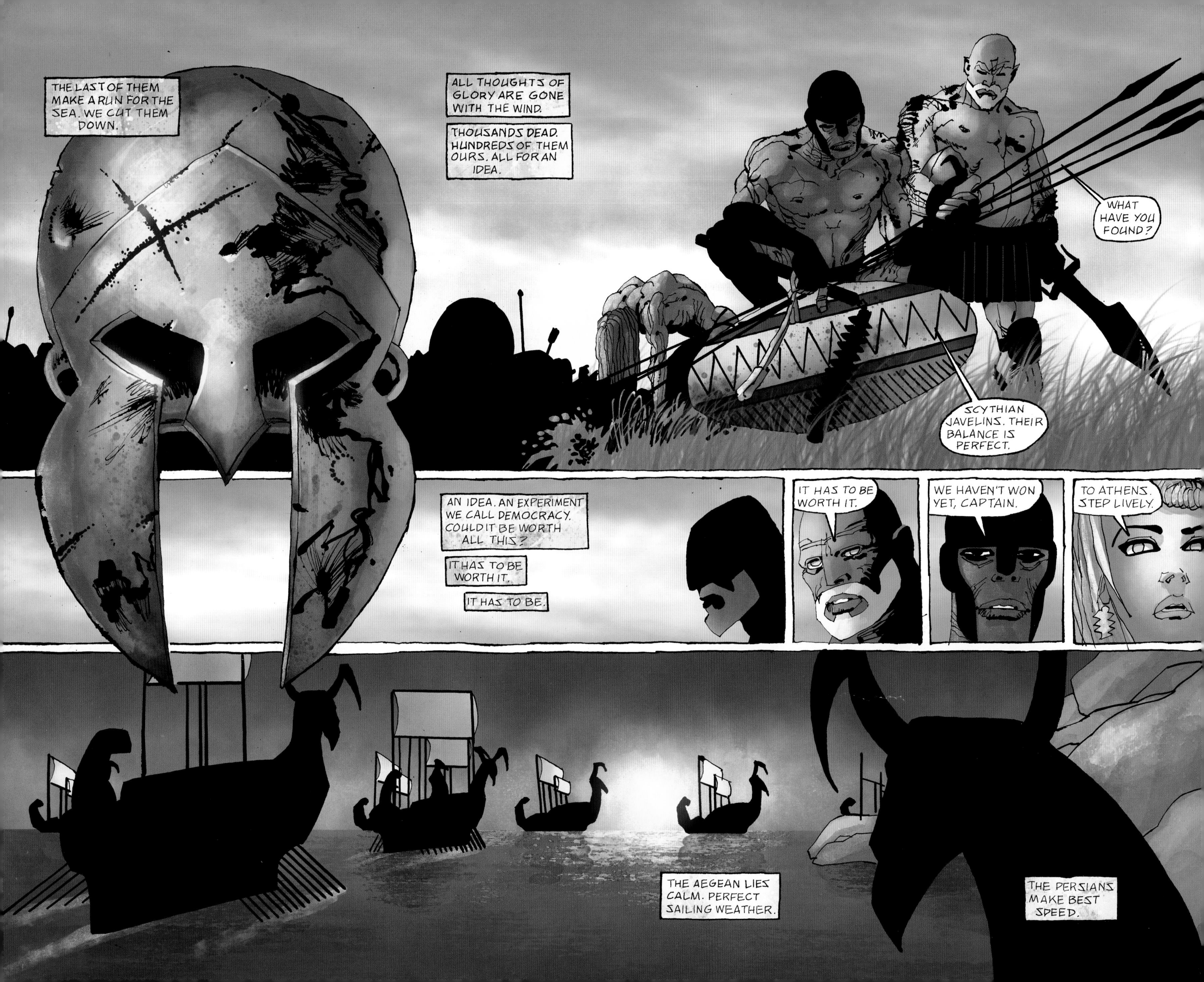

THE LAST OF THEM MAKE A RUN FOR THE SEA. WE CUT THEM DOWN.
ALL THOUGHTS OF GLORY ARE GONE WITH THE WIND.
THOUSANDS DEAD. HUNDREDS OF THEM OURS. ALL FOR AN IDEA.
WHAT HAVE YOU FOUND?
SCYTHIAN JAVELINS. THEIR BALANCE IS PERFECT.
AN IDEA. AN EXPERIMENT WE CALL DEMOCRACY. COULD IT BE WORTH ALL THIS?
IT HAS TO BE WORTH IT.
IT HAS TO BE.
IT HAS TO BE WORTH IT.
WE HAVEN'T WON YET, CAPTAIN.
TO ATHENS. STEP LIVELY.
THE AEGEAN LIES CALM. PERFECT SAILING WEATHER.
THE PERSIANS MAKE BEST SPEED.

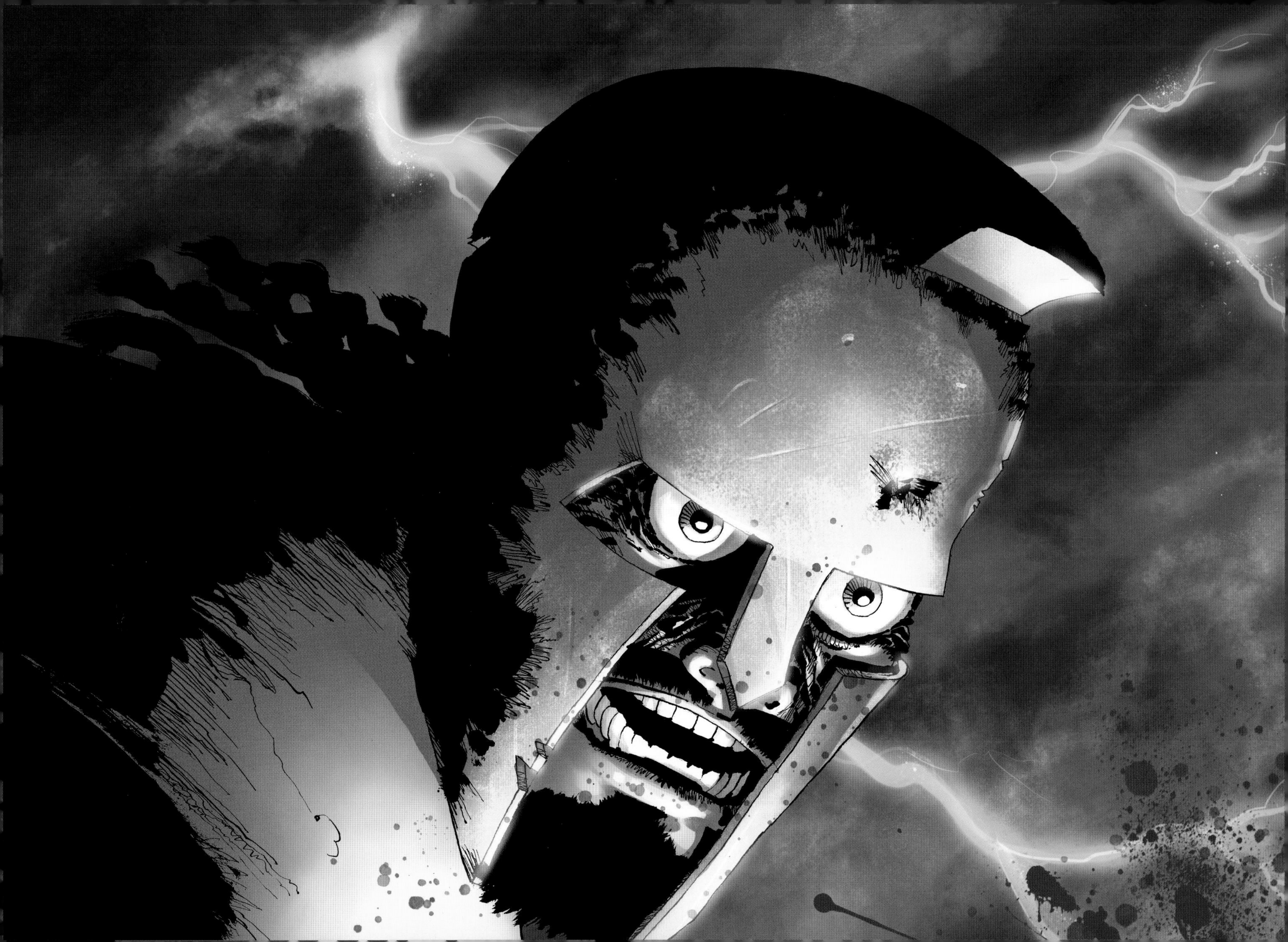

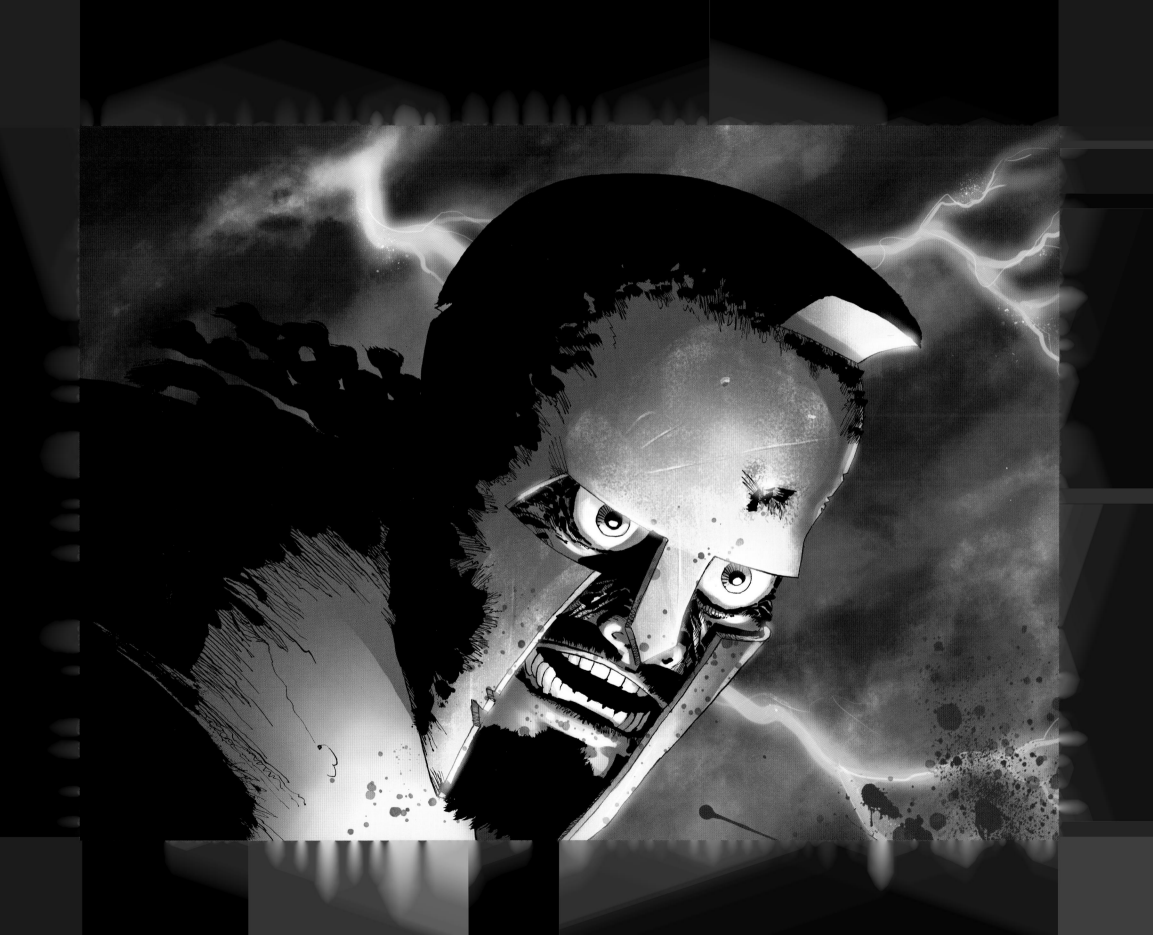

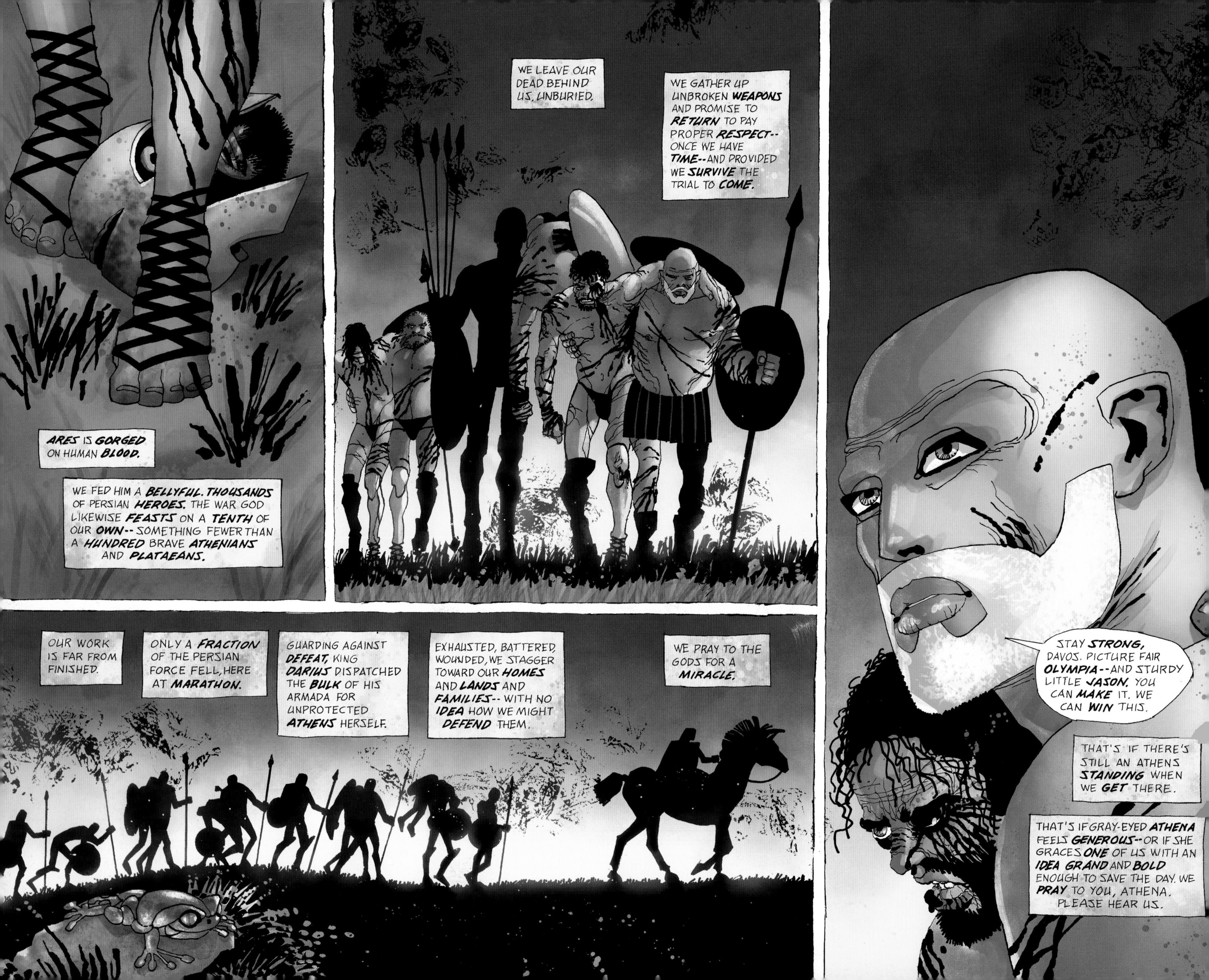
ARES IS GORGED ON HUMAN BLOOD.
WE FED HIM A BELLYFUL. THOUSANDS OF PERSIAN HEROES. THE WAR GOD LIKEWISE FEASTS ON A TENTH OF OUR OWN-- SOMETHING FEWER THAN A HUNDRED BRAVE ATHENIANS AND PLATAEANS.
WE LEAVE OUR DEAD BEHIND US, UNBURIED.
WE GATHER UP UNBROKEN WEAPONS AND PROMISE TO RETURN TO PAY PROPER RESPECT-- ONCE WE HAVE TIME--AND PROVIDED WE SURVIVE THE TRIAL TO COME.
STAY STRONG, DAVOS. PICTURE FAIR OLYMPIA--AND STURDY LITTLE JASON. YOU CAN MAKE IT. WE CAN WIN THIS.
THAT'S IF THERE'S STILL AN ATHENS STANDING WHEN WE GET THERE.
THAT'S IF GRAY-EYED ATHENA FEELS GENEROUS--OR IF SHE GRACES ONE OF US WITH AN IDEA GRAND AND BOLD ENOUGH TO SAVE THE DAY. WE PRAY TO YOU, ATHENA. PLEASE HEAR US.
OUR WORK IS FAR FROM FINISHED.
ONLY A FRACTION OF THE PERSIAN FORCE FELL, HERE AT MARATHON.
GUARDING AGAINST DEFEAT, KING DARIUS DISPATCHED THE BULK OF HIS ARMADA FOR UNPROTECTED ATHENS HERSELF.
EXHAUSTED, BATTERED, WOUNDED, WE STAGGER TOWARD OUR HOMES AND LANDS AND FAMILIES-- WITH NO IDEA HOW WE MIGHT DEFEND THEM.
WE PRAY TO THE GODS FOR A MIRACLE.

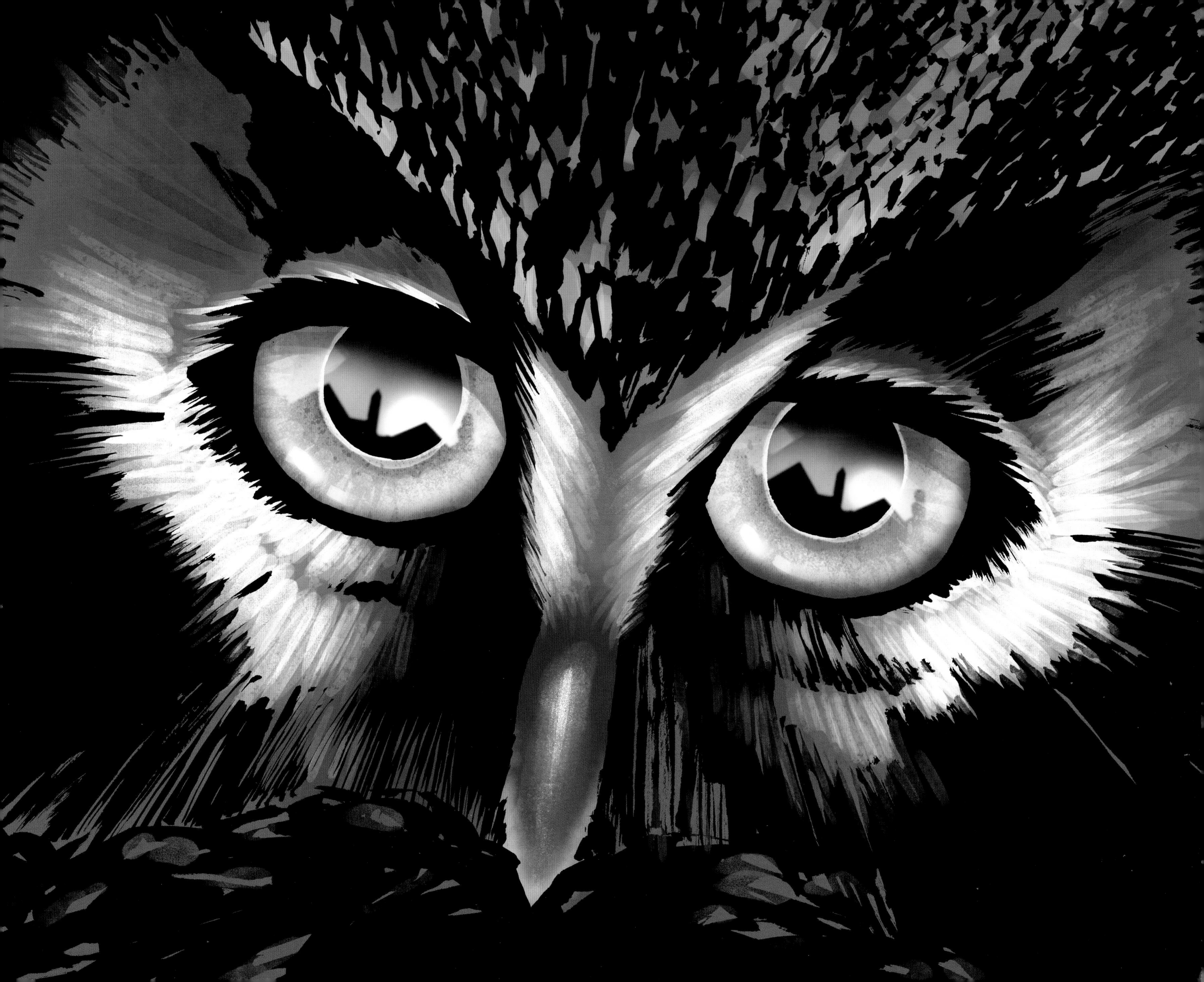

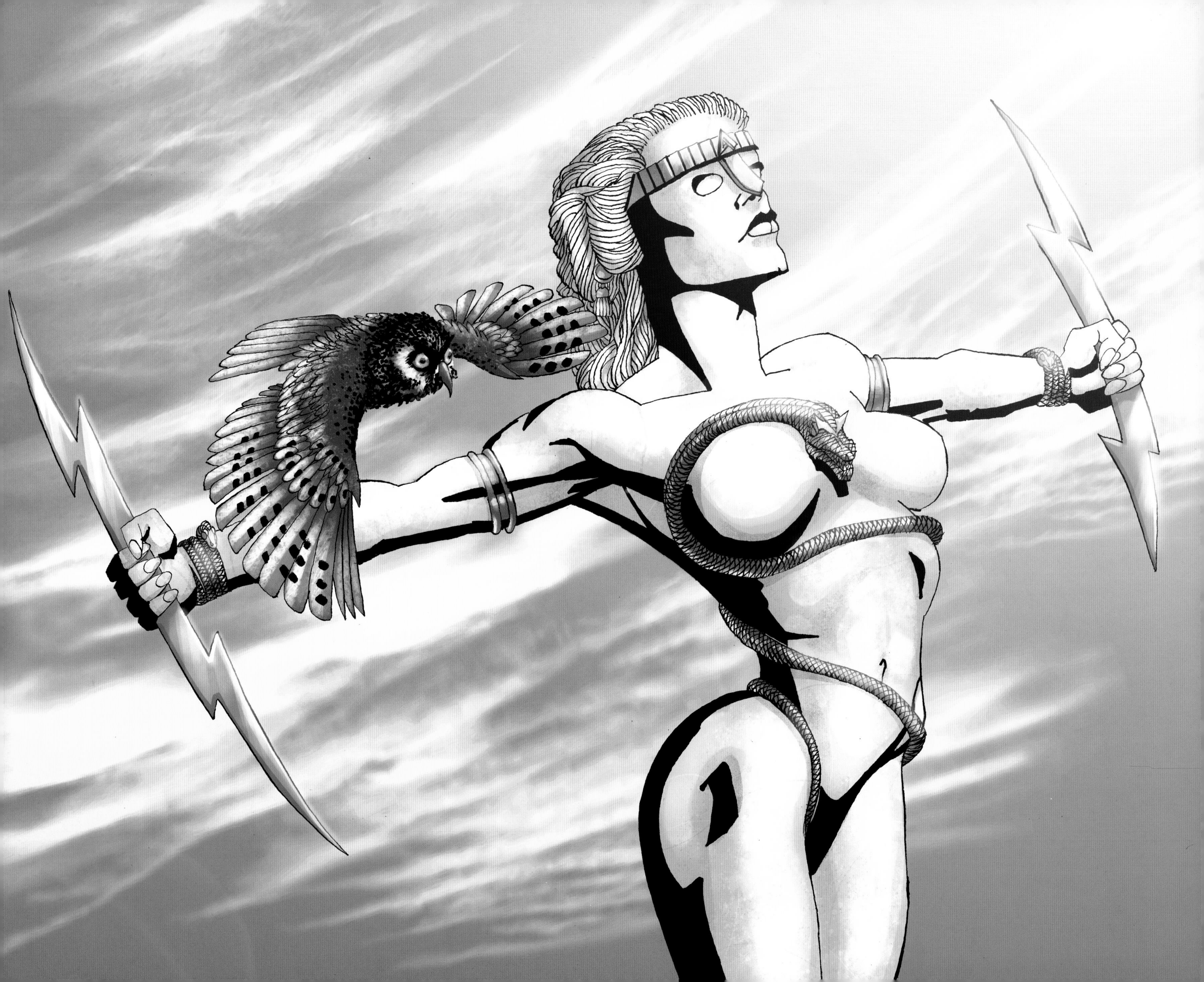

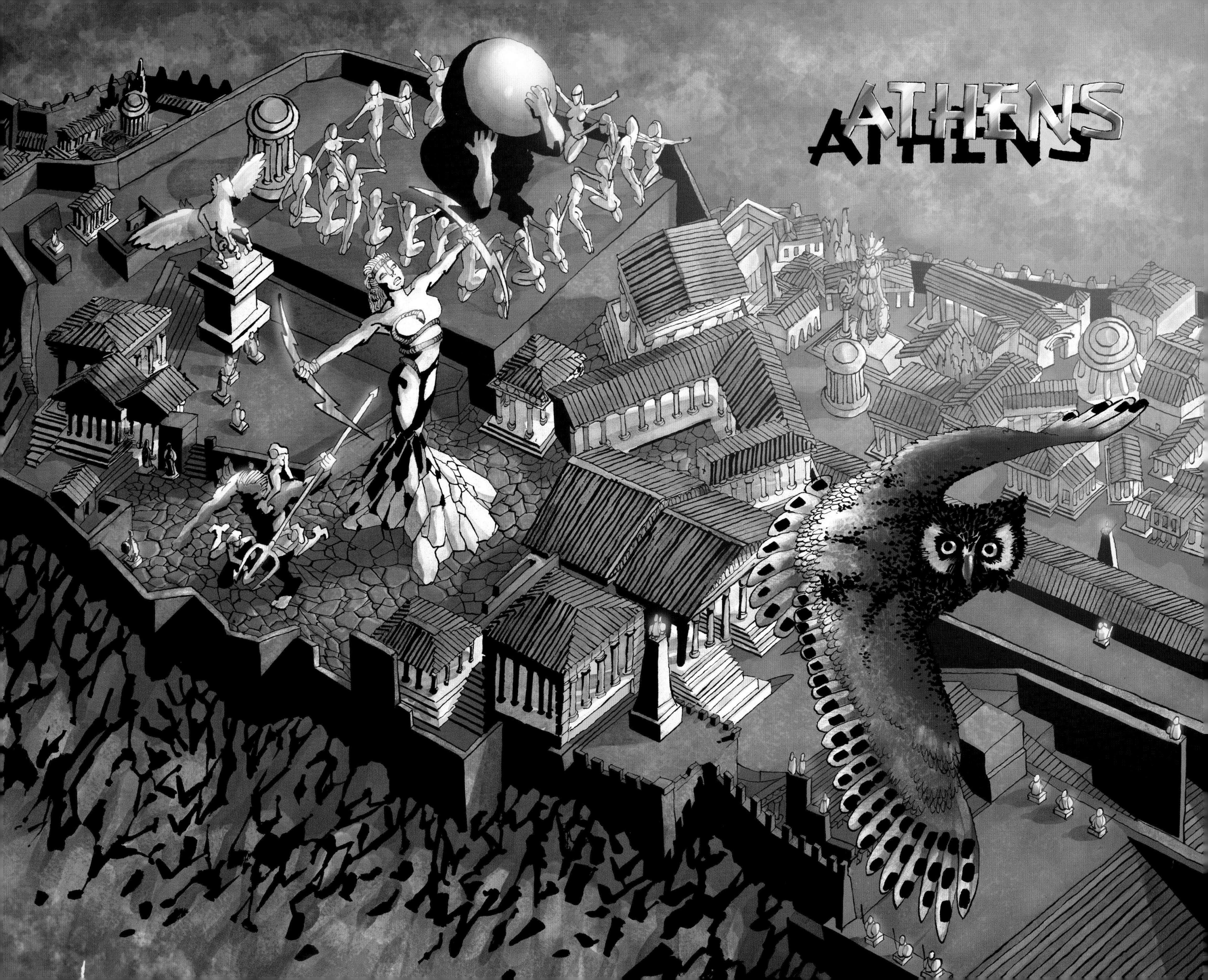
ATHENS

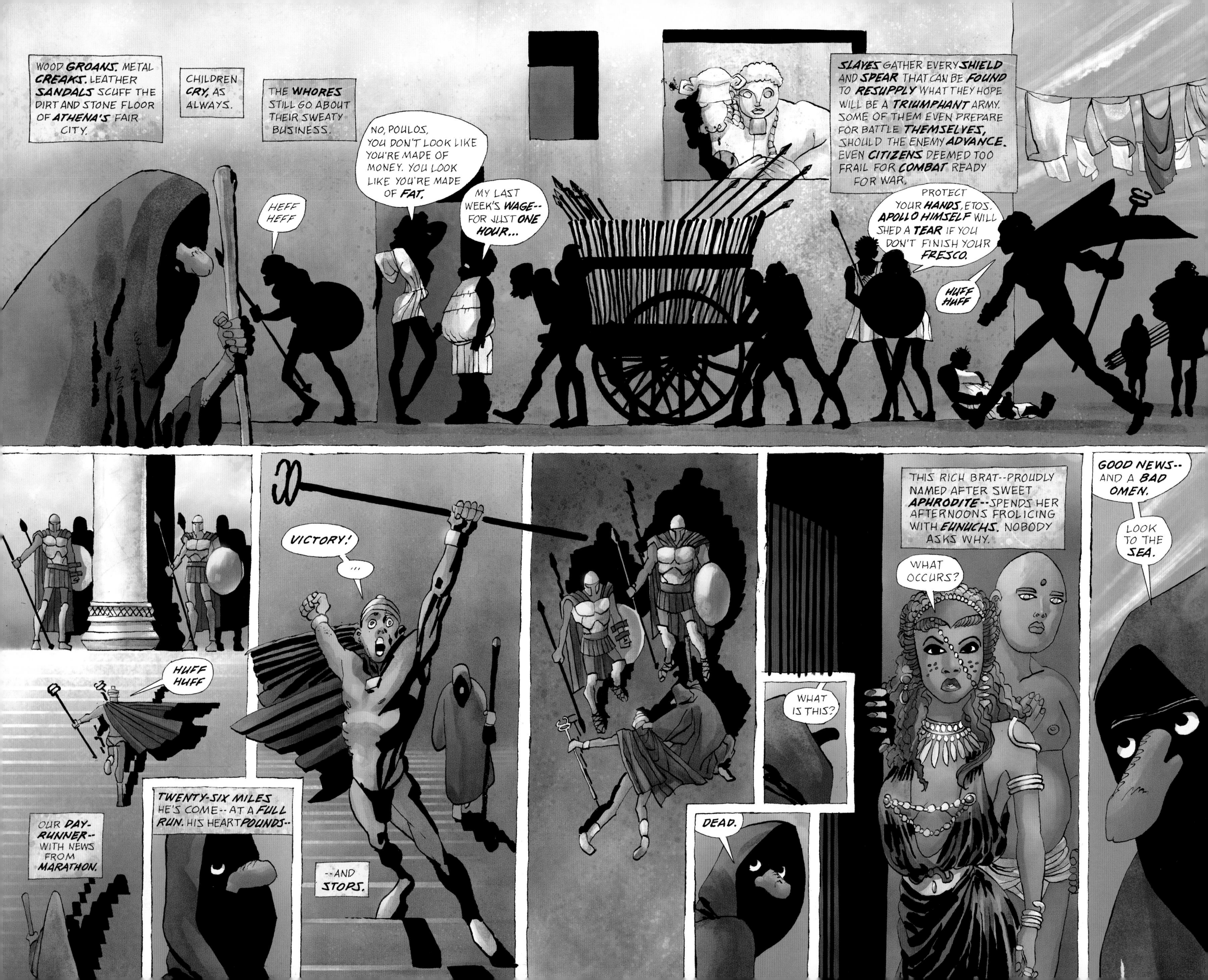
WOOD GROANS. METAL CREAKS. LEATHER SANDALS SCUFF THE DIRT AND STONE FLOOR OF ATHENA'S FAIR CITY.
CHILDREN CRY, AS ALWAYS.
THE WHORES STILL GO ABOUT THEIR SWEATY BUSINESS.
HEFF HEFF
NO, POULOS, YOU DON'T LOOK LIKE YOU'RE MADE OF MONEY. YOU LOOK LIKE YOU'RE MADE OF FAT.
MY LAST WEEK'S WAGE-- FOR JUST ONE HOUR...
SLAVES GATHER EVERY SHIELD AND SPEAR THAT CAN BE FOUND TO RESUPPLY WHAT THEY HOPE WILL BE A TRIUMPHANT ARMY. SOME OF THEM EVEN PREPARE FOR BATTLE THEMSELVES, SHOULD THE ENEMY ADVANCE. EVEN CITIZENS DEEMED TOO FRAIL FOR COMBAT READY FOR WAR.
PROTECT YOUR HANDS, ETOS. APOLLO HIMSELF WILL SHED A TEAR IF YOU DON'T FINISH YOUR FRESCO.
HUFF HUFF
HUFF HUFF
OUR DAY-RUNNER-- WITH NEWS FROM MARATHON.
TWENTY-SIX MILES HE'S COME-- AT A FULL RUN. HIS HEART POUNDS--
VICTORY!
...
--AND STOPS.
WHAT IS THIS?
DEAD.
THIS RICH BRAT--PROUDLY NAMED AFTER SWEET APHRODITE--SPENDS HER AFTERNOONS FROLICING WITH EUNUCHS. NOBODY ASKS WHY.
WHAT OCCURS?
GOOD NEWS-- AND A BAD OMEN.
LOOK TO THE SEA.

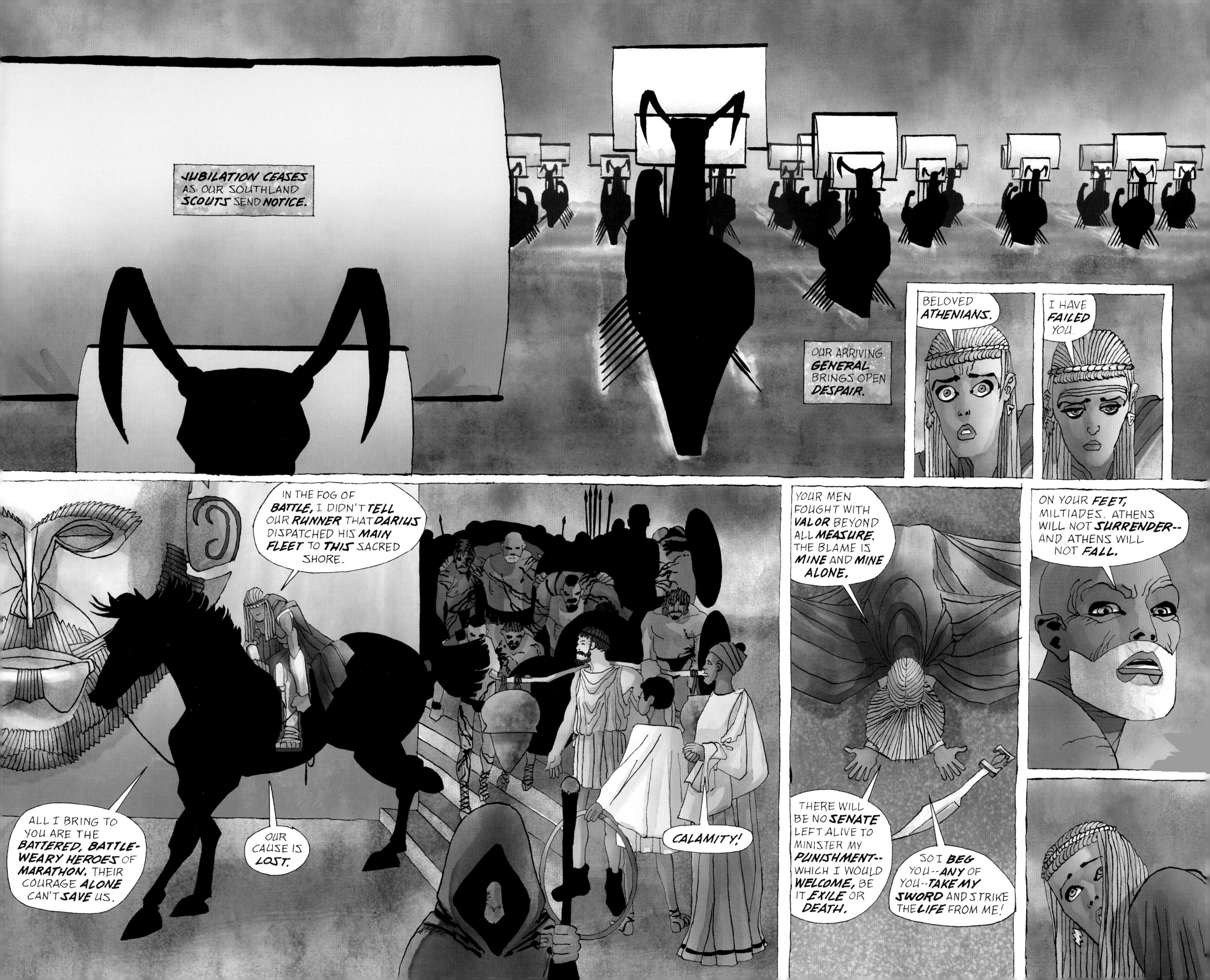

JUBILATION CEASES AS OUR SOUTHLAND SCOUTS SEND NOTICE.
OUR ARRIVING GENERAL BRINGS OPEN DESPAIR.
BELOVED ATHENIANS.
I HAVE FAILED YOU.
IN THE FOG OF BATTLE, I DIDN'T TELL OUR RUNNER THAT DARIUS DISPATCHED HIS MAIN FLEET TO THIS SACRED SHORE.
ALL I BRING TO YOU ARE THE BATTERED, BATTLE-WEARY HEROES OF MARATHON. THEIR COURAGE ALONE CAN'T SAVE US.
OUR CAUSE IS LOST.
CALAMITY!
YOUR MEN FOUGHT WITH VALOR BEYOND ALL MEASURE. THE BLAME IS MINE AND MINE ALONE.
THERE WILL BE NO SENATE LEFT ALIVE TO MINISTER MY PUNISHMENT-- WHICH I WOULD WELCOME, BE IT EXILE OR DEATH.
SO I BEG YOU--ANY OF YOU--TAKE MY SWORD AND STRIKE THE LIFE FROM ME!
ON YOUR FEET, MILTIADES. ATHENS WILL NOT SURRENDER-- AND ATHENS WILL NOT FALL.

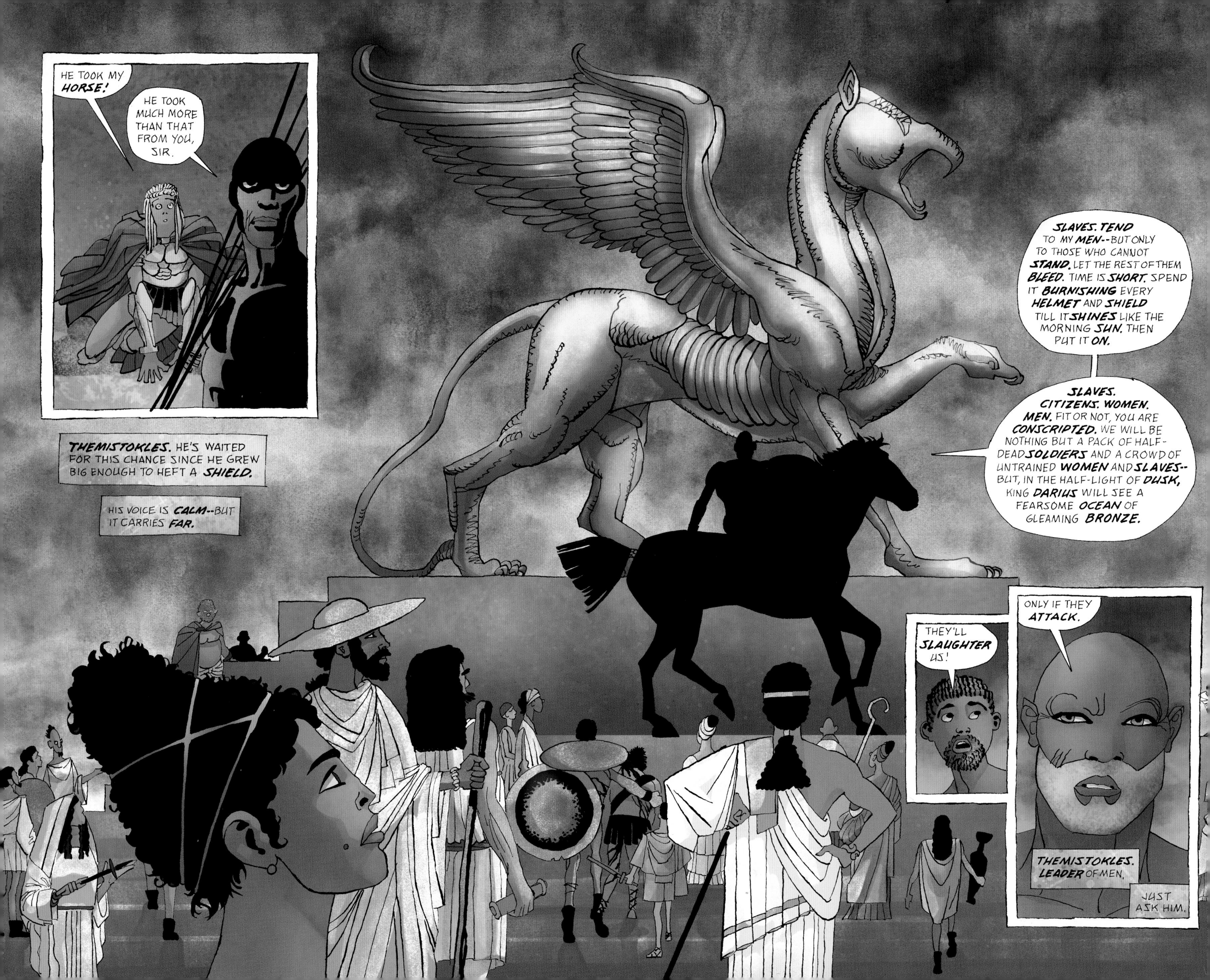

HE TOOK MY HORSE!
HE TOOK MUCH MORE THAN THAT FROM YOU, SIR.
THEMISTOKLES. HE'S WAITED FOR THIS CHANCE SINCE HE GREW BIG ENOUGH TO HEFT A SHIELD.
HIS VOICE IS CALM--BUT IT CARRIES FAR.
SLAVES. TEND TO MY MEN--BUT ONLY TO THOSE WHO CANNOT STAND. LET THE REST OF THEM BLEED. TIME IS SHORT. SPEND IT BURNISHING EVERY HELMET AND SHIELD TILL IT SHINES LIKE THE MORNING SUN. THEN PUT IT ON.
SLAVES. CITIZENS. WOMEN. MEN. FIT OR NOT, YOU ARE CONSCRIPTED. WE WILL BE NOTHING BUT A PACK OF HALF-DEAD SOLDIERS AND A CROWD OF UNTRAINED WOMEN AND SLAVES--BUT, IN THE HALF-LIGHT OF DUSK, KING DARIUS WILL SEE A FEARSOME OCEAN OF GLEAMING BRONZE.
THEY'LL SLAUGHTER US!
ONLY IF THEY ATTACK.
THEMISTOKLES. LEADER OF MEN.
JUST ASK HIM.

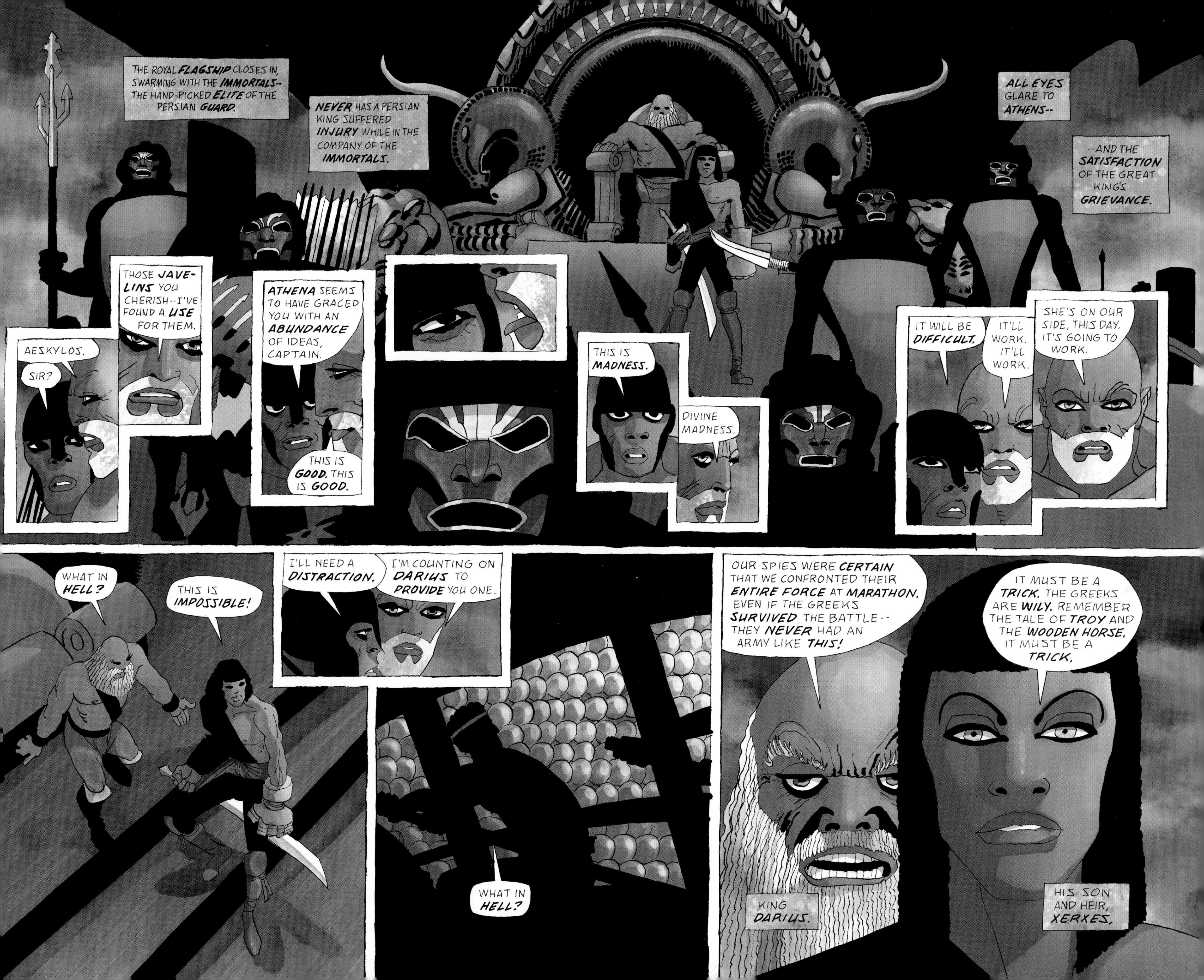
THE ROYAL FLAGSHIP CLOSES IN, SWARMING WITH THE IMMORTALS-- THE HAND-PICKED ELITE OF THE PERSIAN GUARD.
NEVER HAS A PERSIAN KING SUFFERED INJURY WHILE IN THE COMPANY OF THE IMMORTALS.
ALL EYES GLARE TO ATHENS--
--AND THE SATISFACTION OF THE GREAT KING'S GRIEVANCE.
AESKYLOS.
SIR?
THOSE JAVELINS YOU CHERISH--I'VE FOUND A USE FOR THEM.
ATHENA SEEMS TO HAVE GRACED YOU WITH AN ABUNDANCE OF IDEAS, CAPTAIN.
THIS IS GOOD. THIS IS GOOD.
THIS IS MADNESS.
DIVINE MADNESS.
IT WILL BE DIFFICULT.
IT'LL WORK. IT'LL WORK.
SHE'S ON OUR SIDE, THIS DAY. IT'S GOING TO WORK.
WHAT IN HELL?
THIS IS IMPOSSIBLE!
I'LL NEED A DISTRACTION.
I'M COUNTING ON DARIUS TO PROVIDE YOU ONE.
WHAT IN HELL?
OUR SPIES WERE CERTAIN THAT WE CONFRONTED THEIR ENTIRE FORCE AT MARATHON. EVEN IF THE GREEKS SURVIVED THE BATTLE-- THEY NEVER HAD AN ARMY LIKE THIS!
KING DARIUS.
IT MUST BE A TRICK. THE GREEKS ARE WILY. REMEMBER THE TALE OF TROY AND THE WOODEN HORSE. IT MUST BE A TRICK.
HIS SON AND HEIR, XERXES.

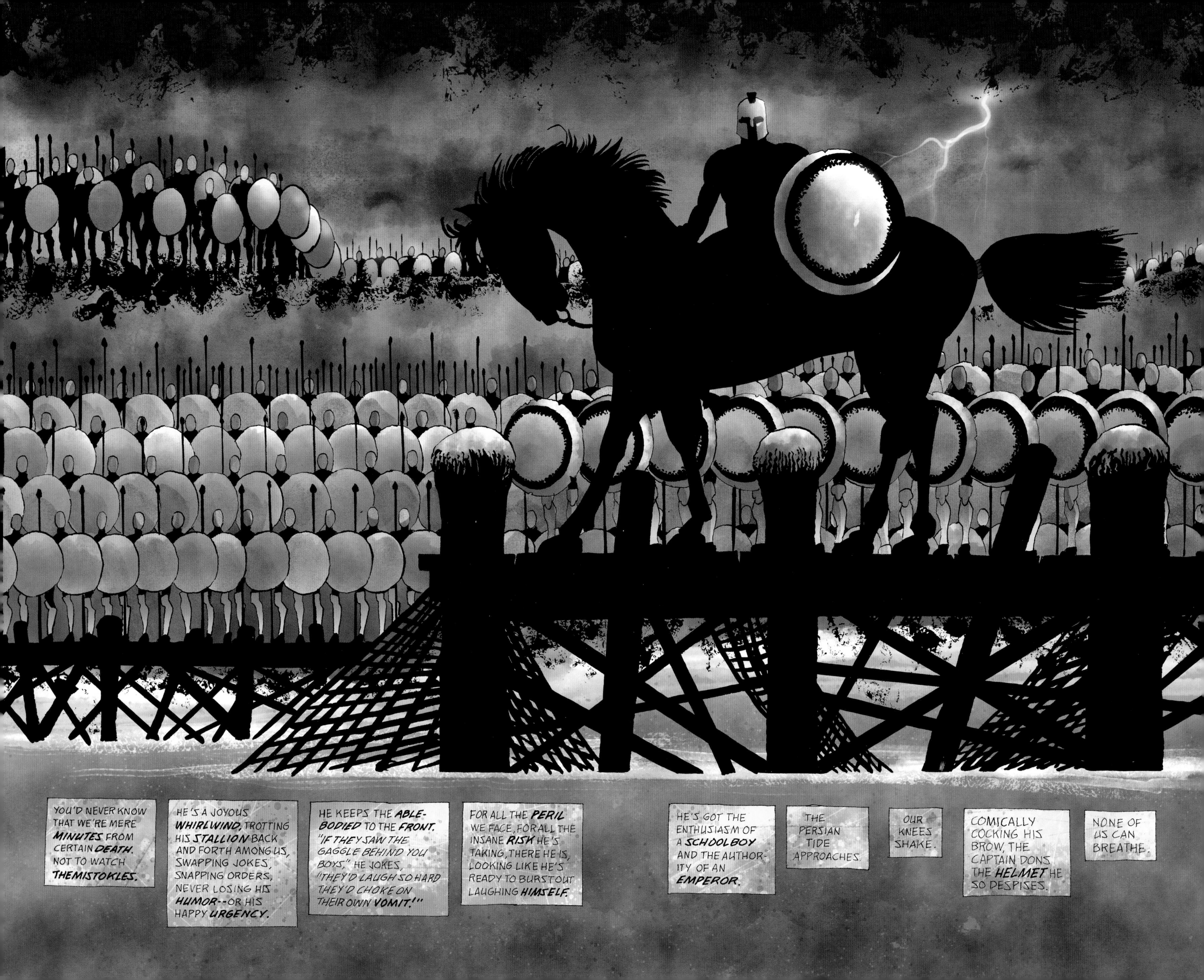
YOU'D NEVER KNOW THAT WE'RE MERE MINUTES FROM CERTAIN DEATH. NOT TO WATCH THEMISTOKLES.
HE'S A JOYOUS WHIRLWIND, TROTTING HIS STALLION BACK AND FORTH AMONG US, SWAPPING JOKES, SNAPPING ORDERS, NEVER LOSING HIS HUMOR--OR HIS HAPPY URGENCY.
HE KEEPS THE ABLE-BODIED TO THE FRONT. "IF THEY SAW THE GAGGLE BEHIND YOU BOYS," HE JOKES, "THEY'D LAUGH SO HARD THEY'D CHOKE ON THEIR OWN VOMIT!"
FOR ALL THE PERIL WE FACE, FOR ALL THE INSANE RISK HE'S TAKING, THERE HE IS, LOOKING LIKE HE'S READY TO BURST OUT LAUGHING HIMSELF.
HE'S GOT THE ENTHUSIASM OF A SCHOOLBOY AND THE AUTHORITY OF AN EMPEROR.
THE PERSIAN TIDE APPROACHES.
OUR KNEES SHAKE.
COMICALLY COCKING HIS BROW, THE CAPTAIN DONS THE HELMET HE SO DESPISES.
NONE OF US CAN BREATHE.

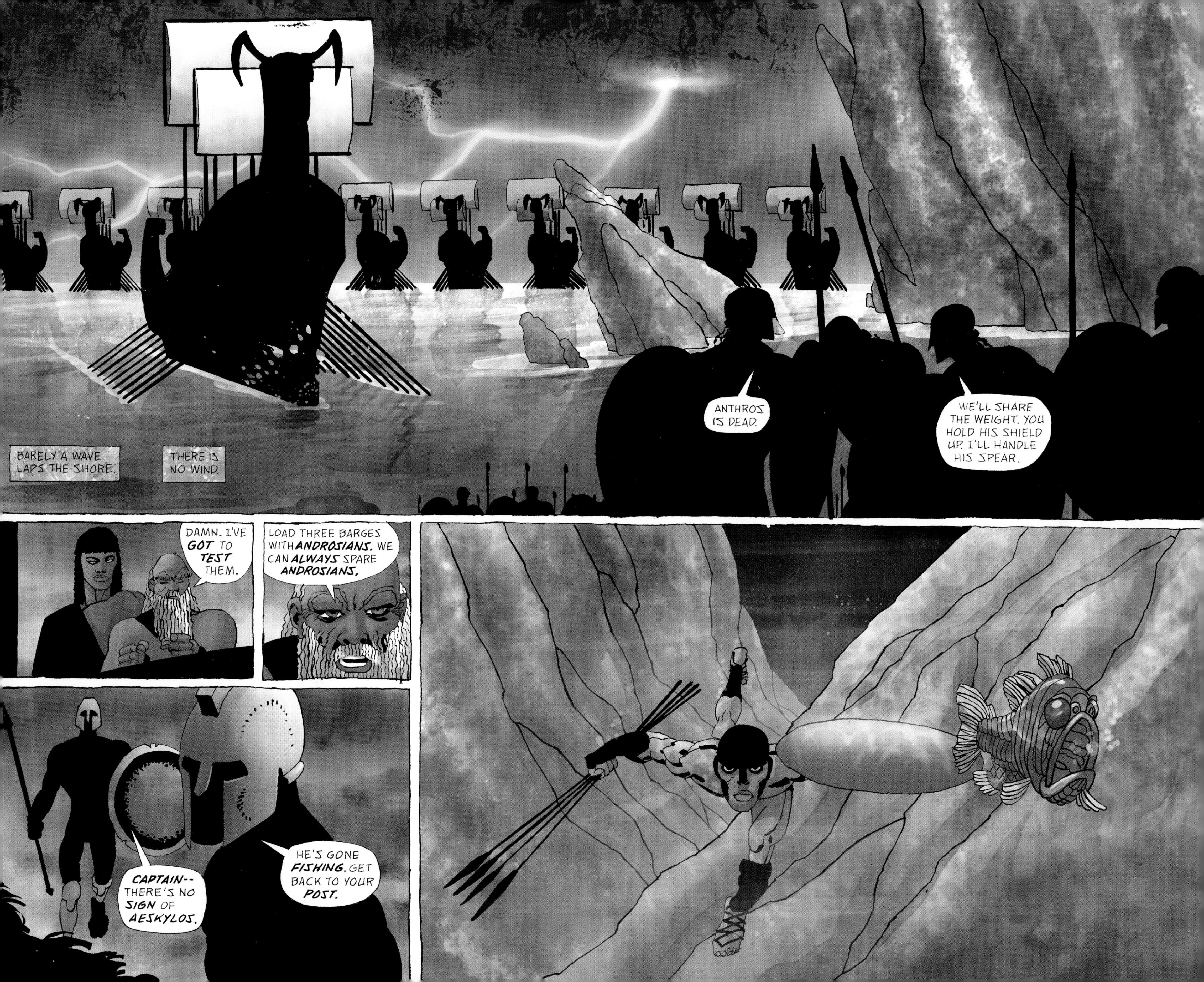
BARELY A WAVE LAPS THE SHORE.
THERE IS NO WIND.
ANTHROS IS DEAD.
WE'LL SHARE THE WEIGHT. YOU HOLD HIS SHIELD UP. I'LL HANDLE HIS SPEAR.
DAMN. I'VE GOT TO TEST THEM.
LOAD THREE BARGES WITH ANDROSIANS. WE CAN ALWAYS SPARE ANDROSIANS.
CAPTAIN-- THERE'S NO SIGN OF AESKYLOS.
HE'S GONE FISHING. GET BACK TO YOUR POST.

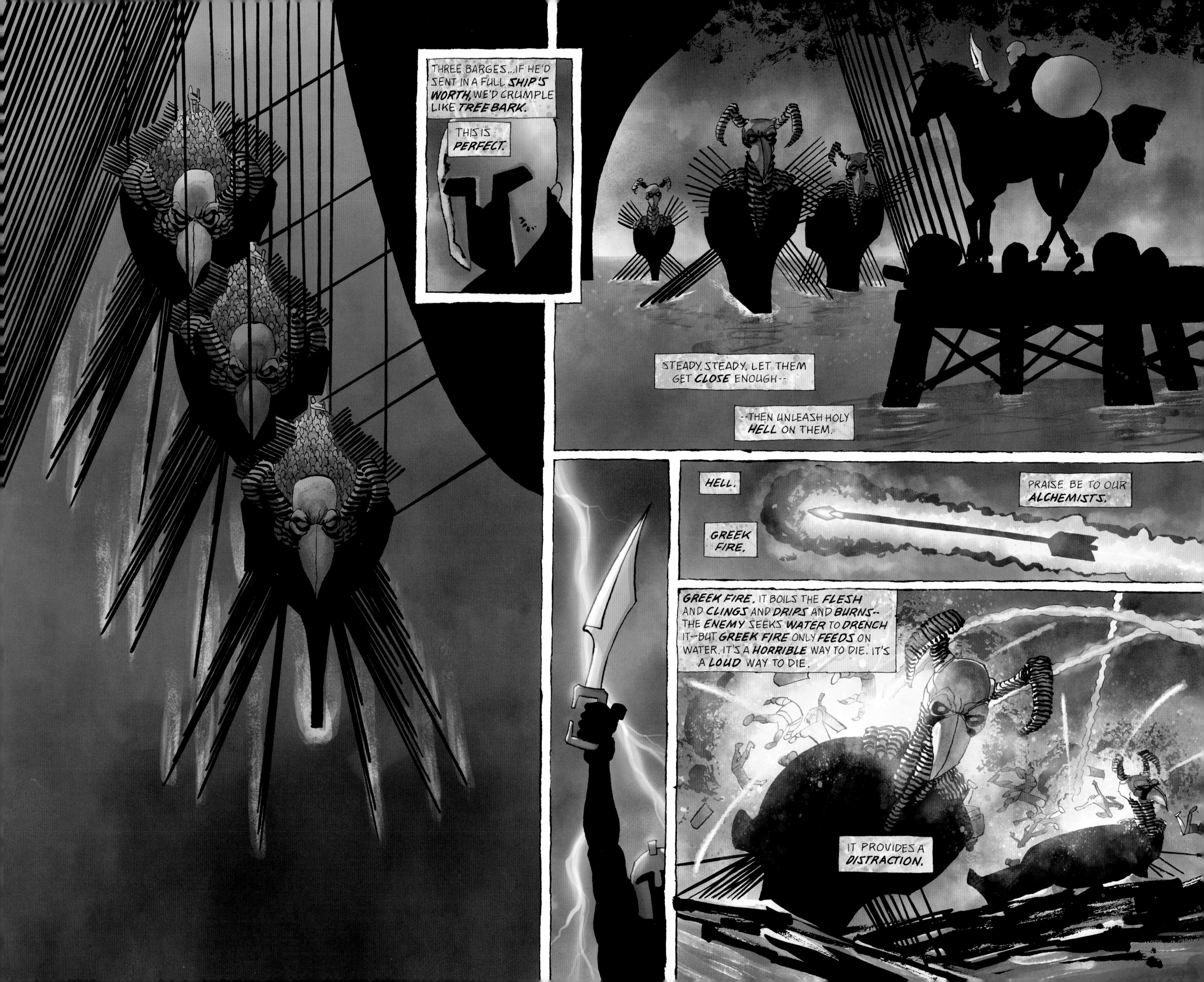
THREE BARGES...IF HE'D SENT IN A FULL SHIP'S WORTH, WE'D CRUMPLE LIKE TREE BARK.
THIS IS PERFECT.
STEADY, STEADY. LET THEM GET CLOSE ENOUGH--
--THEN UNLEASH HOLY HELL ON THEM.
HELL.
GREEK FIRE.
PRAISE BE TO OUR ALCHEMISTS.
GREEK FIRE. IT BOILS THE FLESH AND CLINGS AND DRIPS AND BURNS--THE ENEMY SEEKS WATER TO DRENCH IT--BUT GREEK FIRE ONLY FEEDS ON WATER. IT'S A HORRIBLE WAY TO DIE. IT'S A LOUD WAY TO DIE.
IT PROVIDES A DISTRACTION.

ALL PERSIAN EYES FIX *FORWARD*.

ABOVE AND TO THE SIDE, AESKYLOS FINDS HIS *PERCH*.

MAY *ARTEMIS* GUIDE HIS *HAND*.

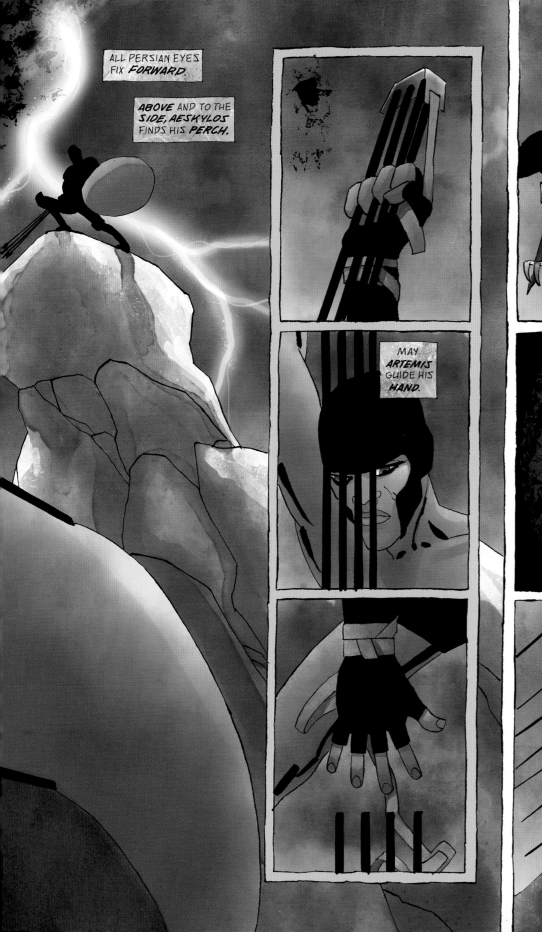

SHE *DOES*.

KUNCH

KUNCH

THUNK

KUNCH

FATHER!

THE WAR IS LOST, XERXES. DON'T LET ME DIE HERE. TAKE ME HOME.

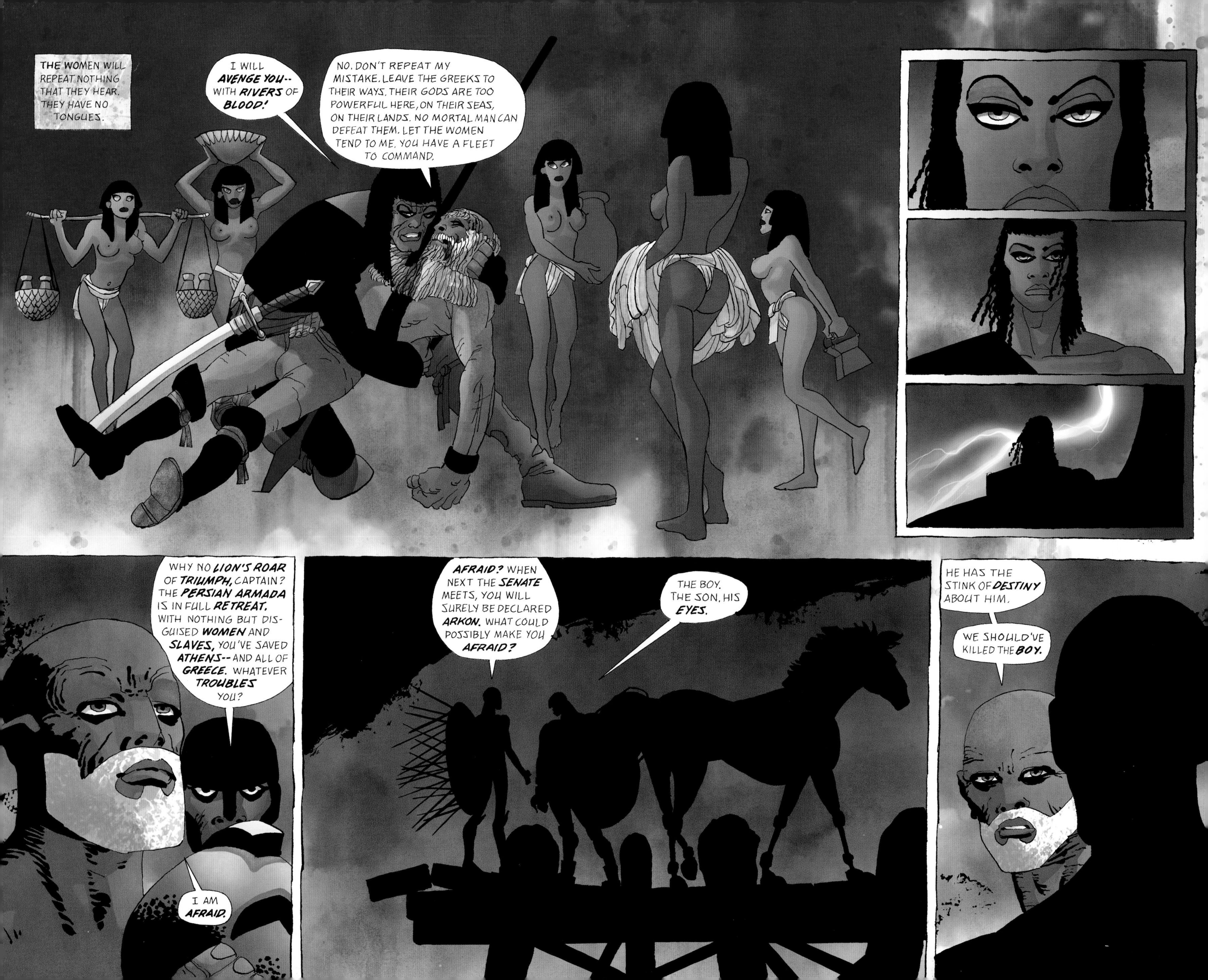
THE WOMEN WILL REPEAT NOTHING THAT THEY HEAR. THEY HAVE NO TONGUES.
I WILL AVENGE YOU-- WITH RIVERS OF BLOOD!
NO. DON'T REPEAT MY MISTAKE. LEAVE THE GREEKS TO THEIR WAYS. THEIR GODS ARE TOO POWERFUL HERE, ON THEIR SEAS, ON THEIR LANDS. NO MORTAL MAN CAN DEFEAT THEM. LET THE WOMEN TEND TO ME. YOU HAVE A FLEET TO COMMAND.
WHY NO LION'S ROAR OF TRIUMPH, CAPTAIN? THE PERSIAN ARMADA IS IN FULL RETREAT. WITH NOTHING BUT DISGUISED WOMEN AND SLAVES, YOU'VE SAVED ATHENS-- AND ALL OF GREECE. WHATEVER TROUBLES YOU?
I AM AFRAID.
AFRAID? WHEN NEXT THE SENATE MEETS, YOU WILL SURELY BE DECLARED ARKON. WHAT COULD POSSIBLY MAKE YOU AFRAID?
THE BOY. THE SON. HIS EYES.
HE HAS THE STINK OF DESTINY ABOUT HIM.
WE SHOULD'VE KILLED THE BOY.

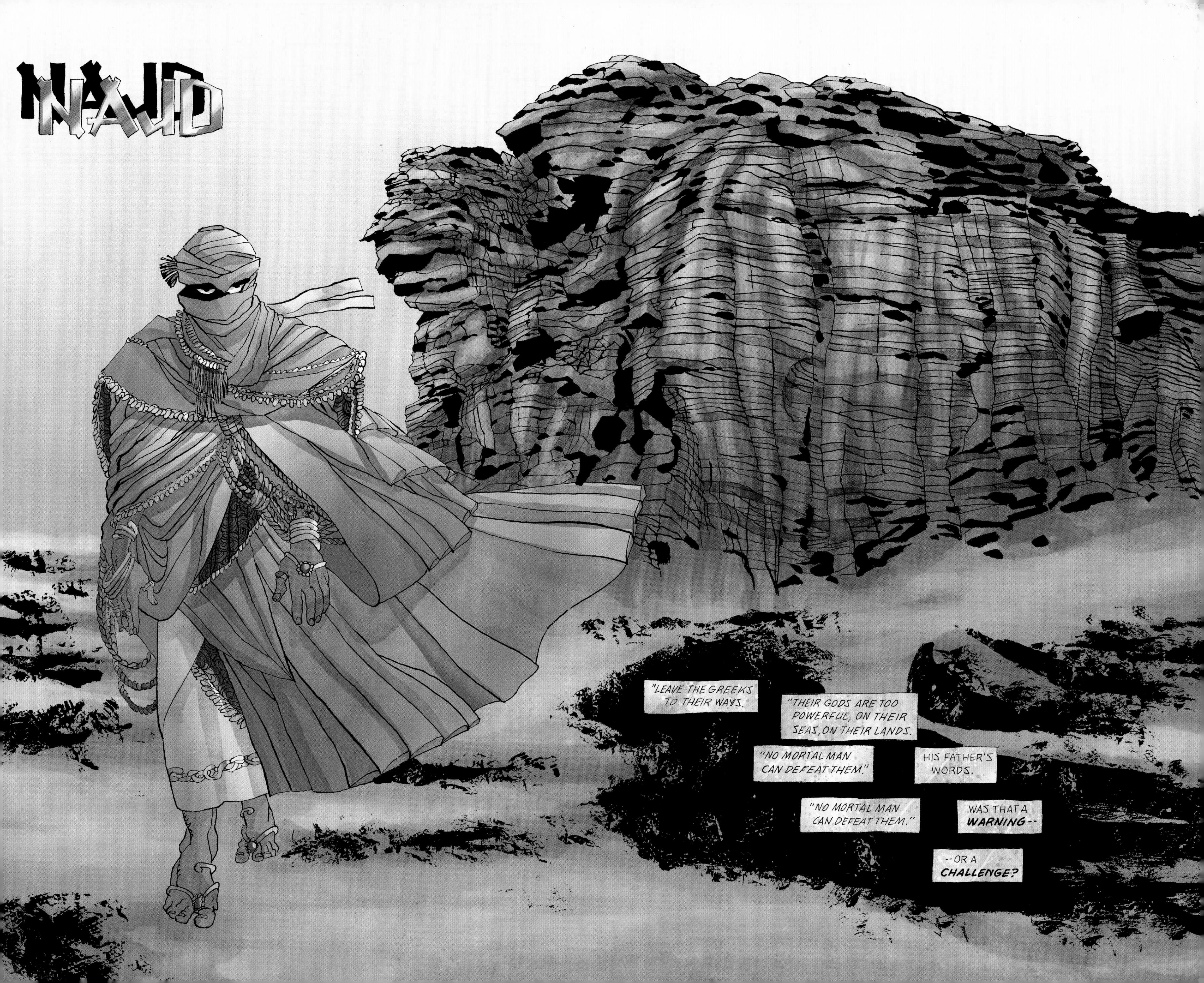
NAJD
"LEAVE THE GREEKS TO THEIR WAYS.
"THEIR GODS ARE TOO POWERFUL, ON THEIR SEAS, ON THEIR LANDS.
"NO MORTAL MAN CAN DEFEAT THEM."
HIS FATHER'S WORDS.
"NO MORTAL MAN CAN DEFEAT THEM."
WAS THAT A WARNING--
--OR A CHALLENGE?

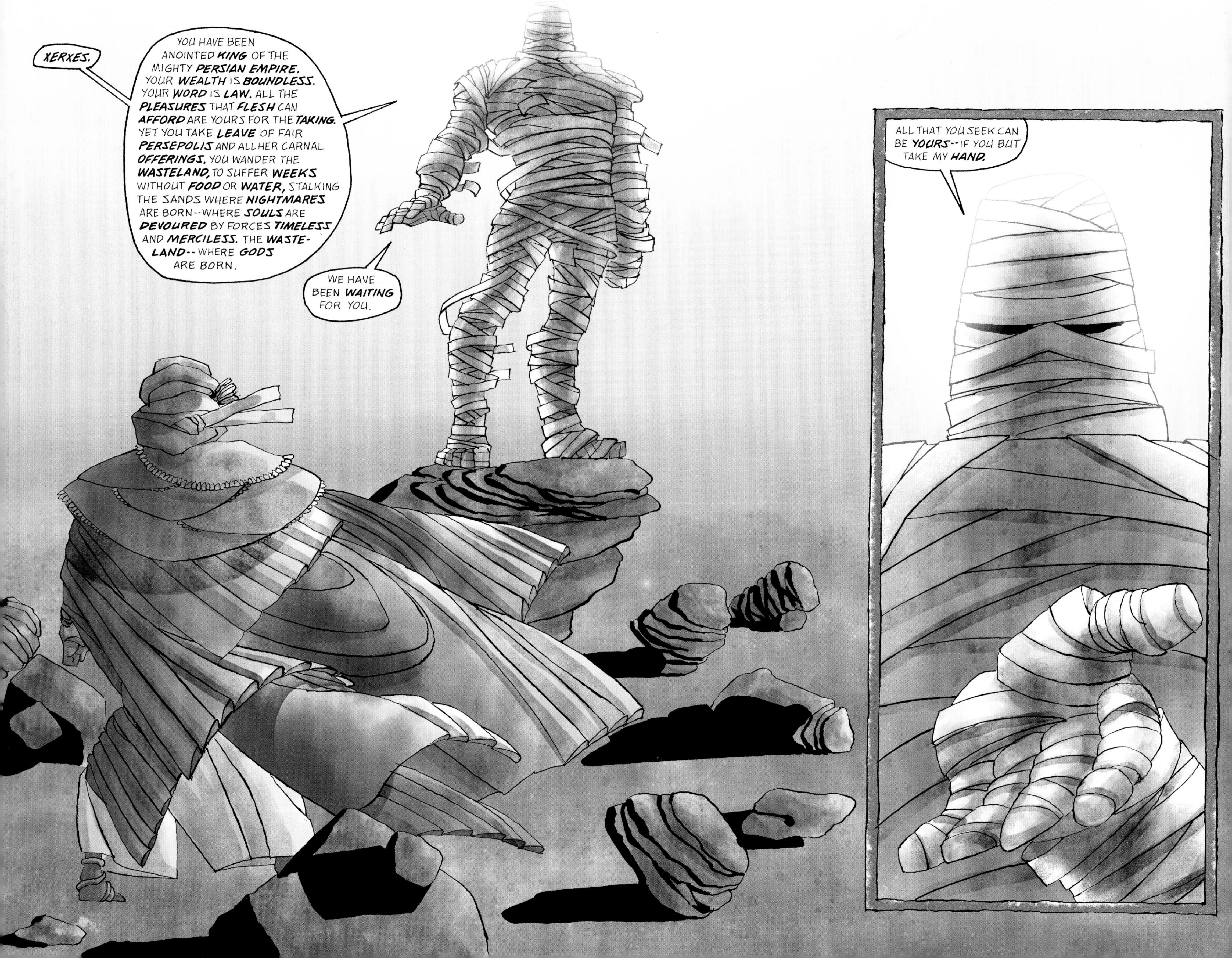
XERXES.
YOU HAVE BEEN ANOINTED KING OF THE MIGHTY PERSIAN EMPIRE. YOUR WEALTH IS BOUNDLESS. YOUR WORD IS LAW. ALL THE PLEASURES THAT FLESH CAN AFFORD ARE YOURS FOR THE TAKING. YET YOU TAKE LEAVE OF FAIR PERSEPOLIS AND ALL HER CARNAL OFFERINGS. YOU WANDER THE WASTELAND, TO SUFFER WEEKS WITHOUT FOOD OR WATER, STALKING THE SANDS WHERE NIGHTMARES ARE BORN--WHERE SOULS ARE DEVOURED BY FORCES TIMELESS AND MERCILESS. THE WASTE-LAND-- WHERE GODS ARE BORN.
WE HAVE BEEN WAITING FOR YOU.
ALL THAT YOU SEEK CAN BE YOURS-- IF YOU BUT TAKE MY HAND.

CHAPTER THREE

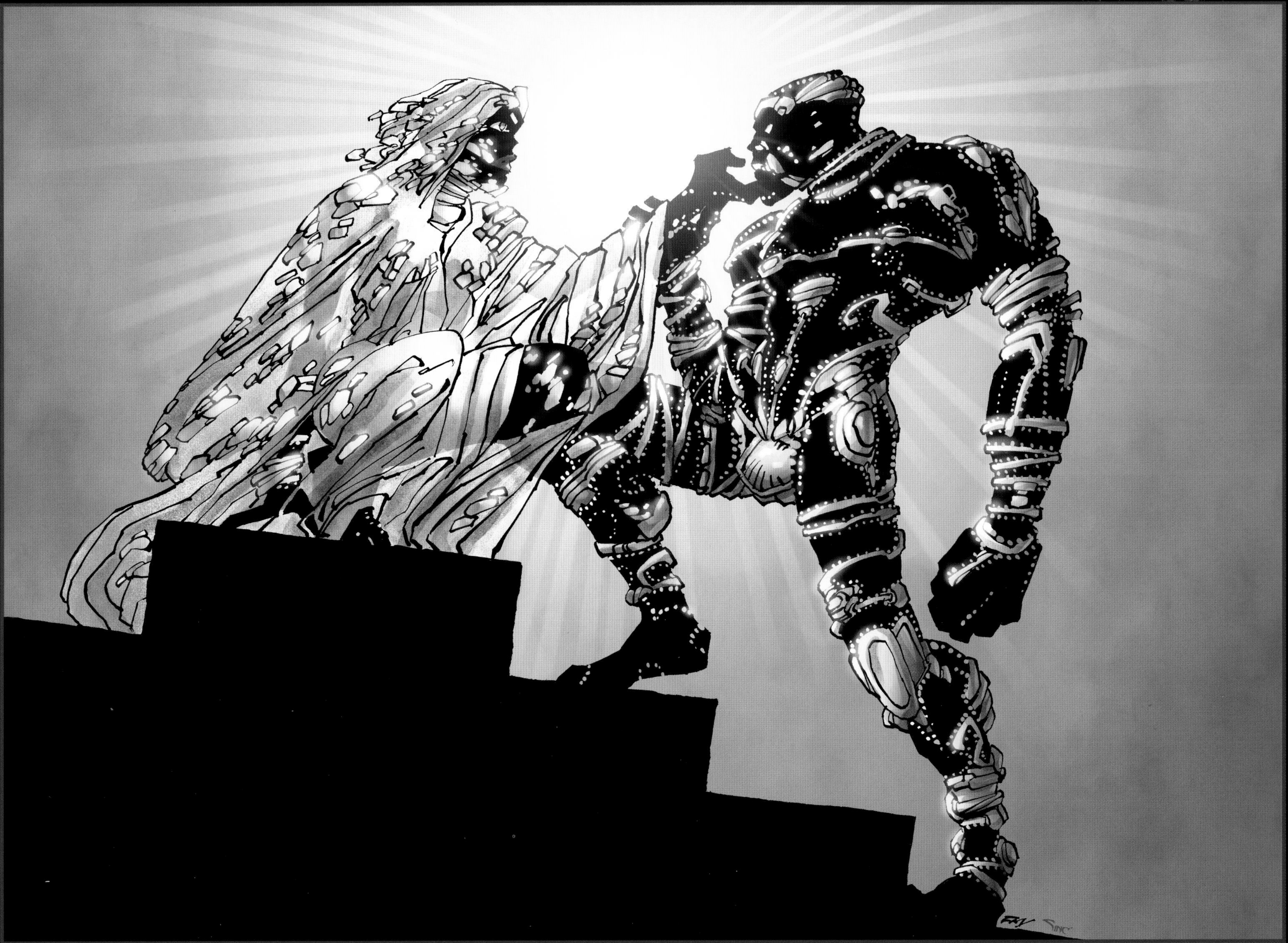

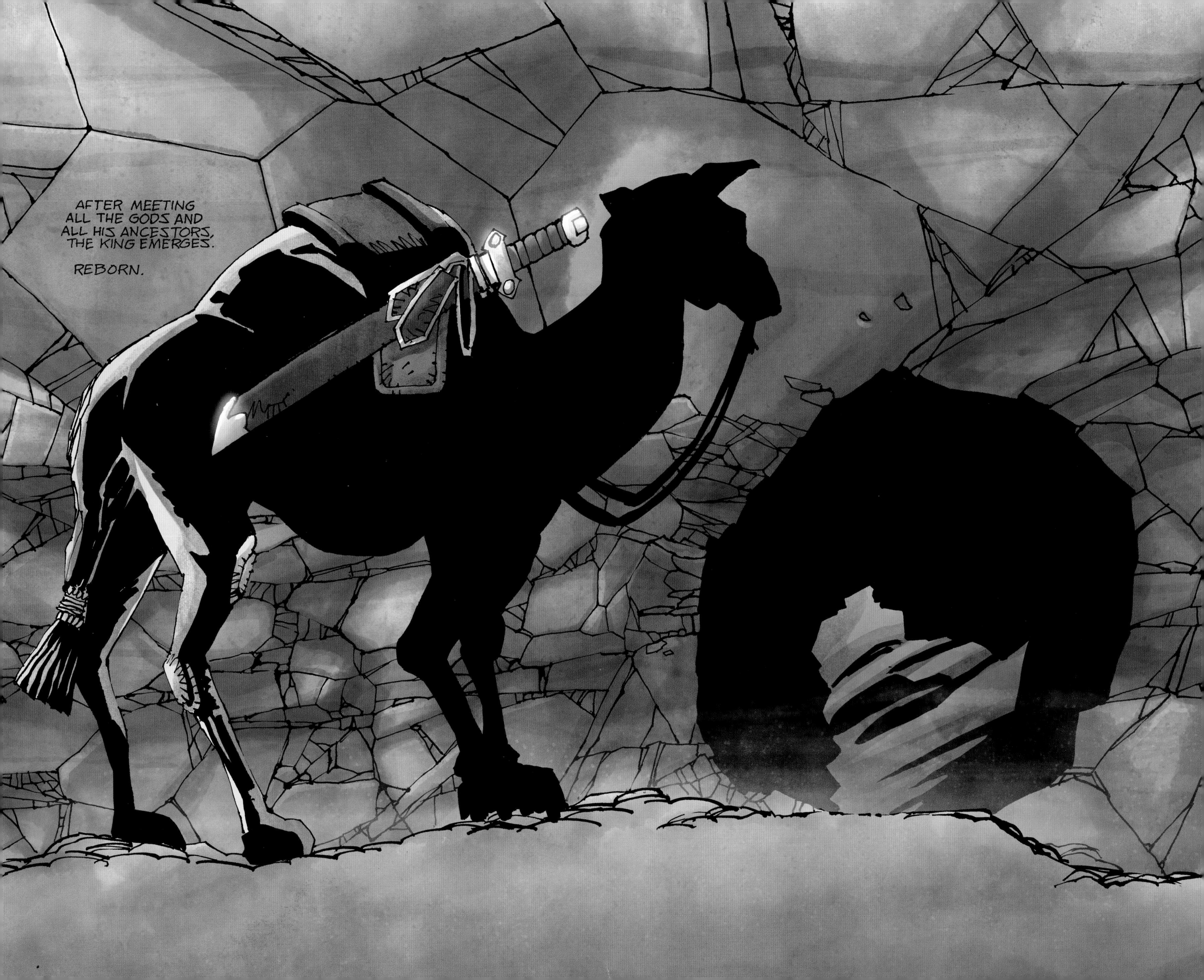
AFTER MEETING ALL THE GODS AND ALL HIS ANCESTORS, THE KING EMERGES.
REBORN.

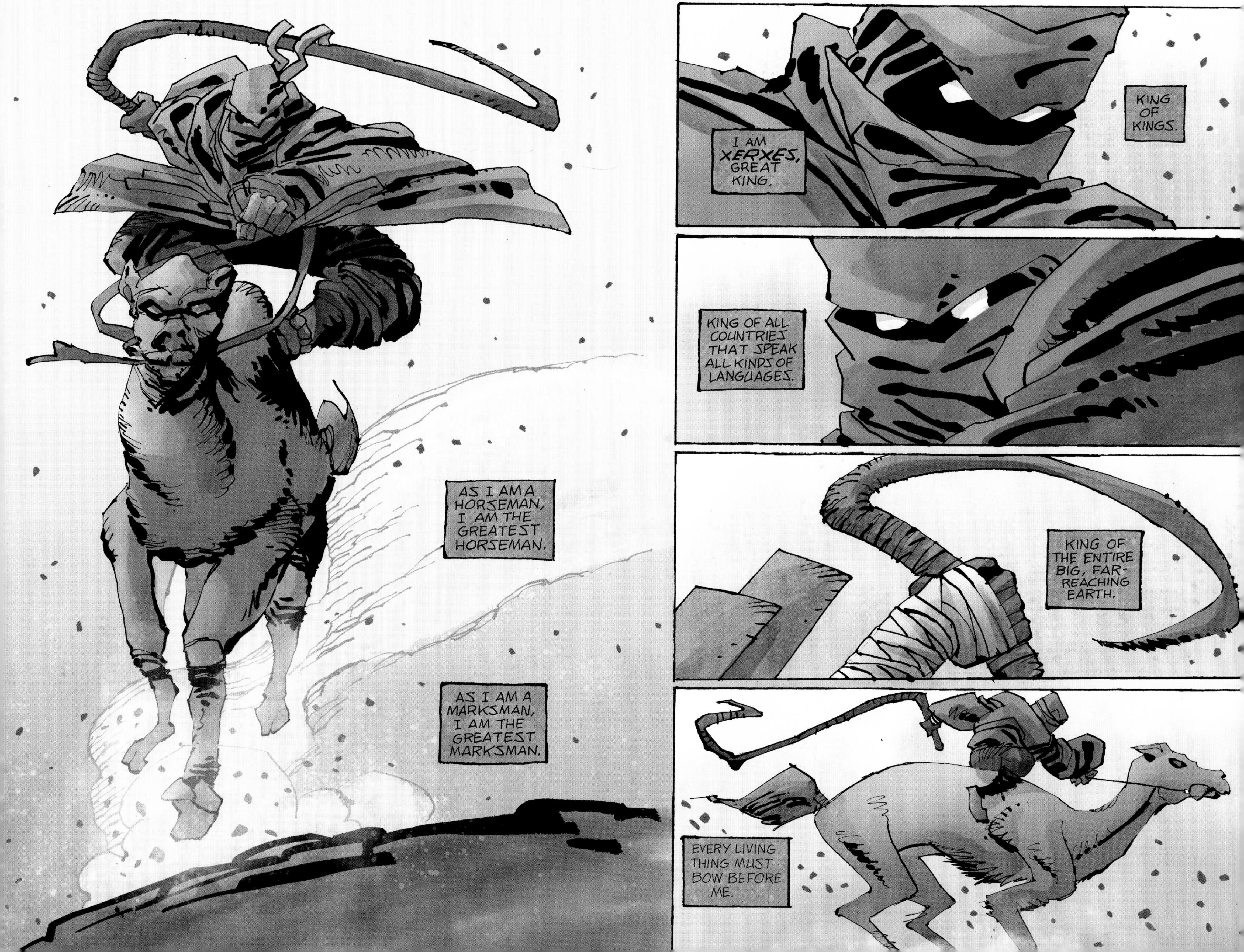
AS I AM A HORSEMAN, I AM THE GREATEST HORSEMAN.
AS I AM A MARKSMAN, I AM THE GREATEST MARKSMAN.
I AM XERXES, GREAT KING.
KING OF KINGS.
KING OF ALL COUNTRIES THAT SPEAK ALL KINDS OF LANGUAGES.
KING OF THE ENTIRE BIG, FAR-REACHING EARTH.
EVERY LIVING THING MUST BOW BEFORE ME.

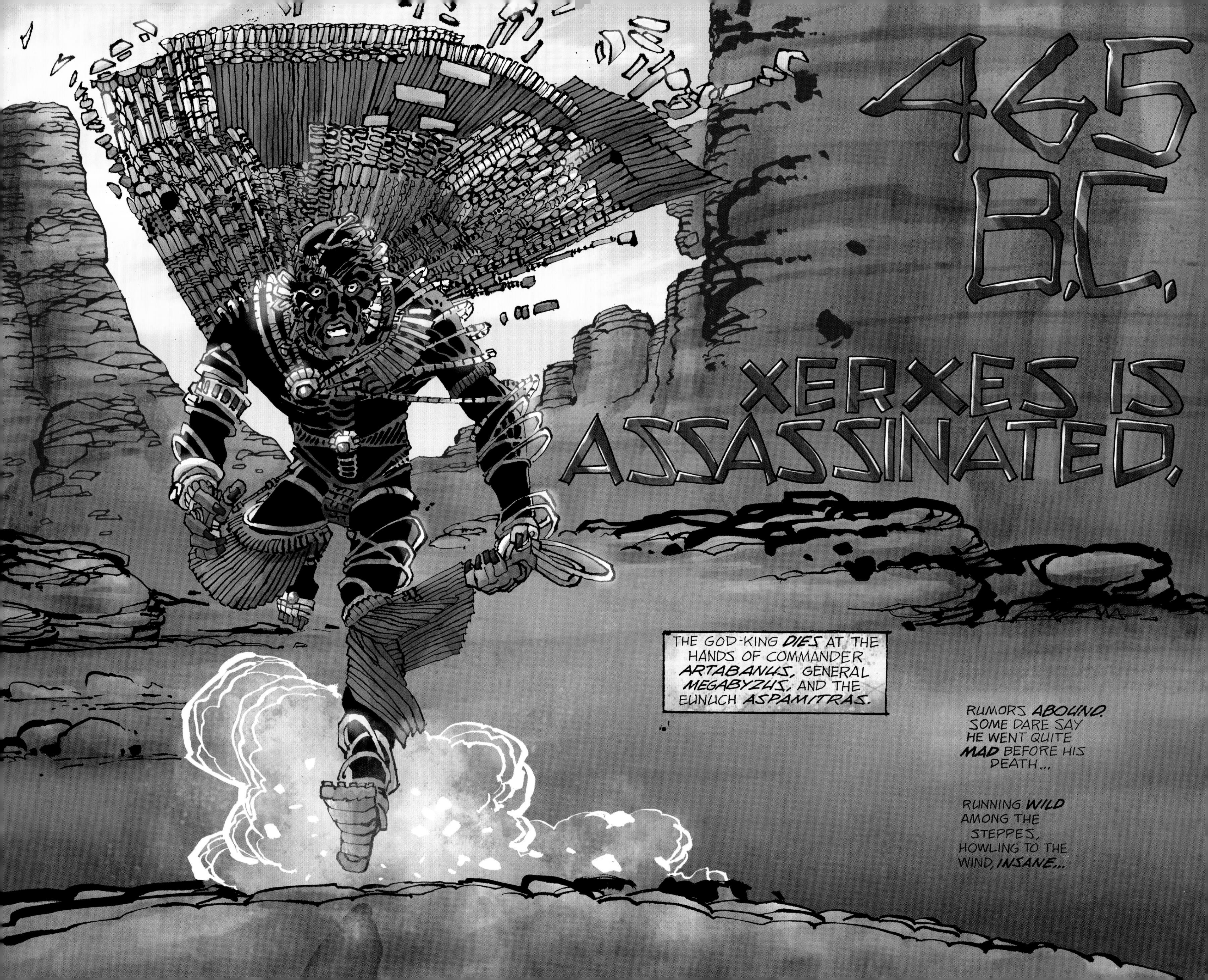
465 B.C.
XERXES IS ASSASSINATED.
THE GOD-KING DIES AT THE HANDS OF COMMANDER ARTABANUS, GENERAL MEGABYZUS, AND THE EUNUCH ASPAMITRAS.
RUMORS ABOUND. SOME DARE SAY HE WENT QUITE MAD BEFORE HIS DEATH...
RUNNING WILD AMONG THE STEPPES, HOWLING TO THE WIND, INSANE...

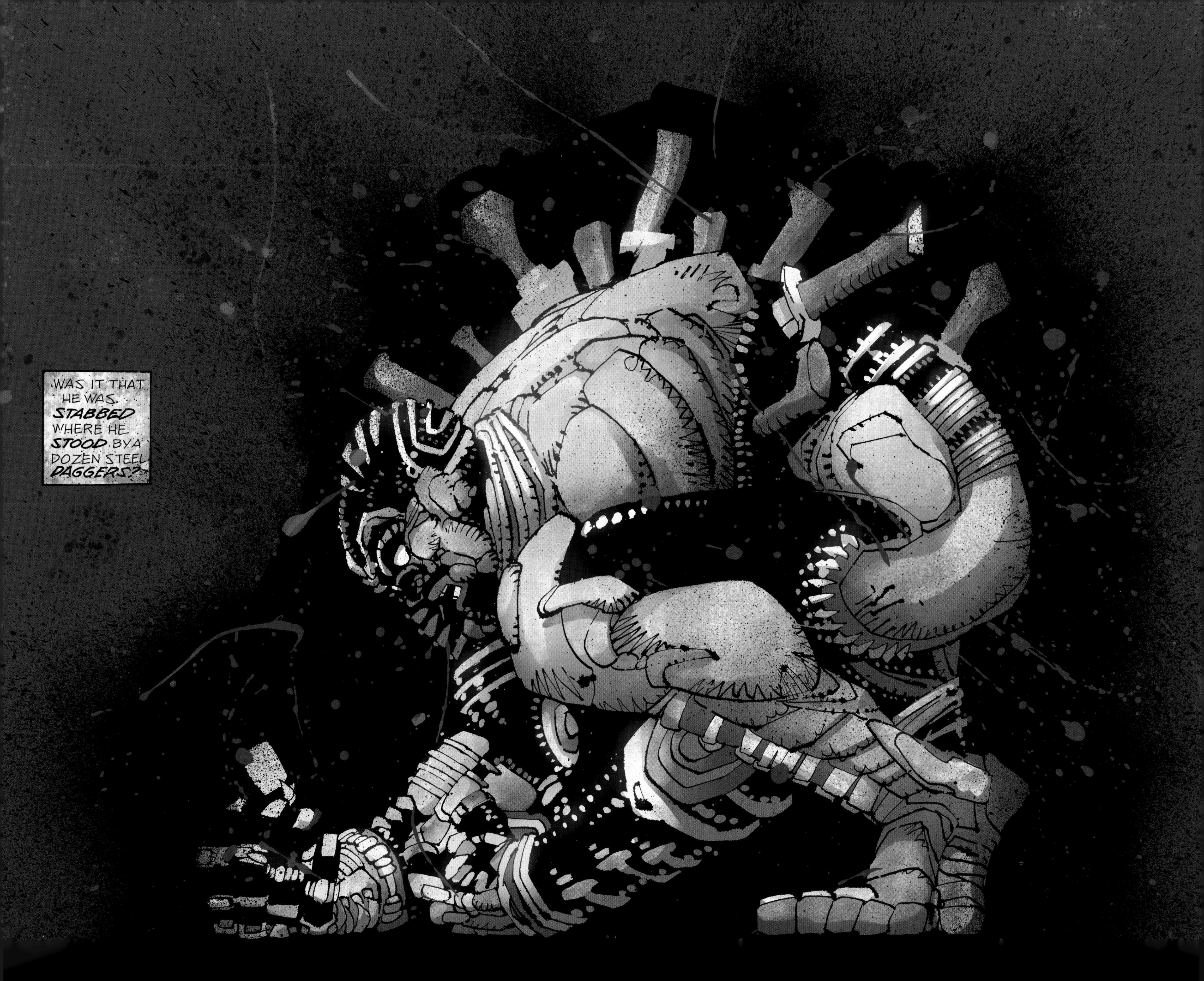
WAS IT THAT HE WAS STABBED WHERE HE STOOD BY A DOZEN STEEL DAGGERS?

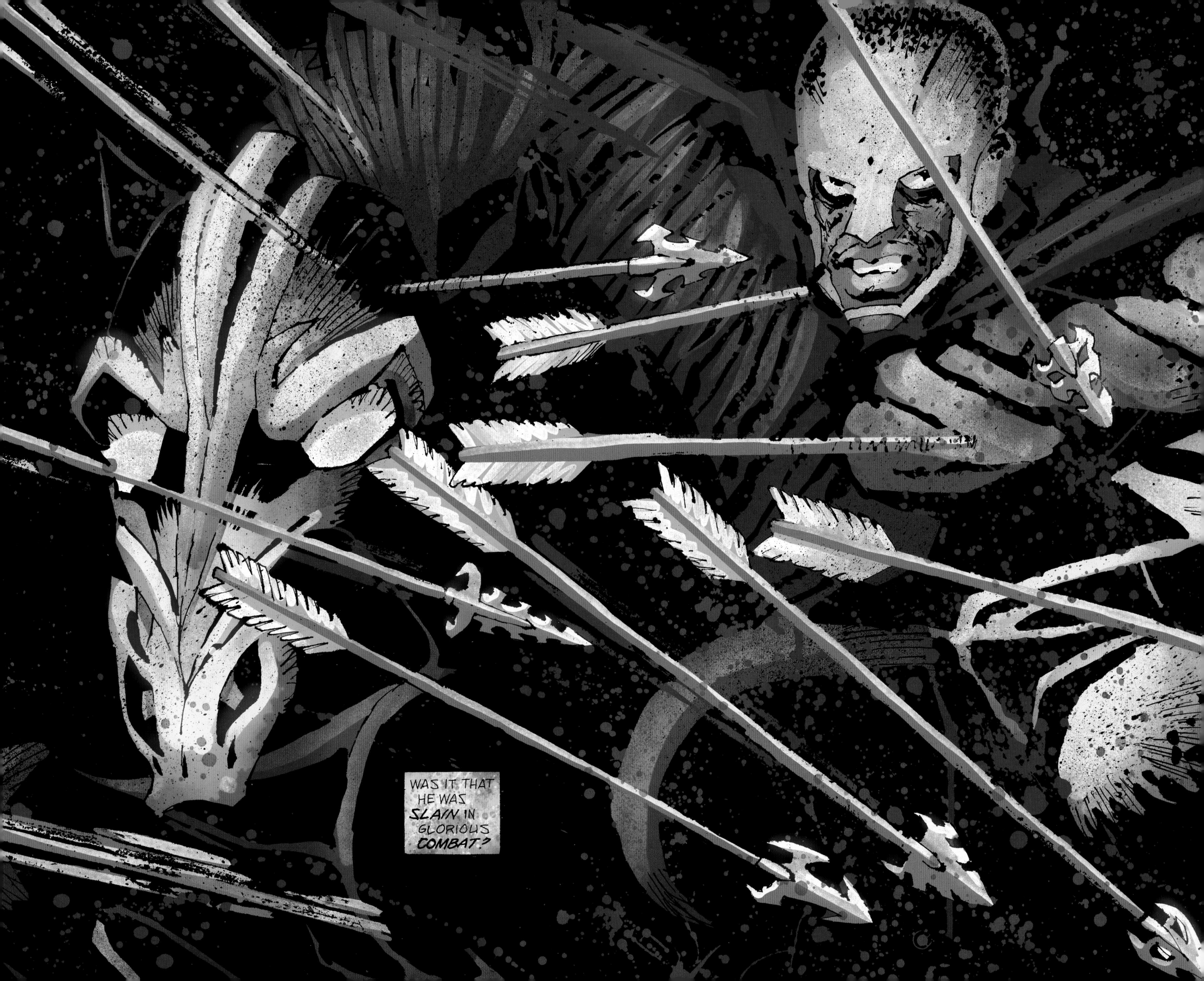
WAS IT THAT HE WAS SLAIN IN GLORIOUS COMBAT?

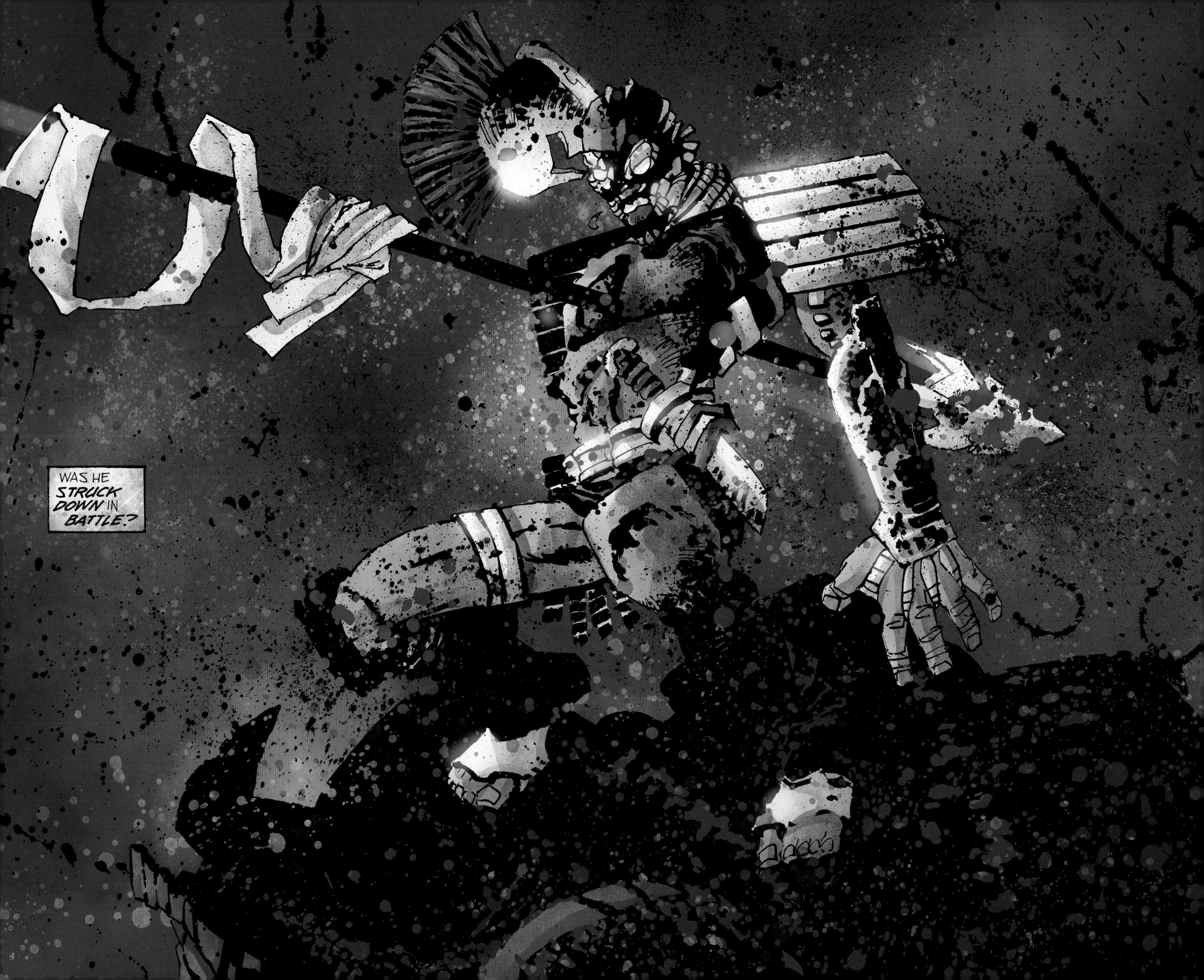
WAS HE STRUCK DOWN IN BATTLE?

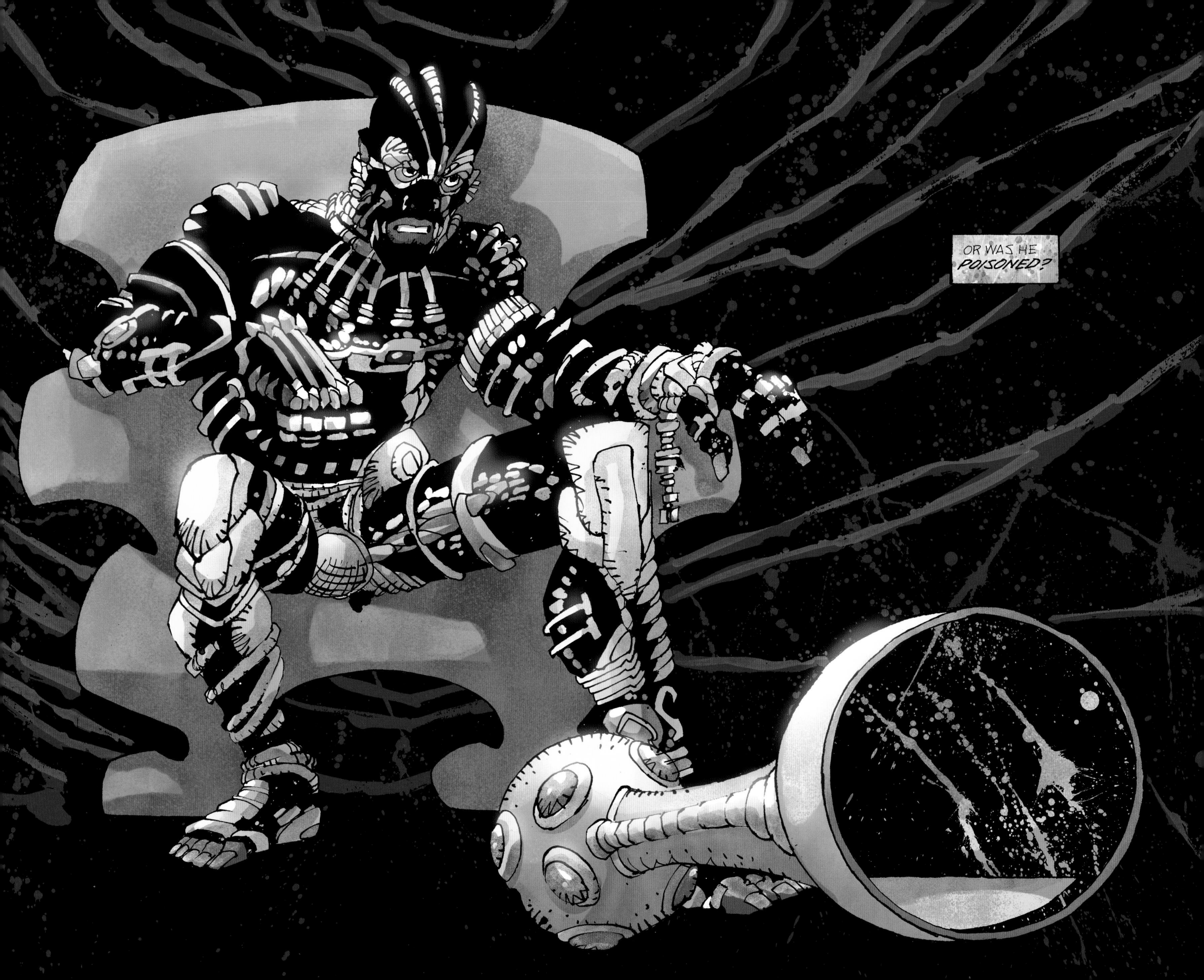
OR WAS HE
POISONED?

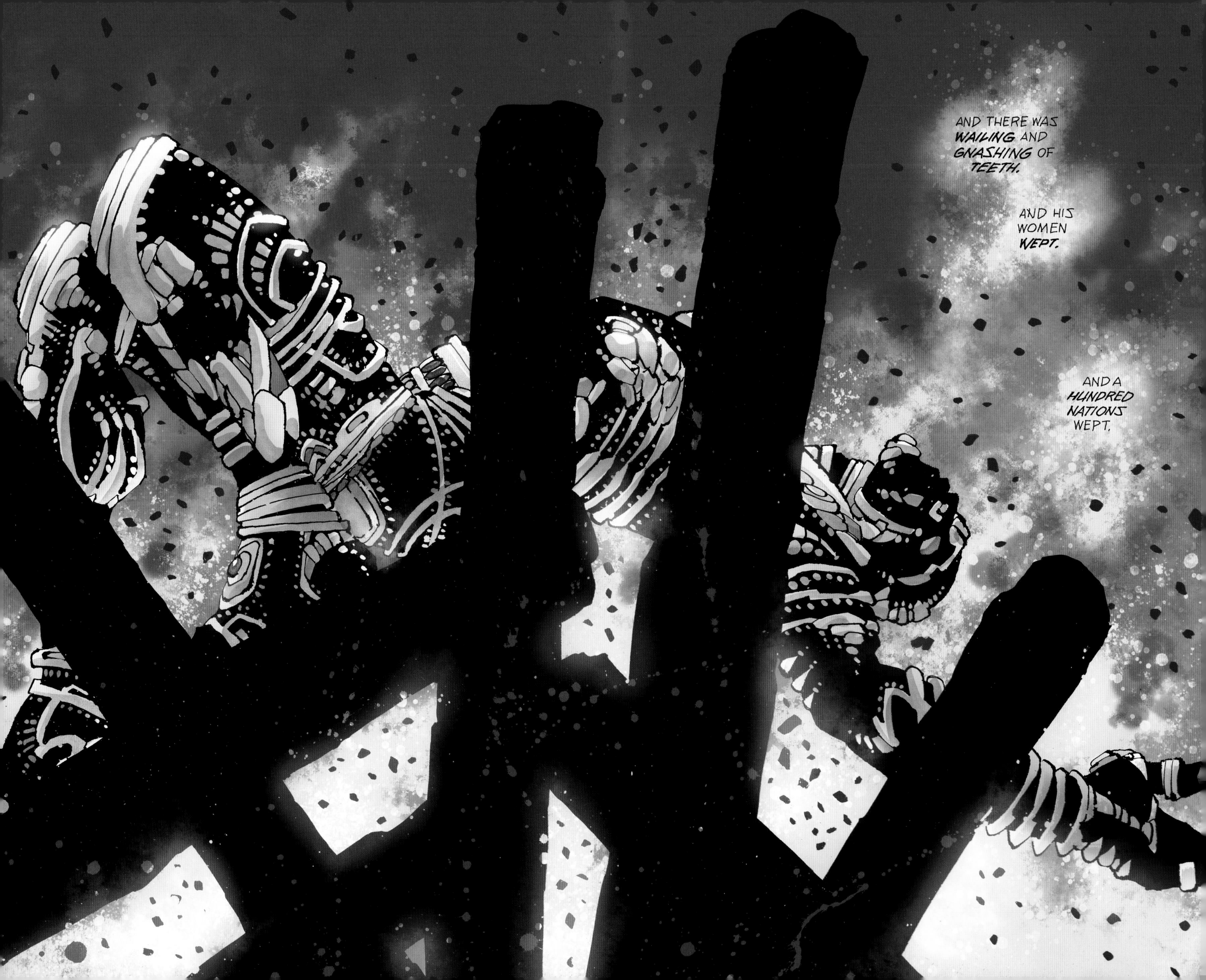
AND THERE WAS WAILING AND GNASHING OF TEETH.
AND HIS WOMEN WEPT.
AND A HUNDRED NATIONS WEPT.

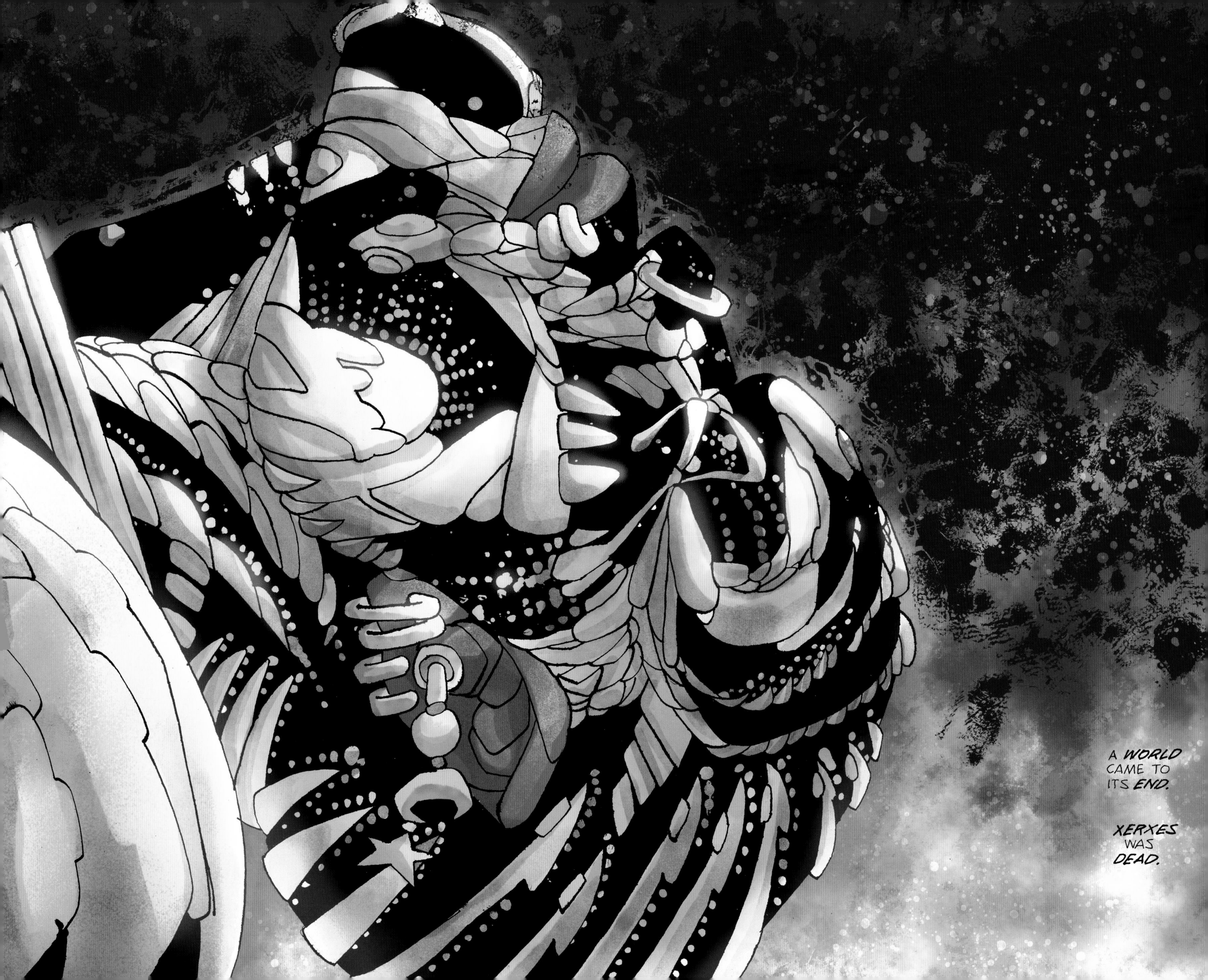
A WORLD CAME TO ITS END.
XERXES WAS DEAD.

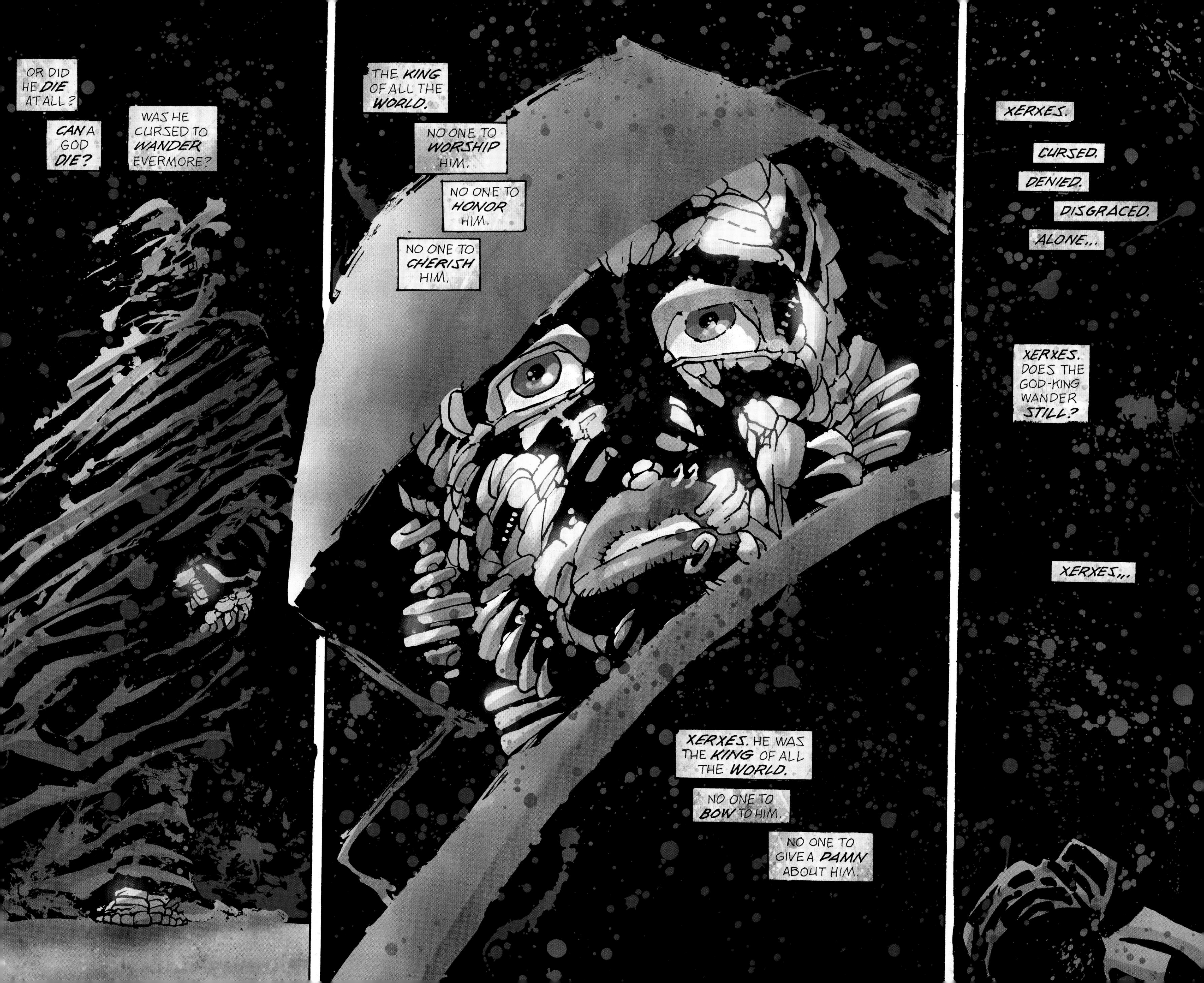
OR DID HE *DIE* AT ALL?
CAN A GOD *DIE?*
WAS HE CURSED TO *WANDER* EVERMORE?
THE *KING* OF ALL THE *WORLD.*
NO ONE TO *WORSHIP* HIM.
NO ONE TO *HONOR* HIM.
NO ONE TO *CHERISH* HIM.
XERXES. HE WAS THE *KING* OF ALL THE *WORLD.*
NO ONE TO *BOW* TO HIM.
NO ONE TO GIVE A *DAMN* ABOUT HIM.
XERXES.
CURSED.
DENIED.
DISGRACED.
ALONE...
XERXES. DOES THE GOD-KING WANDER *STILL?*
XERXES...

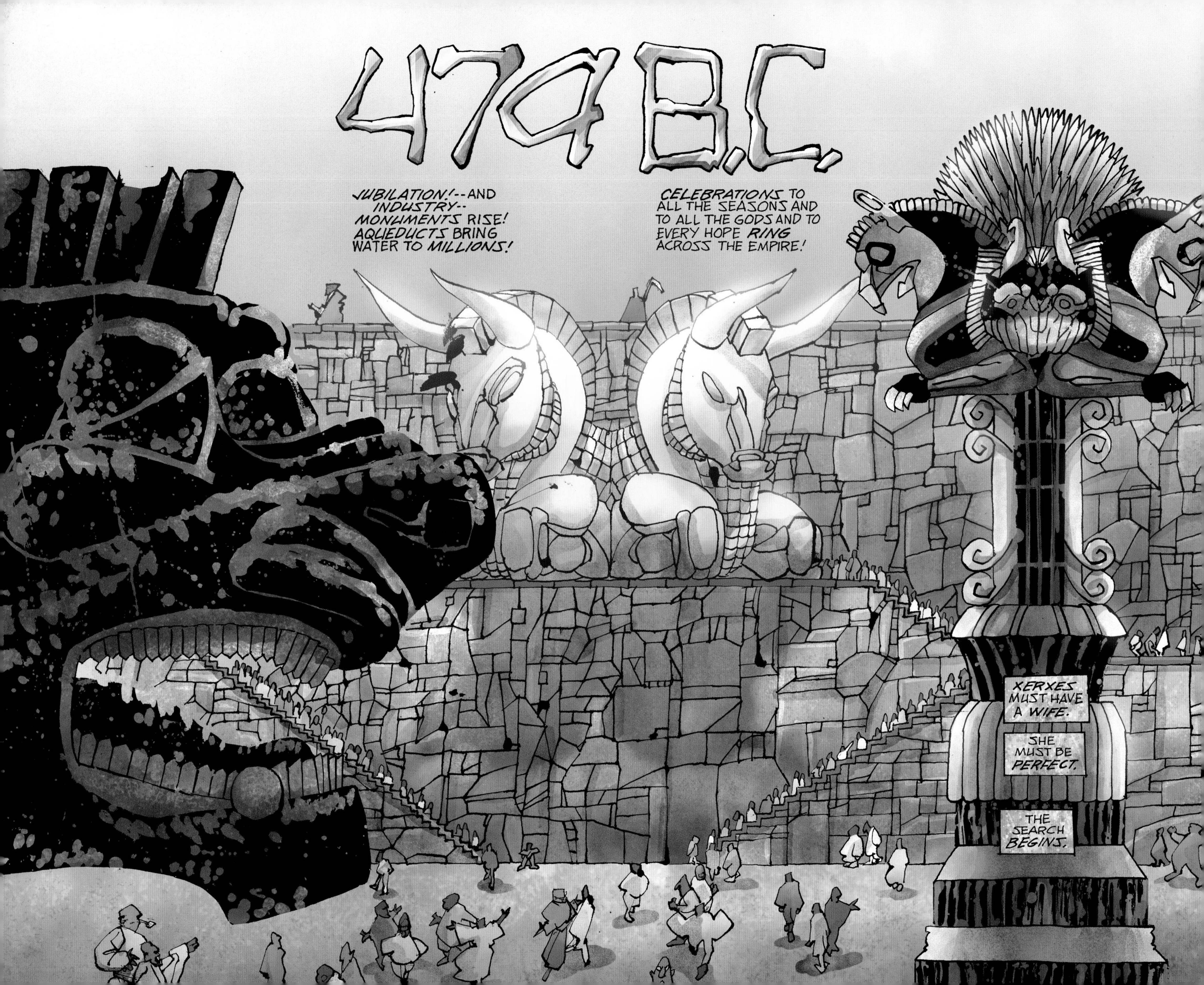
474 B.C.
JUBILATION!--AND INDUSTRY-- MONUMENTS RISE! AQUEDUCTS BRING WATER TO MILLIONS!
CELEBRATIONS TO ALL THE SEASONS AND TO ALL THE GODS AND TO EVERY HOPE RING ACROSS THE EMPIRE!
XERXES MUST HAVE A WIFE.
SHE MUST BE PERFECT.
THE SEARCH BEGINS.

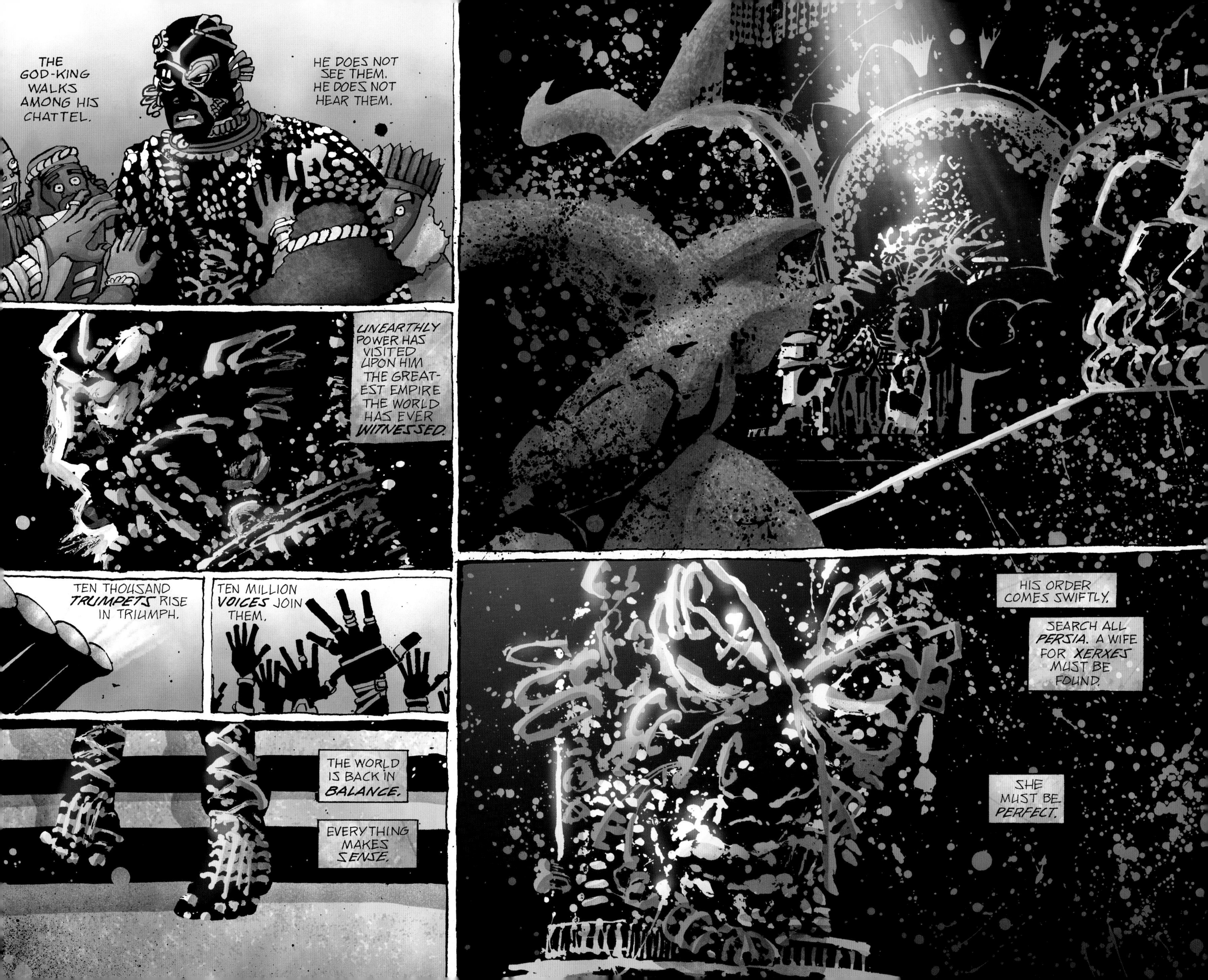
THE GOD-KING WALKS AMONG HIS CHATTEL.
HE DOES NOT SEE THEM. HE DOES NOT HEAR THEM.
UNEARTHLY POWER HAS VISITED UPON HIM THE GREATEST EMPIRE THE WORLD HAS EVER WITNESSED.
TEN THOUSAND TRUMPETS RISE IN TRIUMPH.
TEN MILLION VOICES JOIN THEM.
THE WORLD IS BACK IN BALANCE.
EVERYTHING MAKES SENSE.
HIS ORDER COMES SWIFTLY.
SEARCH ALL PERSIA. A WIFE FOR XERXES MUST BE FOUND.
SHE MUST BE PERFECT.

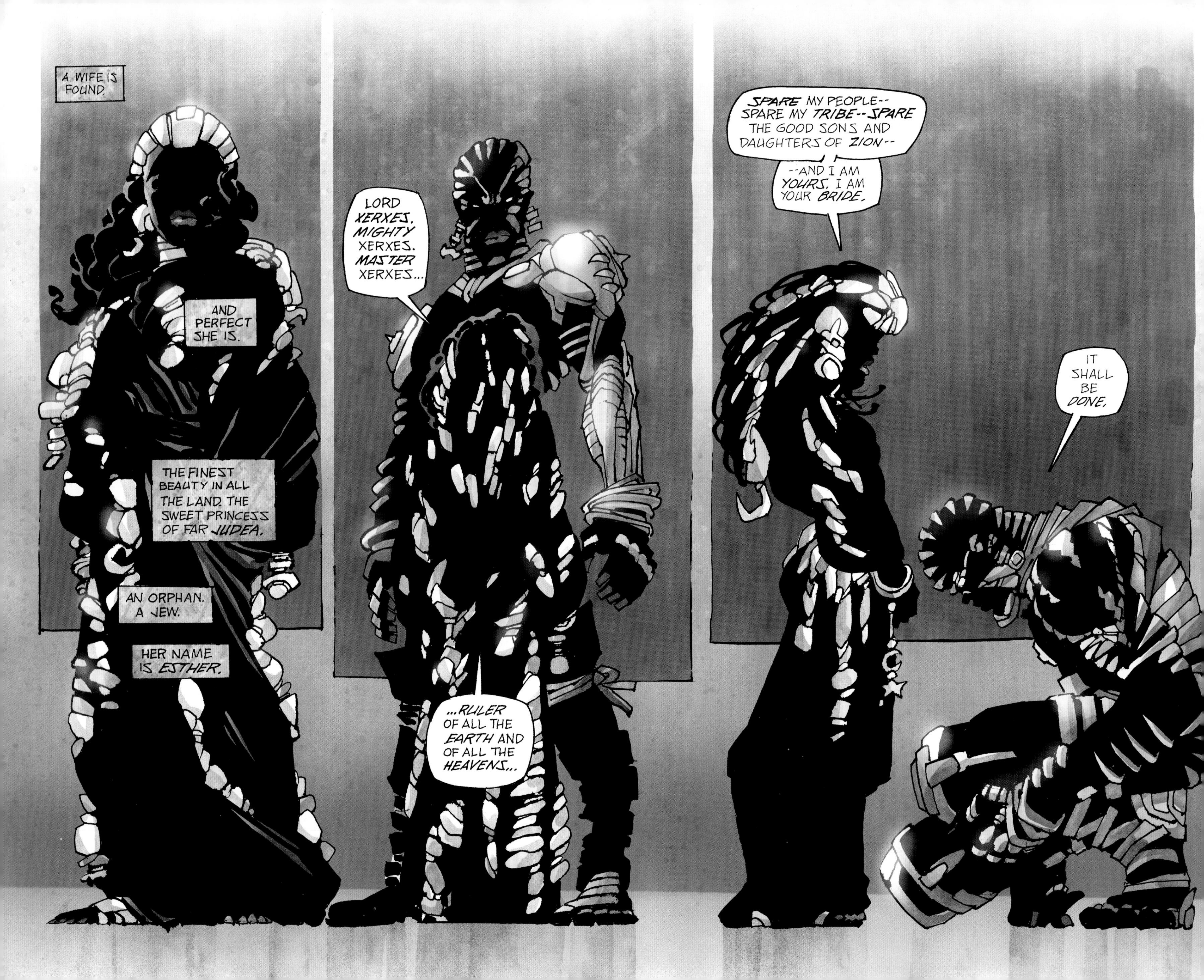
A WIFE IS FOUND.
AND PERFECT SHE IS.
THE FINEST BEAUTY IN ALL THE LAND. THE SWEET PRINCESS OF FAR JUDEA.
AN ORPHAN. A JEW.
HER NAME IS ESTHER.
LORD XERXES. MIGHTY XERXES. MASTER XERXES...
...RULER OF ALL THE EARTH AND OF ALL THE HEAVENS...
SPARE MY PEOPLE-- SPARE MY TRIBE--SPARE THE GOOD SONS AND DAUGHTERS OF ZION--
--AND I AM YOURS. I AM YOUR BRIDE.
IT SHALL BE DONE.

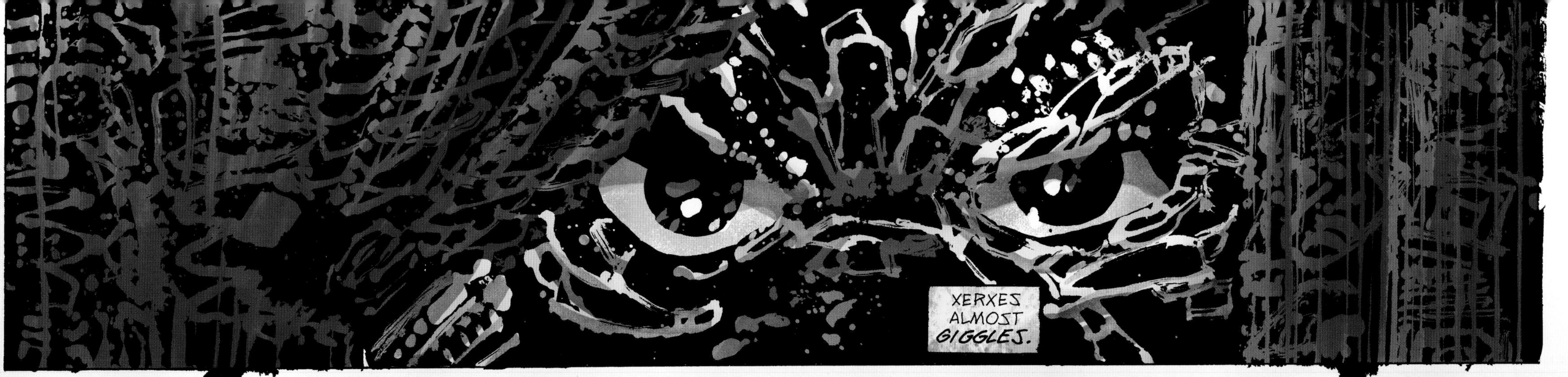
XERXES ALMOST GIGGLES.

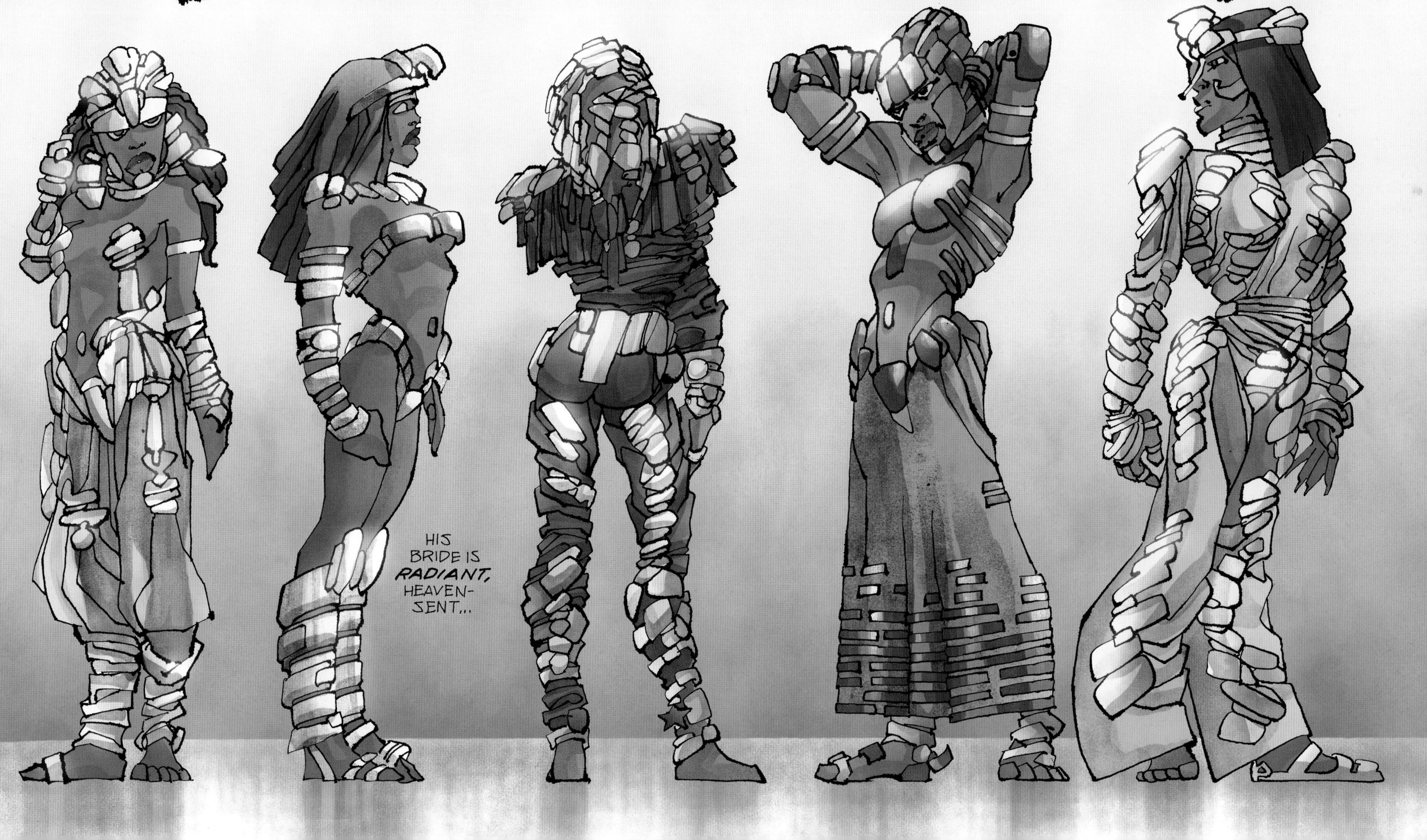
HIS BRIDE IS RADIANT, HEAVEN-SENT...

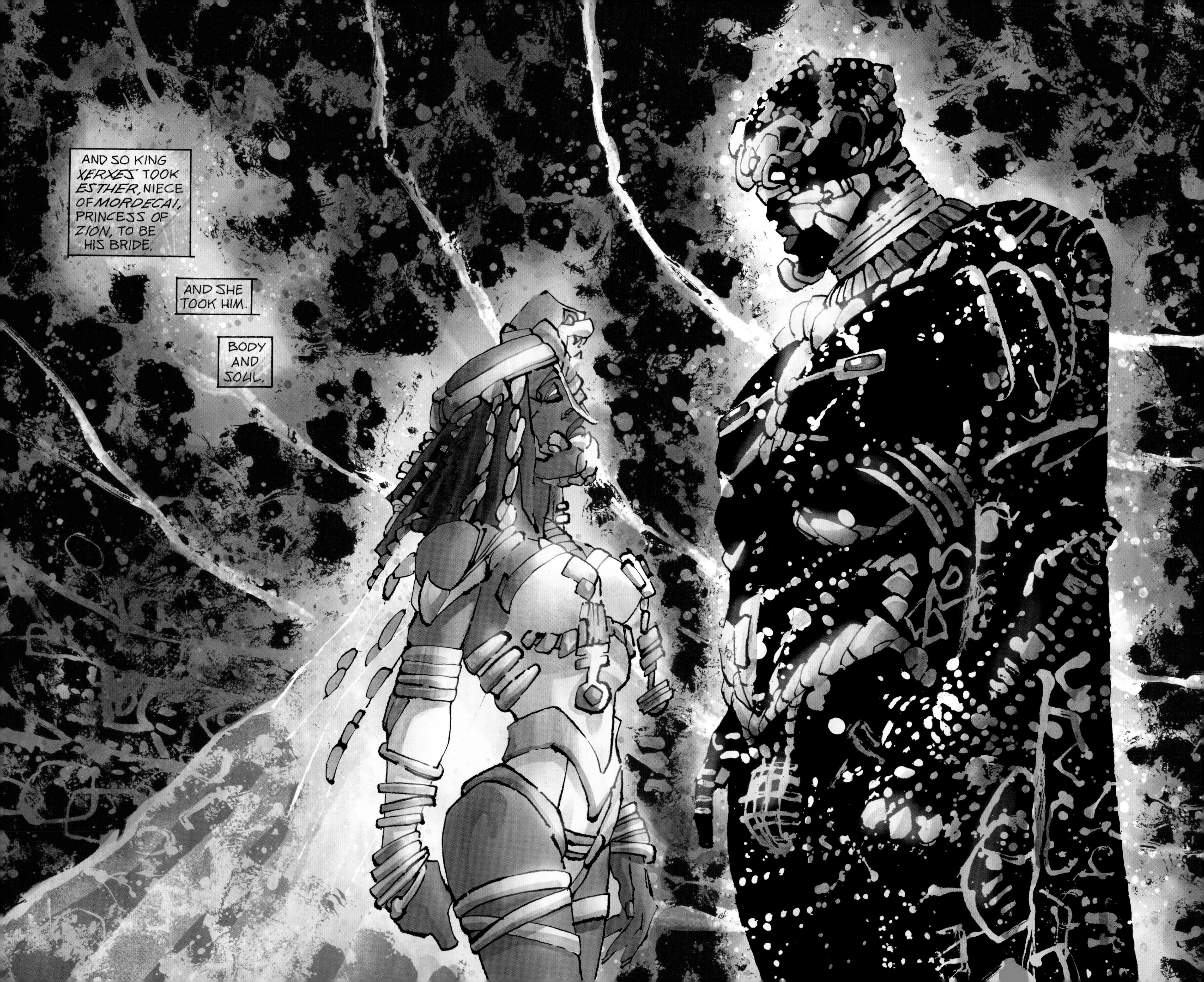
AND SO KING XERXES TOOK ESTHER, NIECE OF MORDECAI, PRINCESS OF ZION, TO BE HIS BRIDE.
AND SHE TOOK HIM.
BODY AND SOUL.

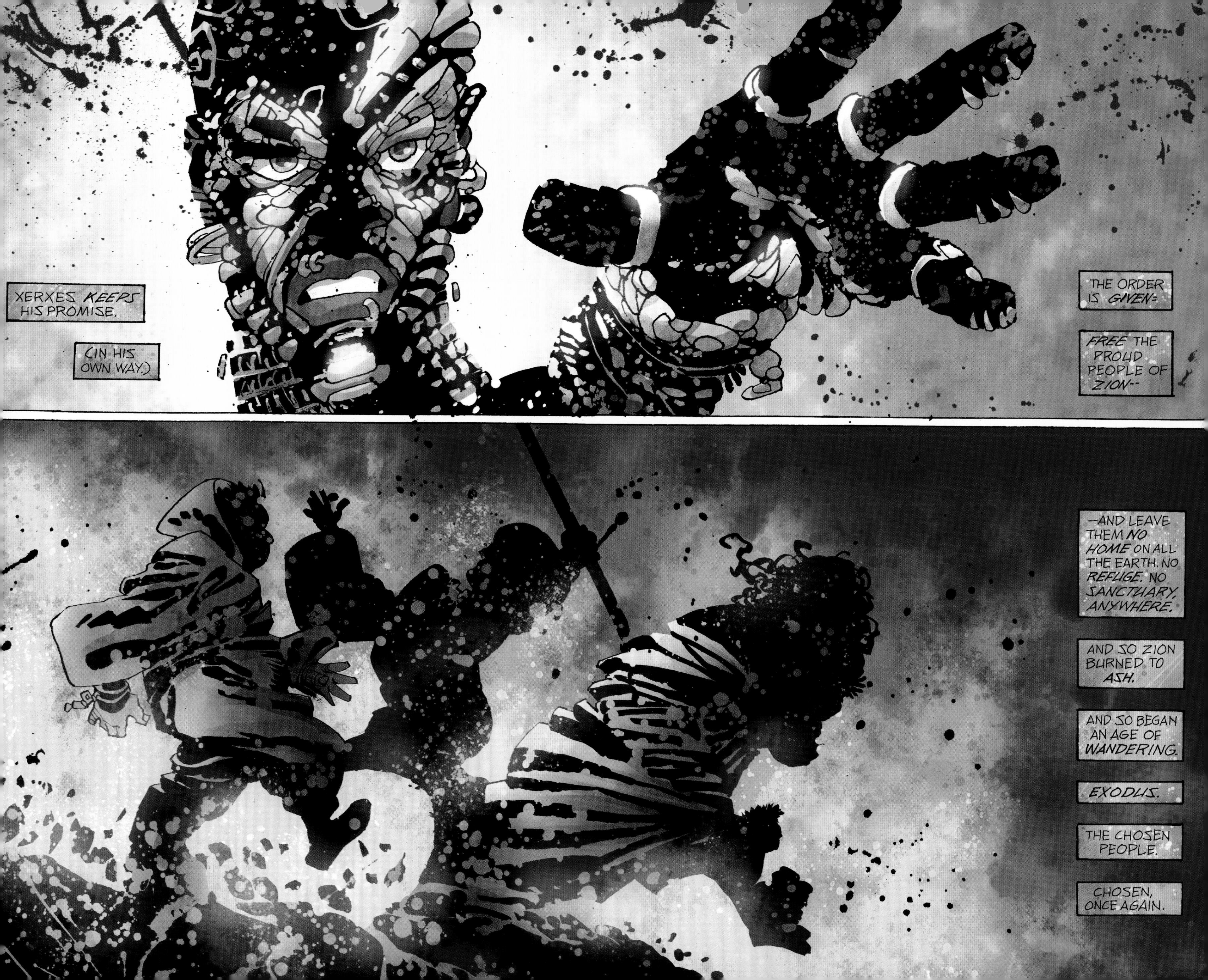
XERXES KEEPS HIS PROMISE.
(IN HIS OWN WAY.)
THE ORDER IS GIVEN:
FREE THE PROUD PEOPLE OF ZION--
--AND LEAVE THEM NO HOME ON ALL THE EARTH. NO REFUGE. NO SANCTUARY, ANYWHERE.
AND SO ZION BURNED TO ASH.
AND SO BEGAN AN AGE OF WANDERING.
EXODUS.
THE CHOSEN PEOPLE.
CHOSEN, ONCE AGAIN.

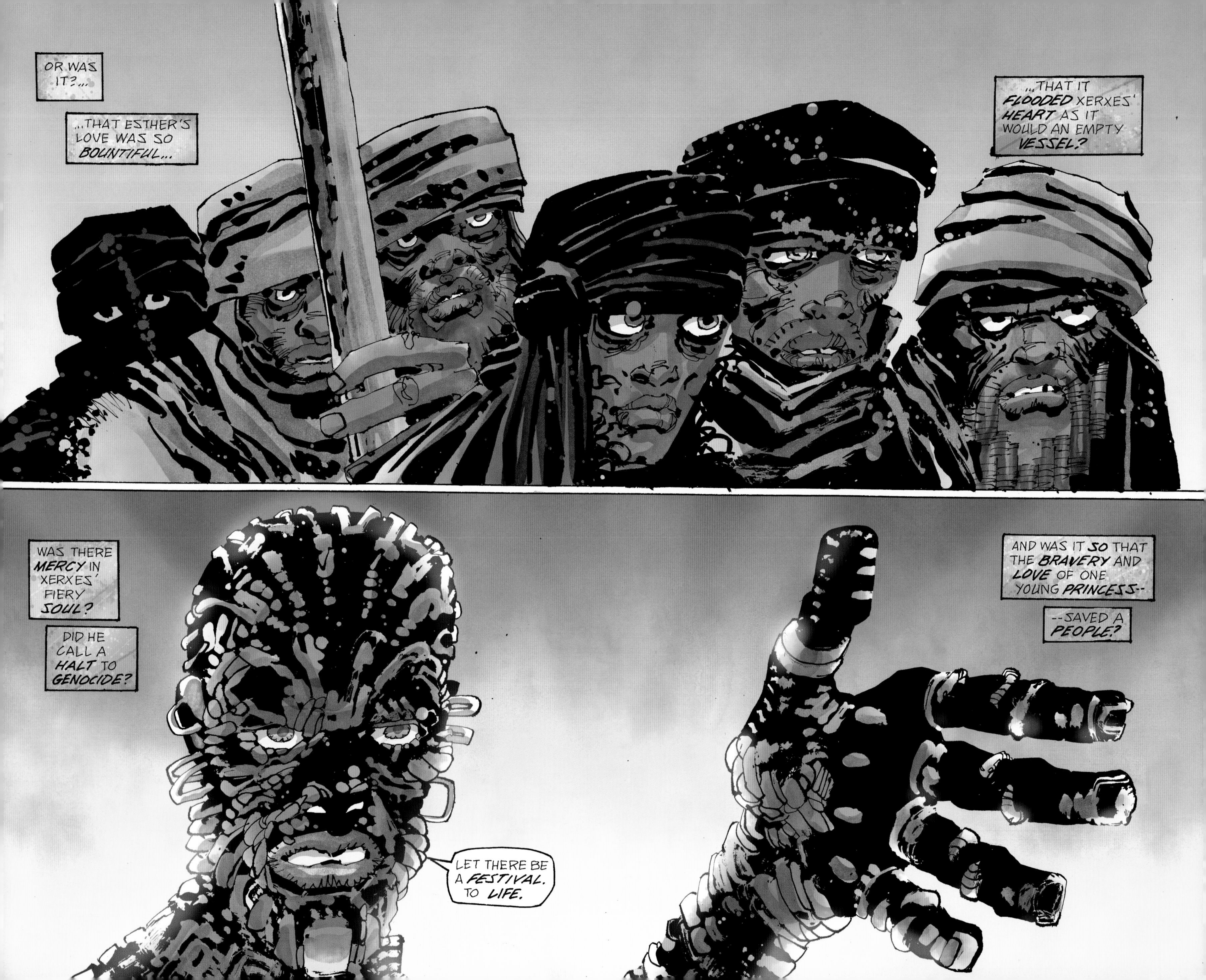
OR WAS IT?...
...THAT ESTHER'S LOVE WAS SO BOUNTIFUL...
...THAT IT FLOODED XERXES' HEART AS IT WOULD AN EMPTY VESSEL?
WAS THERE MERCY IN XERXES' FIERY SOUL?
DID HE CALL A HALT TO GENOCIDE?
AND WAS IT SO THAT THE BRAVERY AND LOVE OF ONE YOUNG PRINCESS--
--SAVED A PEOPLE?
LET THERE BE A FESTIVAL. TO LIFE.

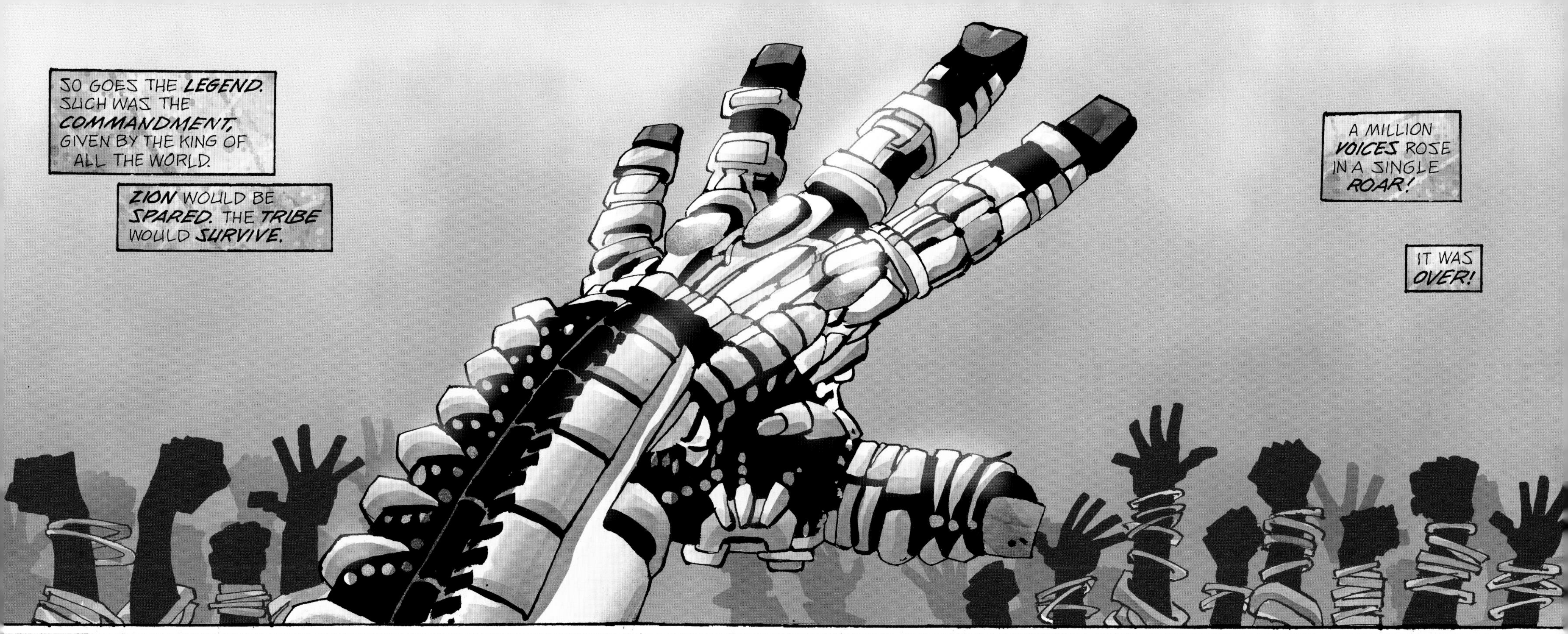
SO GOES THE LEGEND. SUCH WAS THE COMMANDMENT, GIVEN BY THE KING OF ALL THE WORLD.
ZION WOULD BE SPARED. THE TRIBE WOULD SURVIVE.
A MILLION VOICES ROSE IN A SINGLE ROAR!
IT WAS OVER!

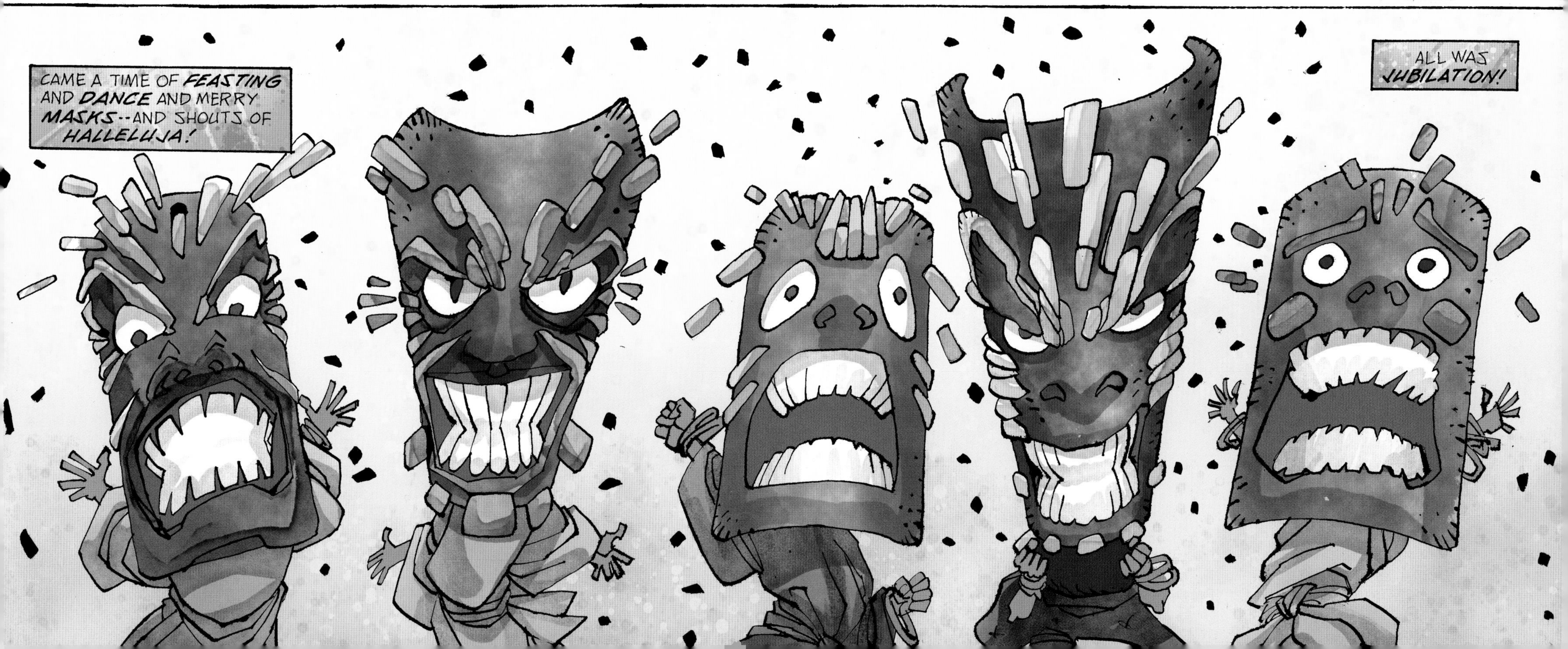
CAME A TIME OF FEASTING AND DANCE AND MERRY MASKS--AND SHOUTS OF HALLELUJA!
ALL WAS JUBILATION!

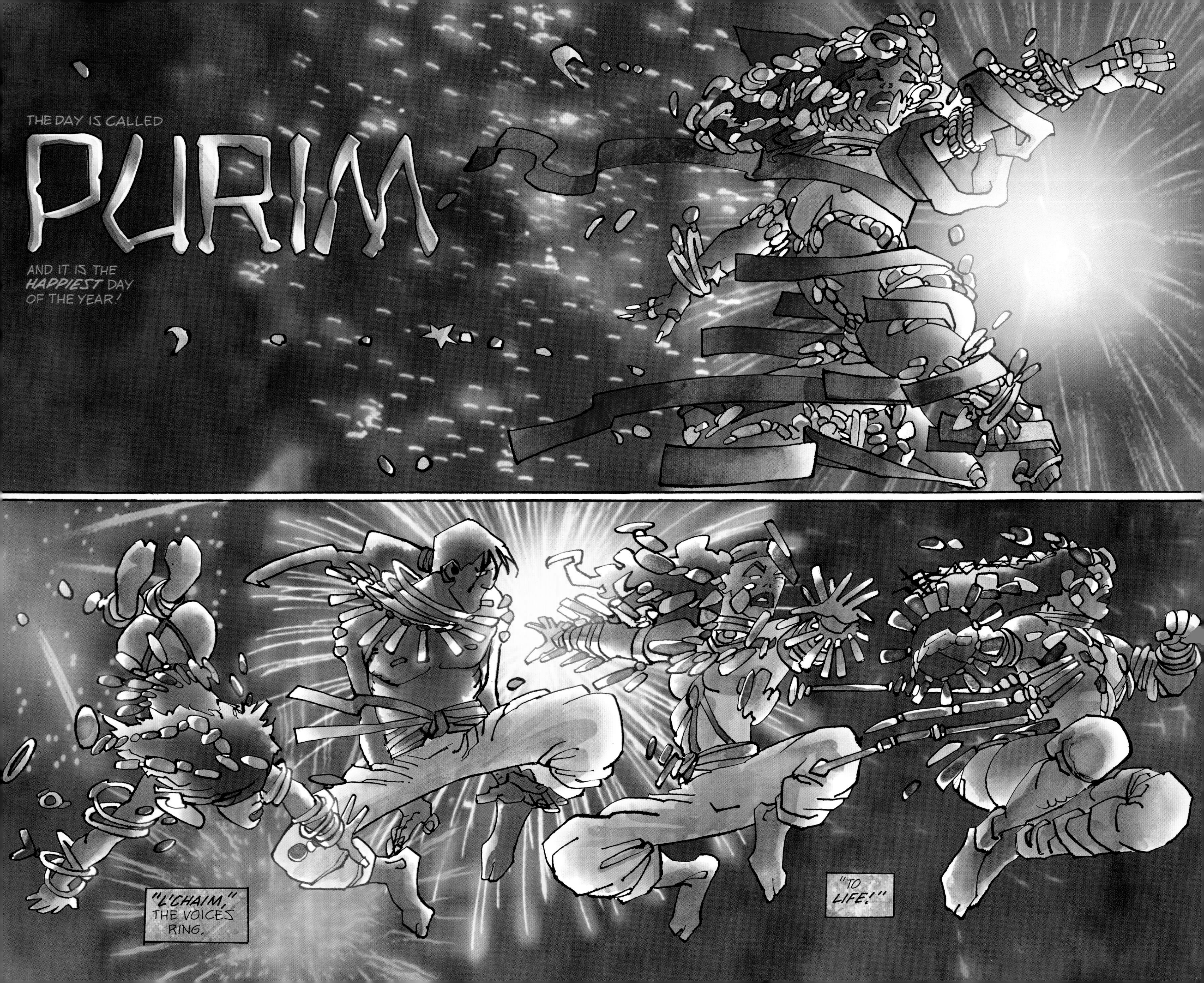
THE DAY IS CALLED
PURIM
AND IT IS THE *HAPPIEST* DAY OF THE YEAR!
"L'CHAIM," THE VOICES RING.
"TO LIFE!"

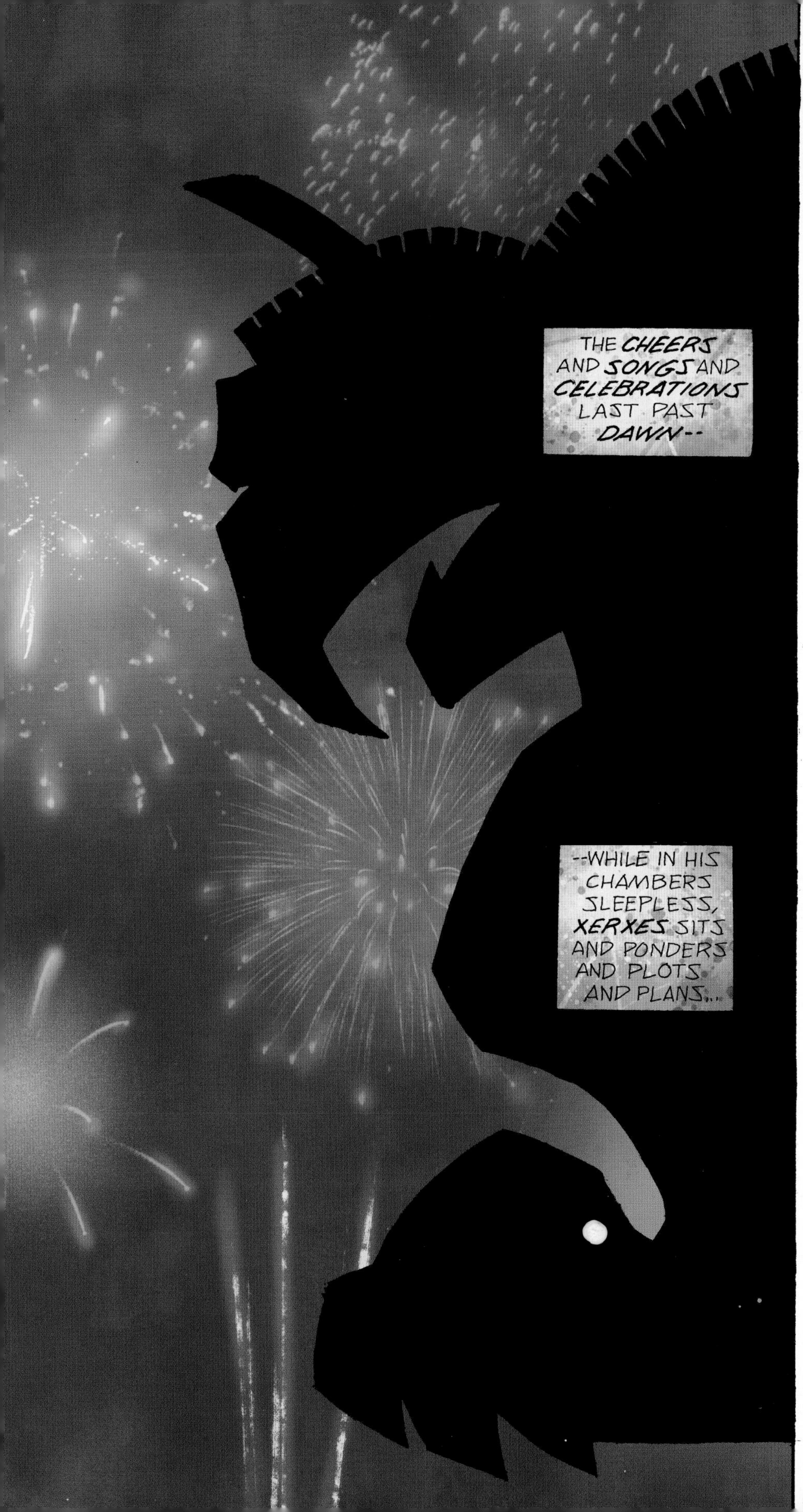
THE CHEERS AND SONGS AND CELEBRATIONS LAST PAST DAWN--
--WHILE IN HIS CHAMBERS SLEEPLESS, XERXES SITS AND PONDERS AND PLOTS AND PLANS...

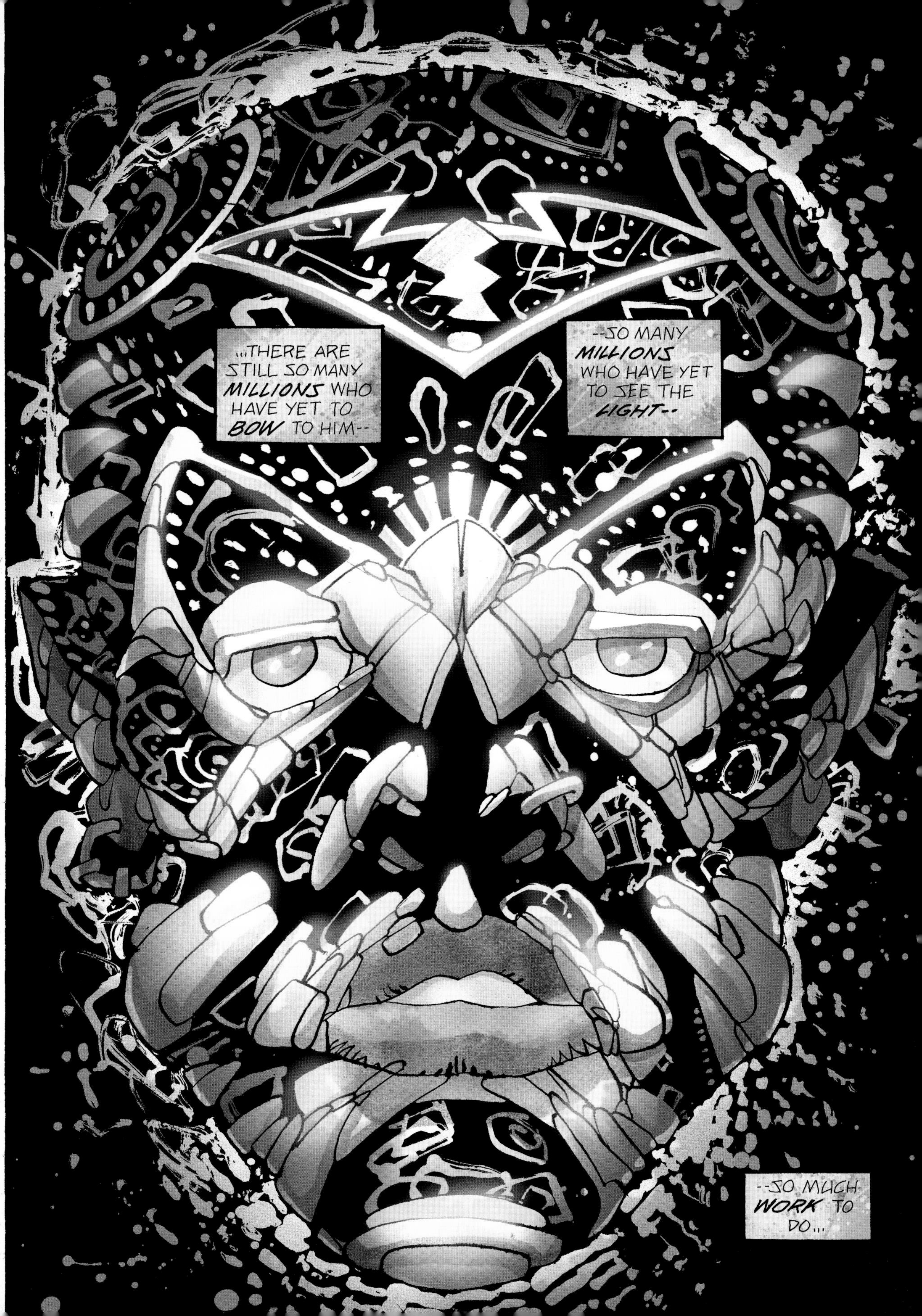
...THERE ARE STILL SO MANY MILLIONS WHO HAVE YET TO BOW TO HIM--
--SO MANY MILLIONS WHO HAVE YET TO SEE THE LIGHT--
--SO MUCH WORK TO DO...

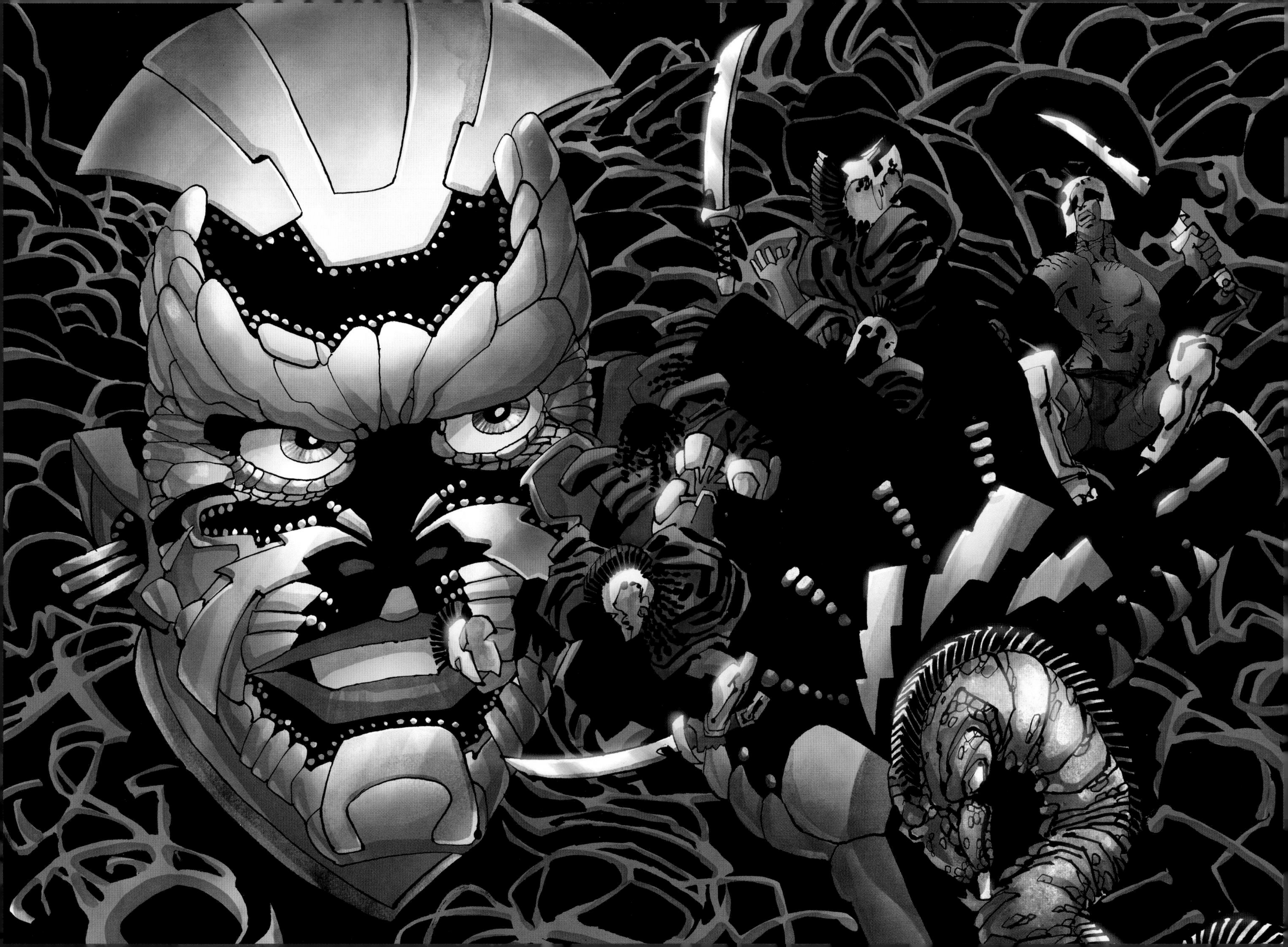

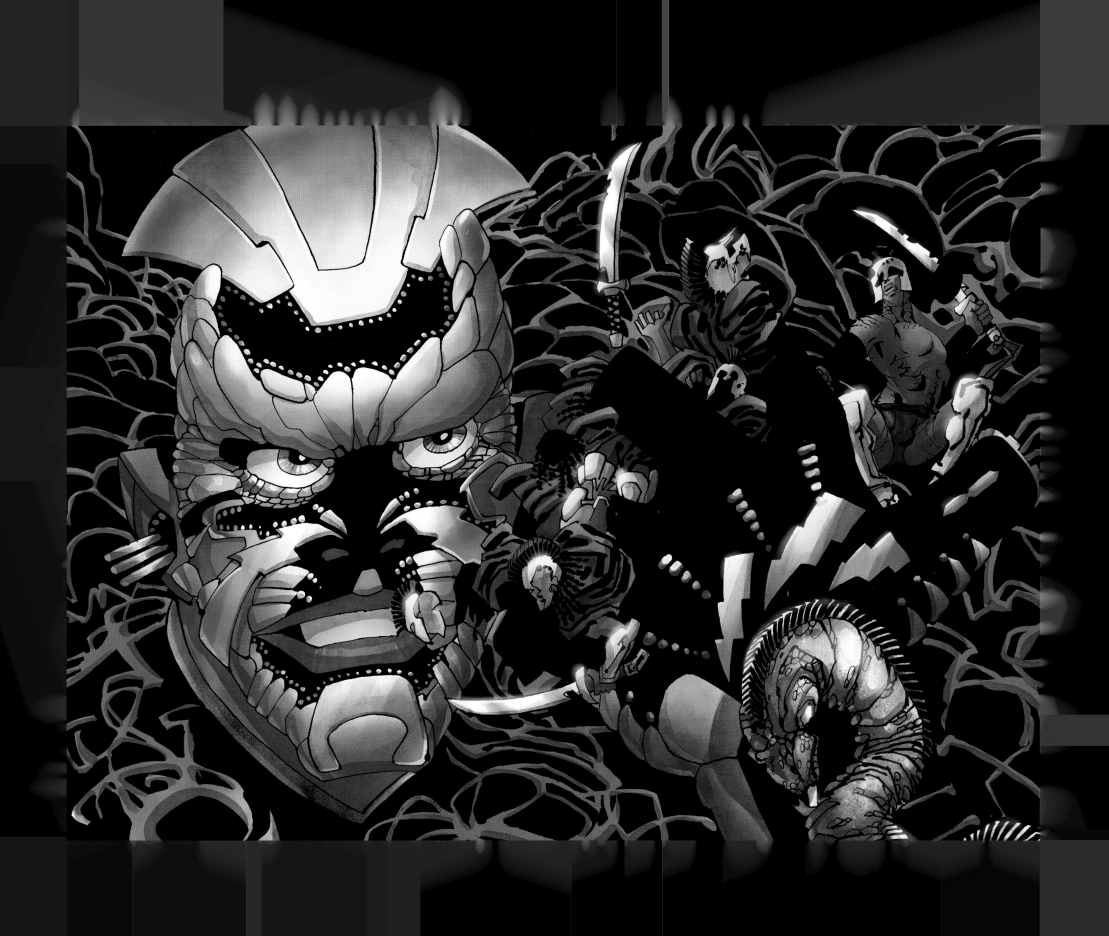

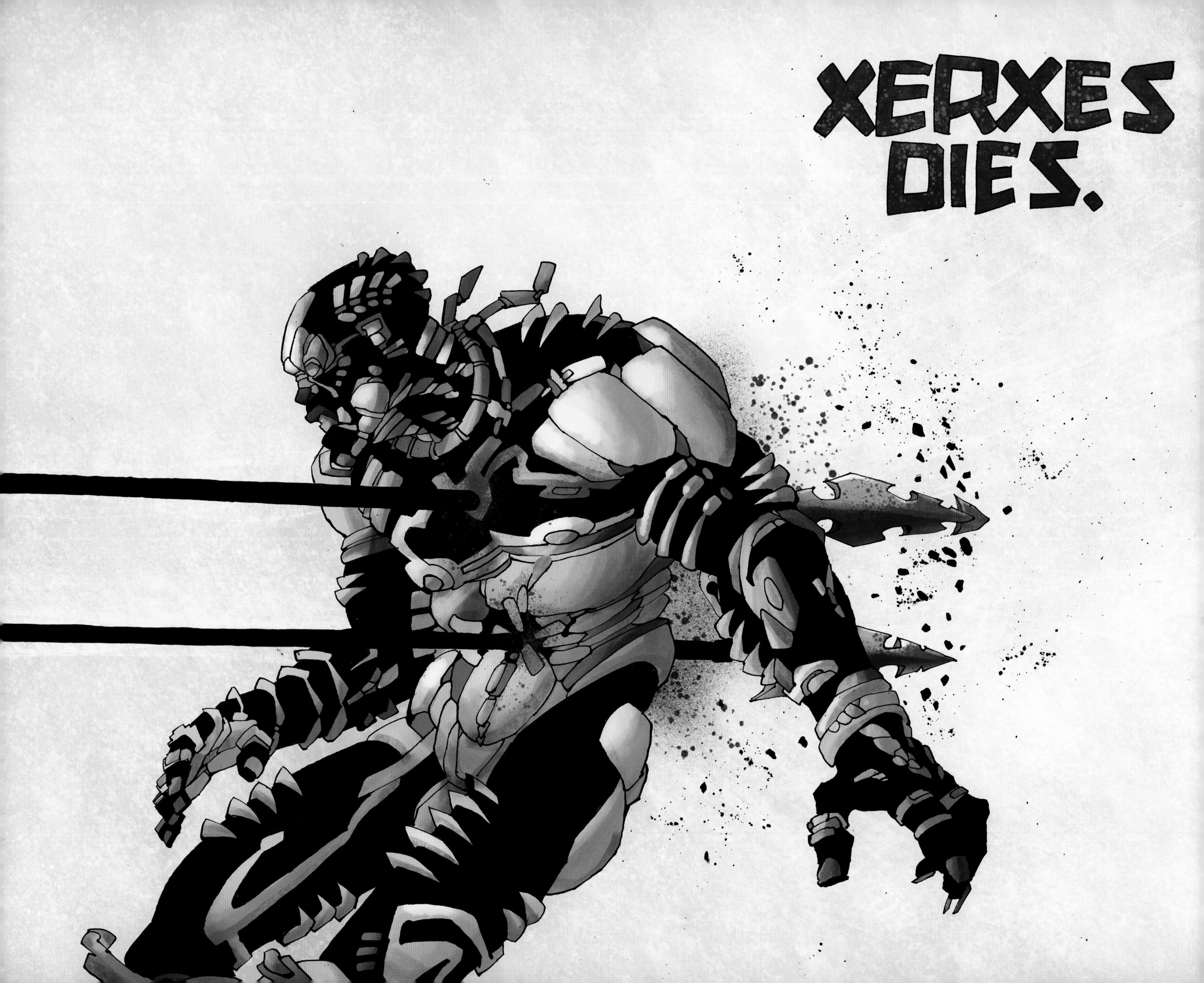
XERXES DIES.

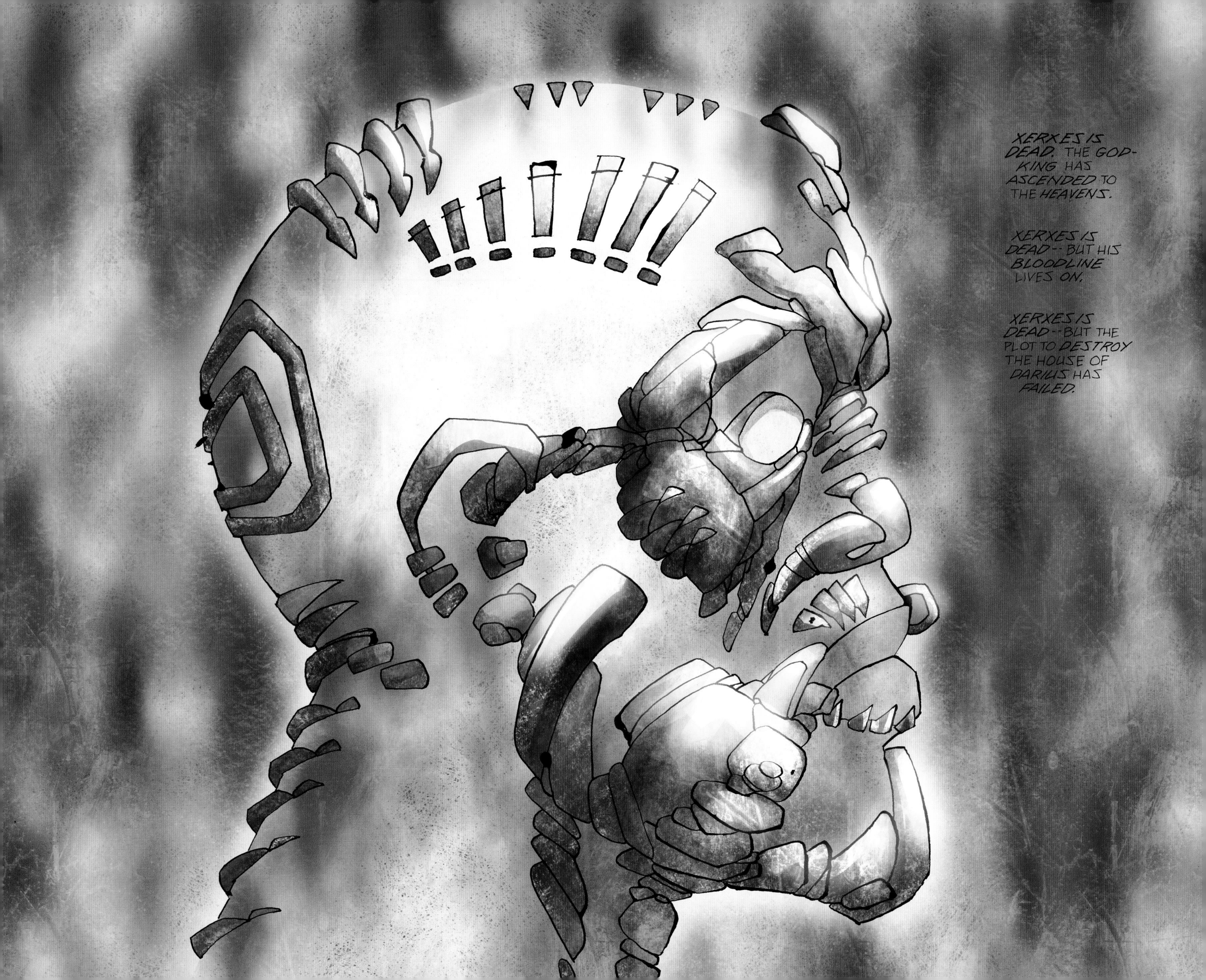
!!!!!!!
XERXES IS DEAD. THE GOD-KING HAS ASCENDED TO THE HEAVENS.
XERXES IS DEAD--BUT HIS BLOODLINE LIVES ON.
XERXES IS DEAD--BUT THE PLOT TO DESTROY THE HOUSE OF DARIUS HAS FAILED.

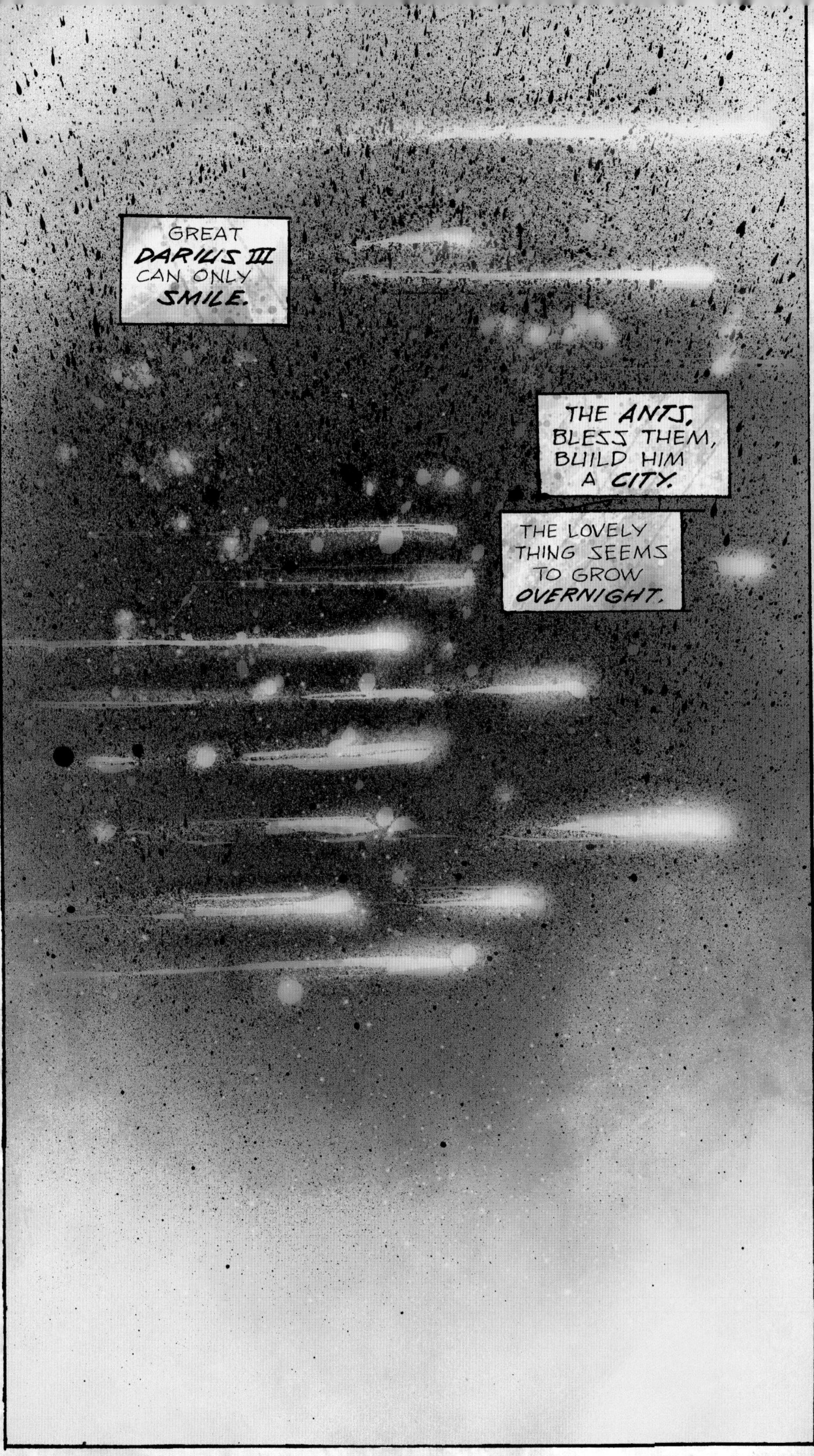
GREAT DARIUS III CAN ONLY SMILE.
THE ANTS, BLESS THEM, BUILD HIM A CITY.
THE LOVELY THING SEEMS TO GROW OVERNIGHT.

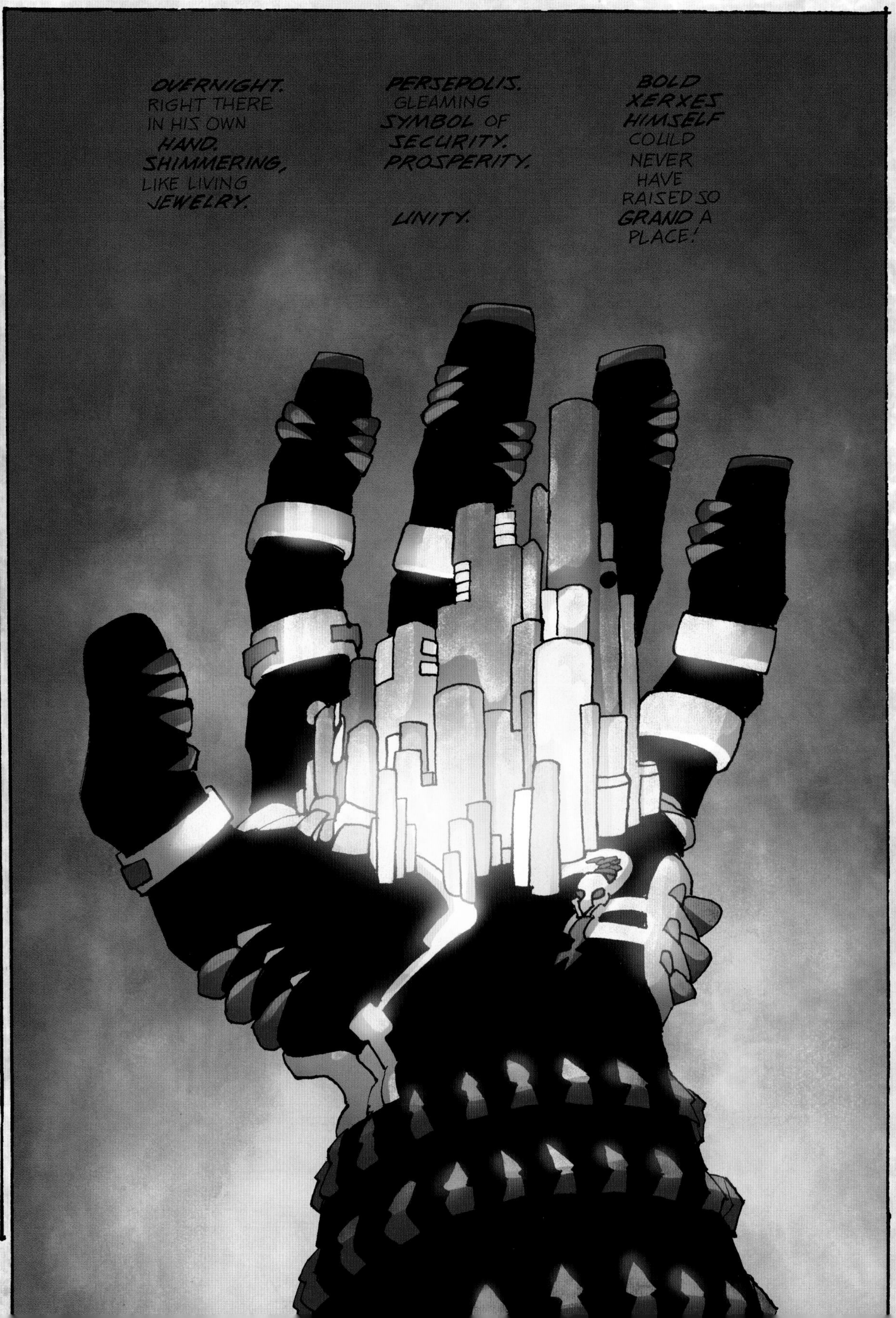
OVERNIGHT. RIGHT THERE IN HIS OWN HAND. SHIMMERING, LIKE LIVING JEWELRY.
PERSEPOLIS. GLEAMING SYMBOL OF SECURITY. PROSPERITY.
UNITY.
BOLD XERXES HIMSELF COULD NEVER HAVE RAISED SO GRAND A PLACE!

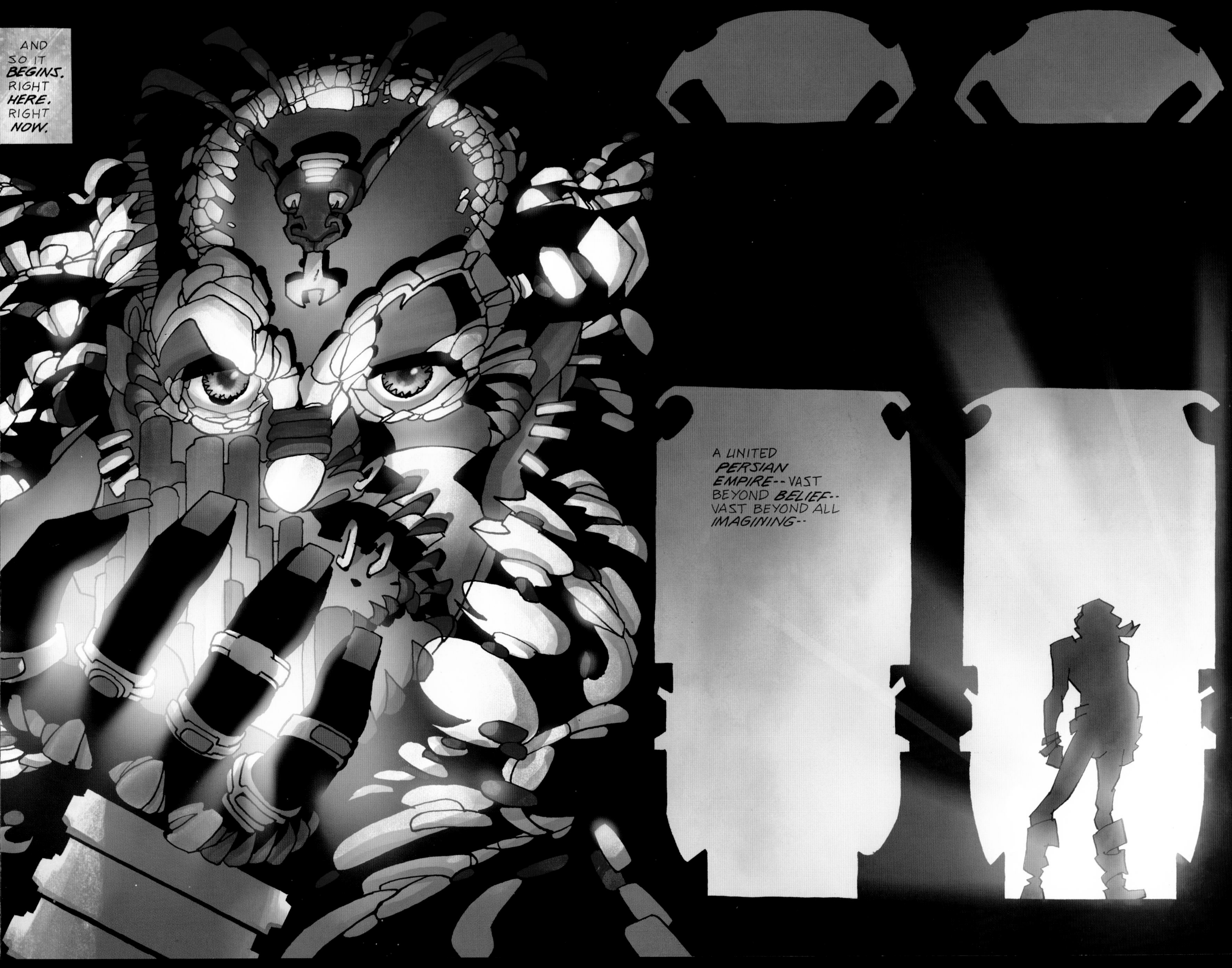
AND SO IT BEGINS. RIGHT HERE. RIGHT NOW.
A UNITED PERSIAN EMPIRE--VAST BEYOND BELIEF--VAST BEYOND ALL IMAGINING--

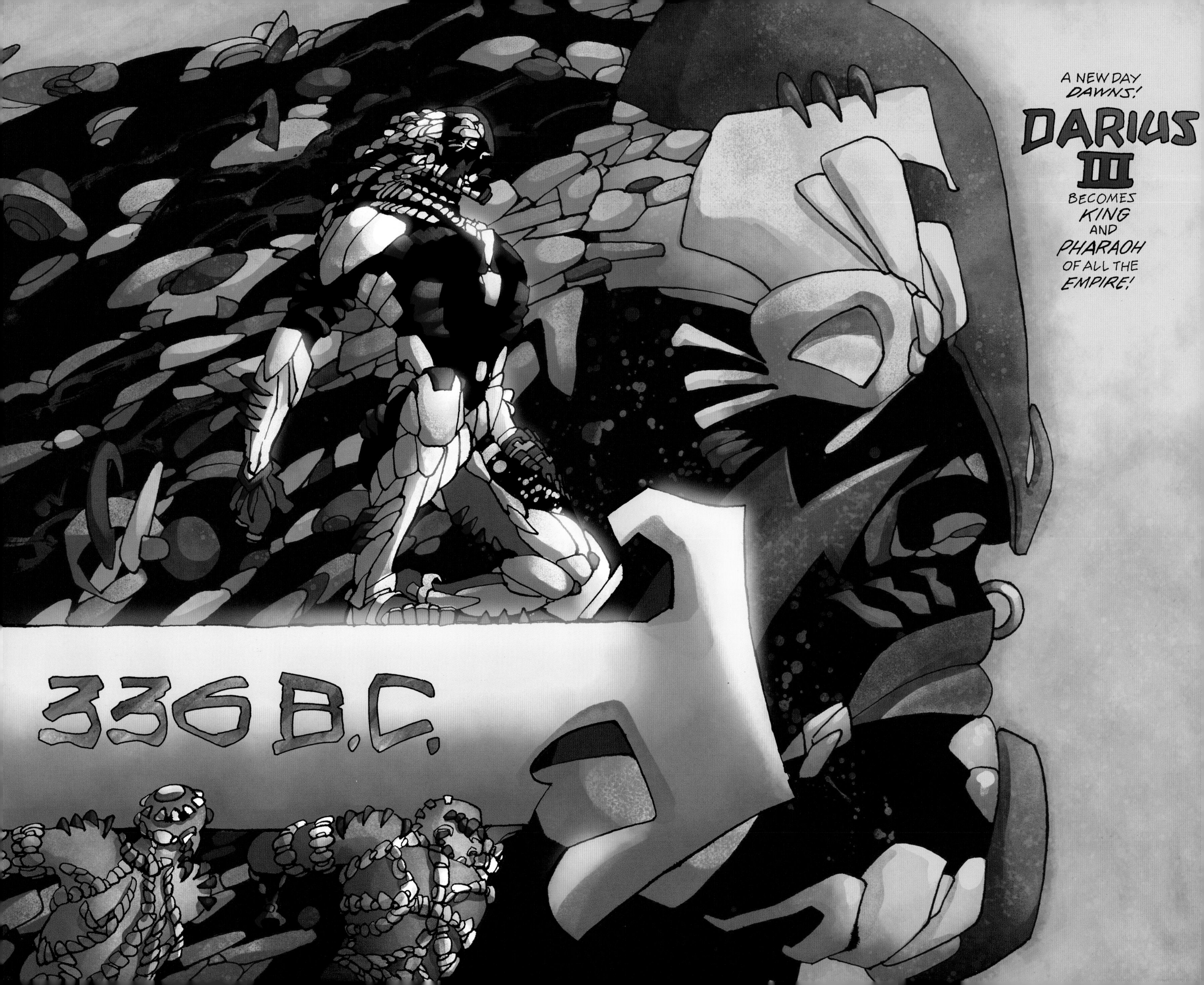

A NEW DAY DAWNS!
DARIUS III
BECOMES KING AND PHARAOH OF ALL THE EMPIRE!
336 B.C.

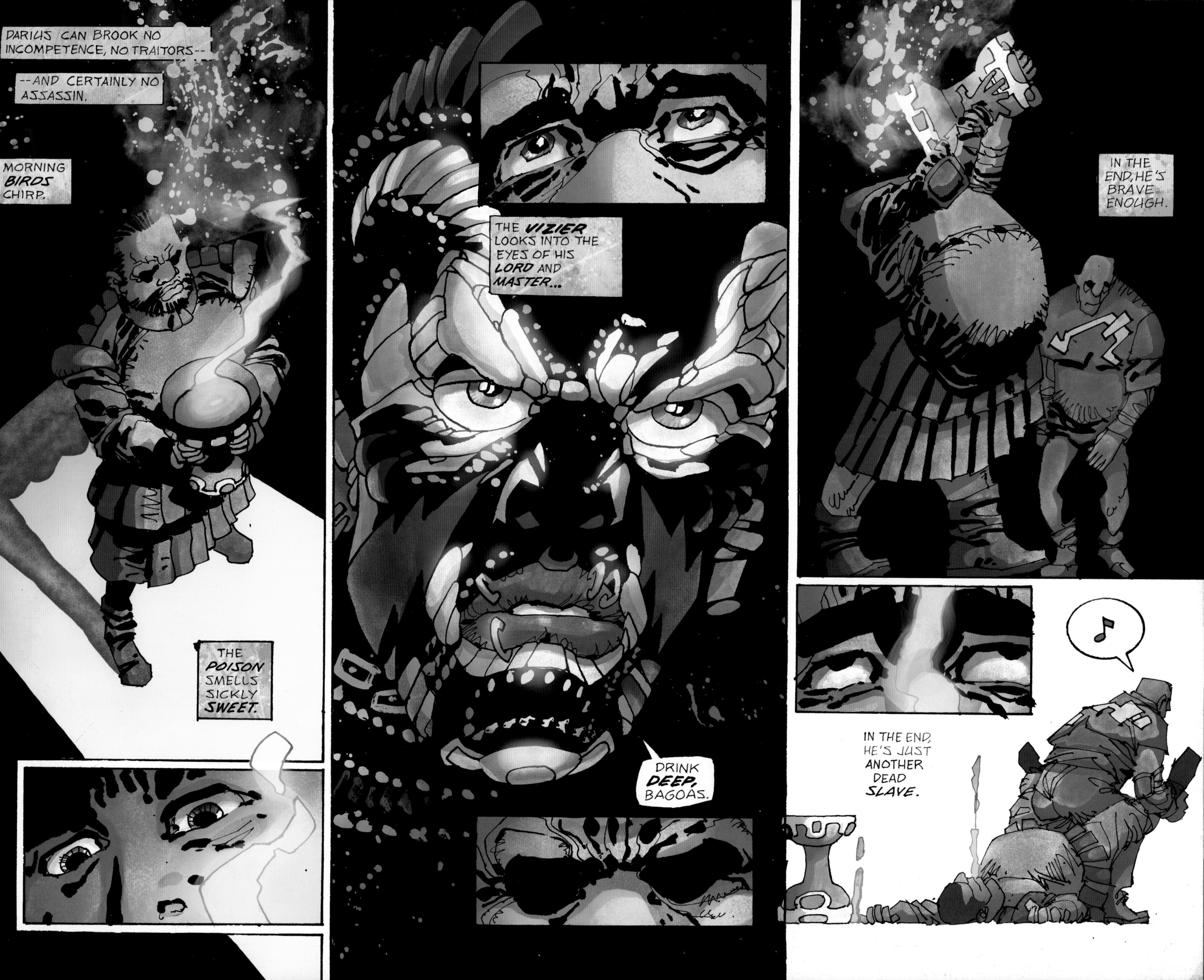
DARIUS CAN BROOK NO INCOMPETENCE, NO TRAITORS--
--AND CERTAINLY NO ASSASSIN.
MORNING BIRDS CHIRP.
THE POISON SMELLS SICKLY SWEET.
THE VIZIER LOOKS INTO THE EYES OF HIS LORD AND MASTER...
DRINK DEEP, BAGOAS.
IN THE END, HE'S BRAVE ENOUGH.
IN THE END, HE'S JUST ANOTHER DEAD SLAVE.

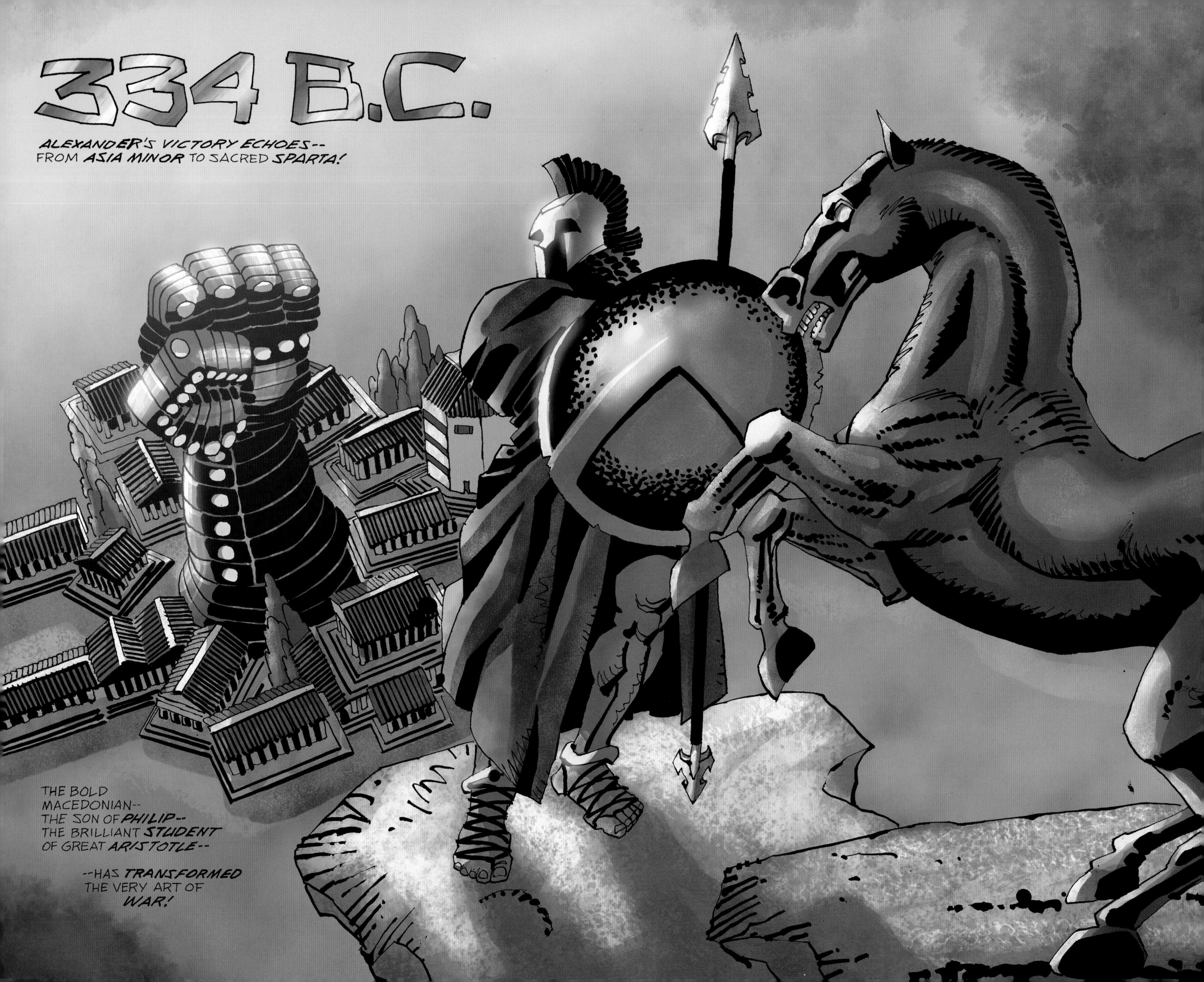
334 B.C.
ALEXANDER'S VICTORY ECHOES-- FROM ASIA MINOR TO SACRED SPARTA!
THE BOLD MACEDONIAN-- THE SON OF PHILIP-- THE BRILLIANT STUDENT OF GREAT ARISTOTLE--
--HAS TRANSFORMED THE VERY ART OF WAR!

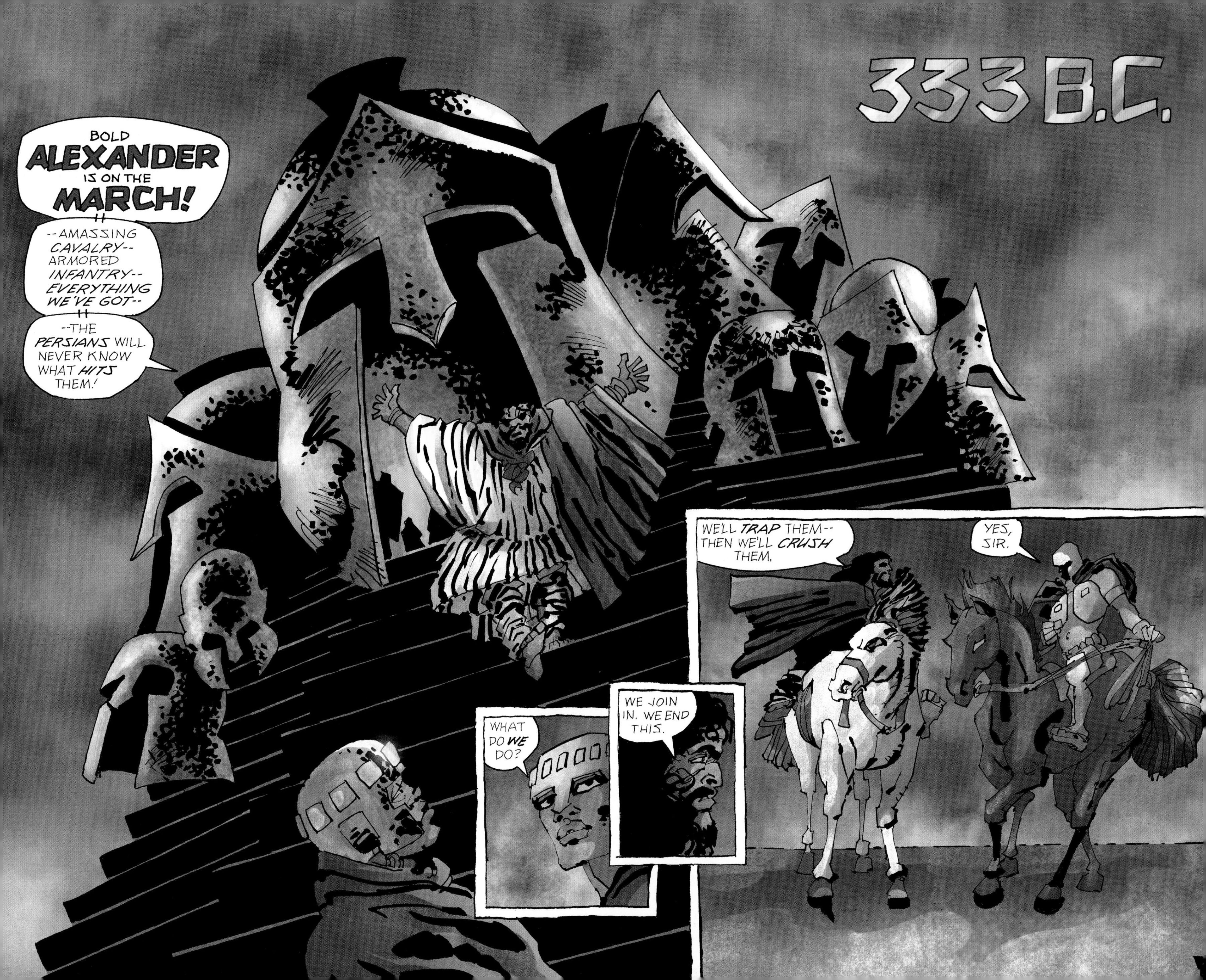
333 B.C.
BOLD ALEXANDER IS ON THE MARCH!
--AMASSING CAVALRY-- ARMORED INFANTRY-- EVERYTHING WE'VE GOT--
--THE PERSIANS WILL NEVER KNOW WHAT HITS THEM!
WE'LL TRAP THEM-- THEN WE'LL CRUSH THEM.
YES, SIR.
WHAT DO WE DO?
WE JOIN IN. WE END THIS.

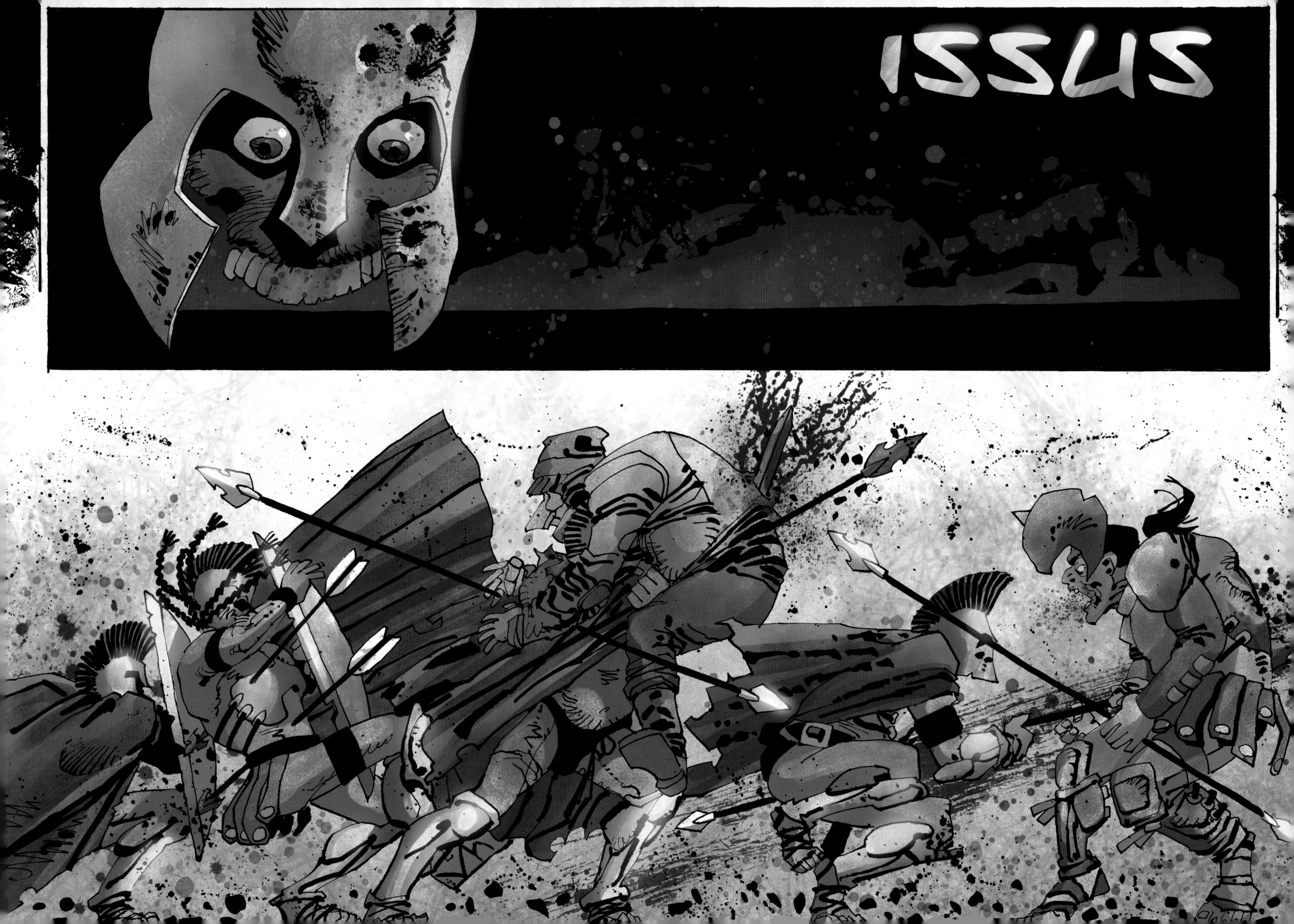
ISSUS

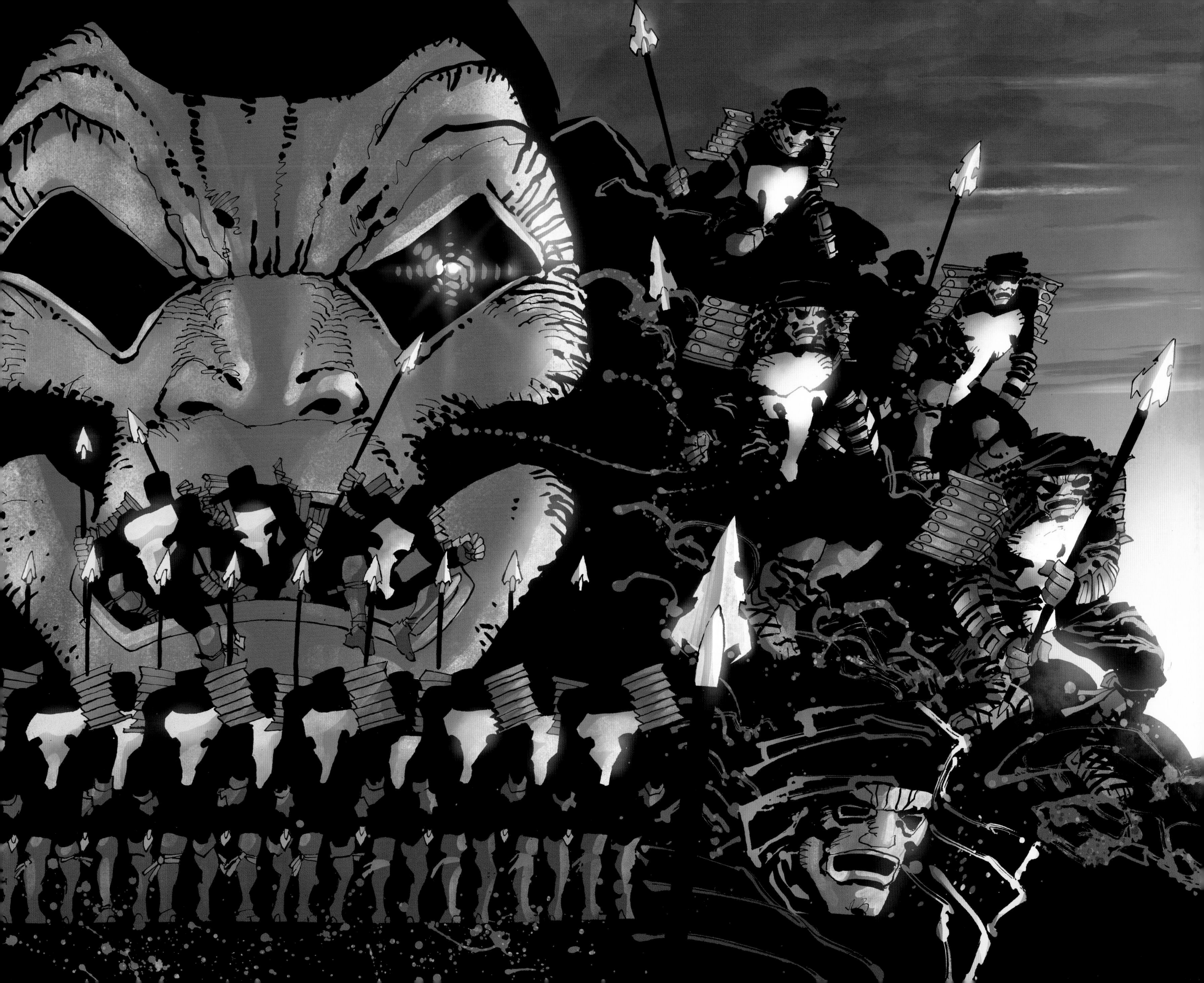

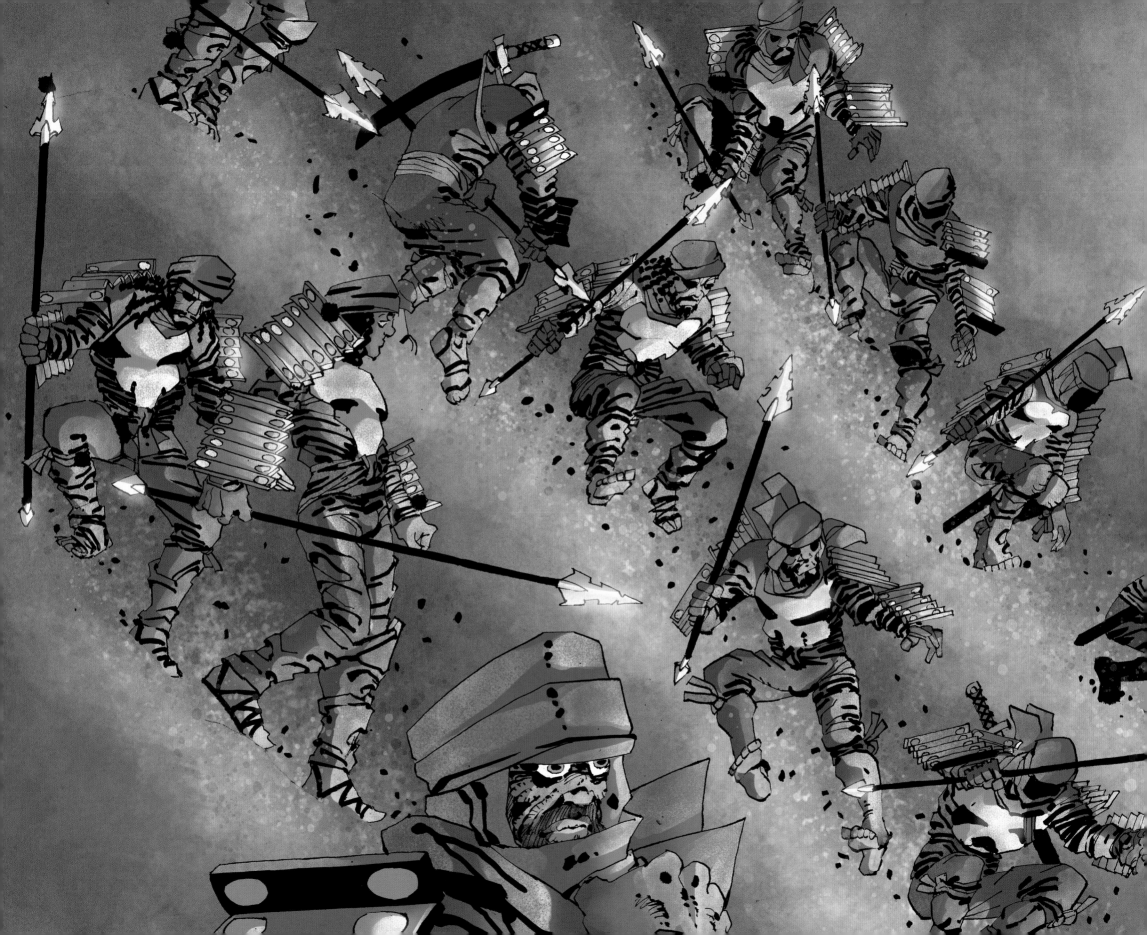

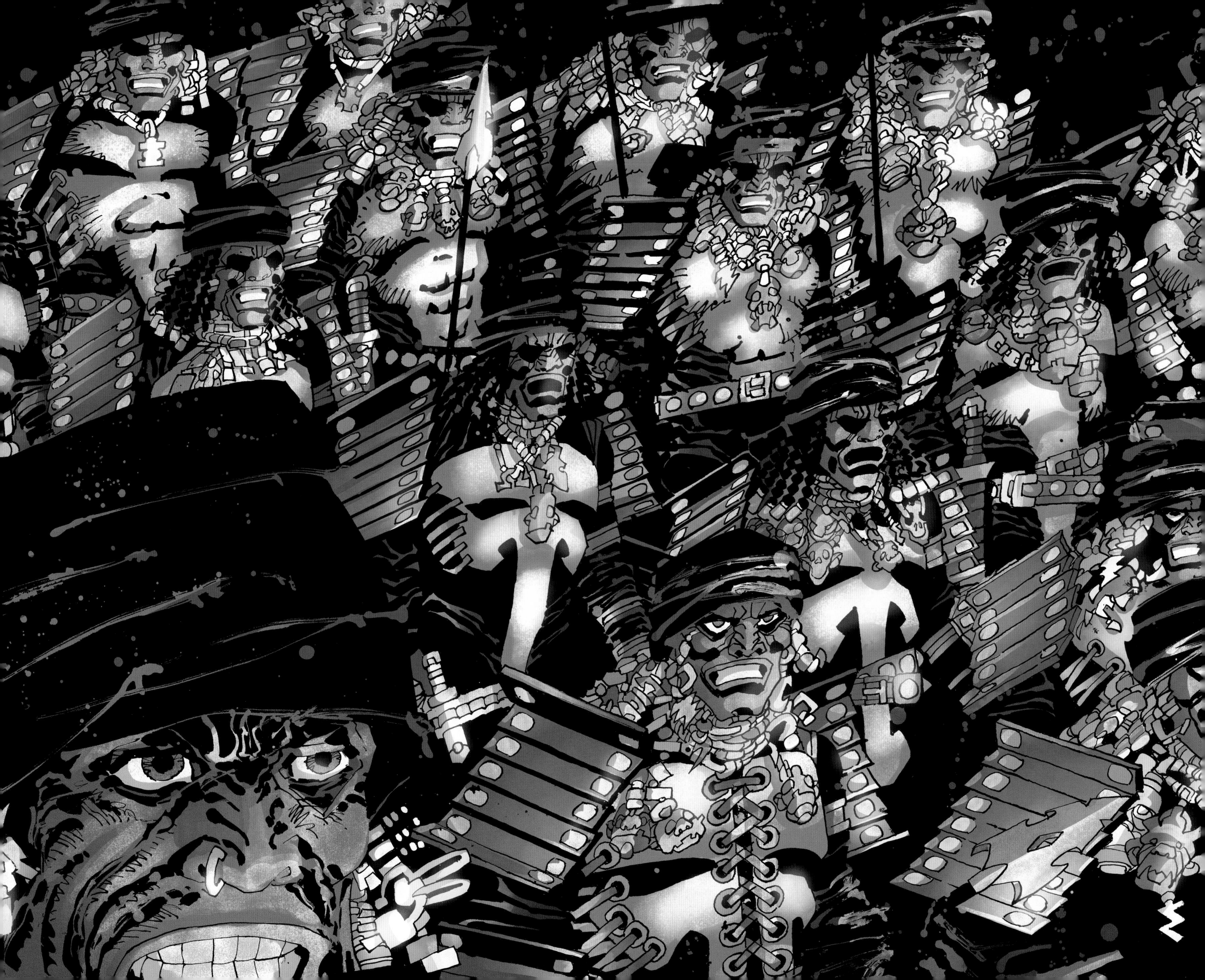

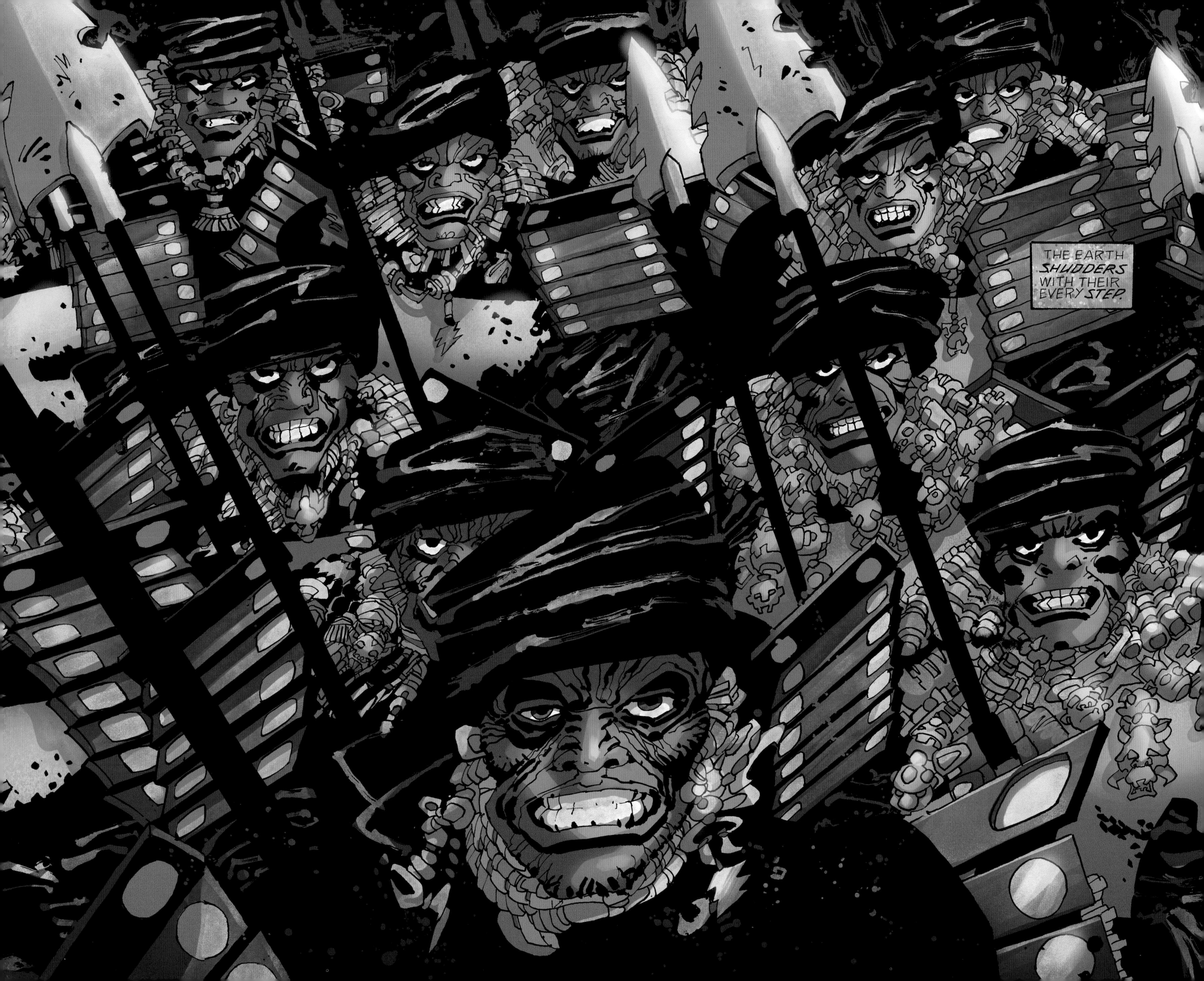
THE EARTH SHUDDERS WITH THEIR EVERY STEP.

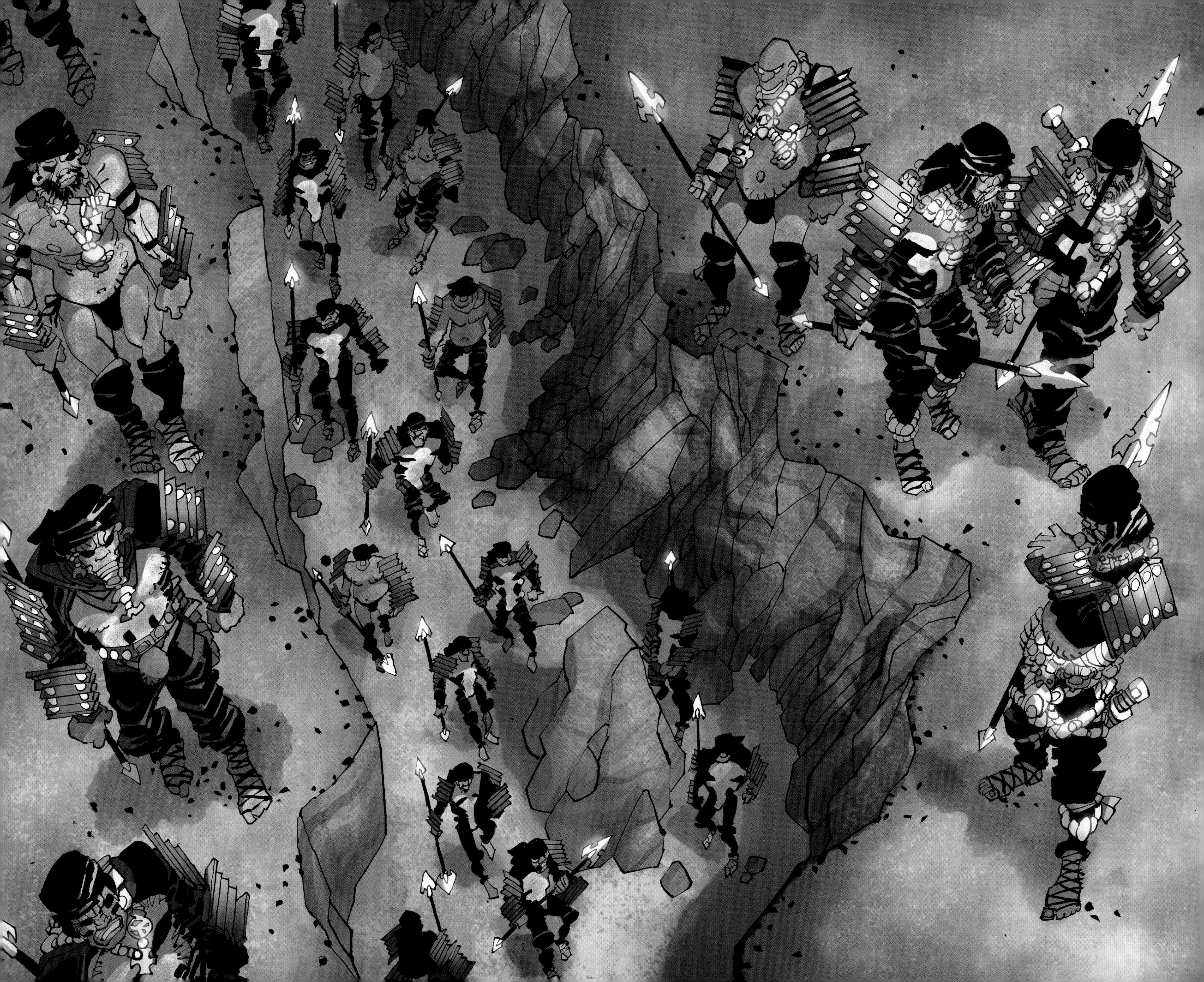

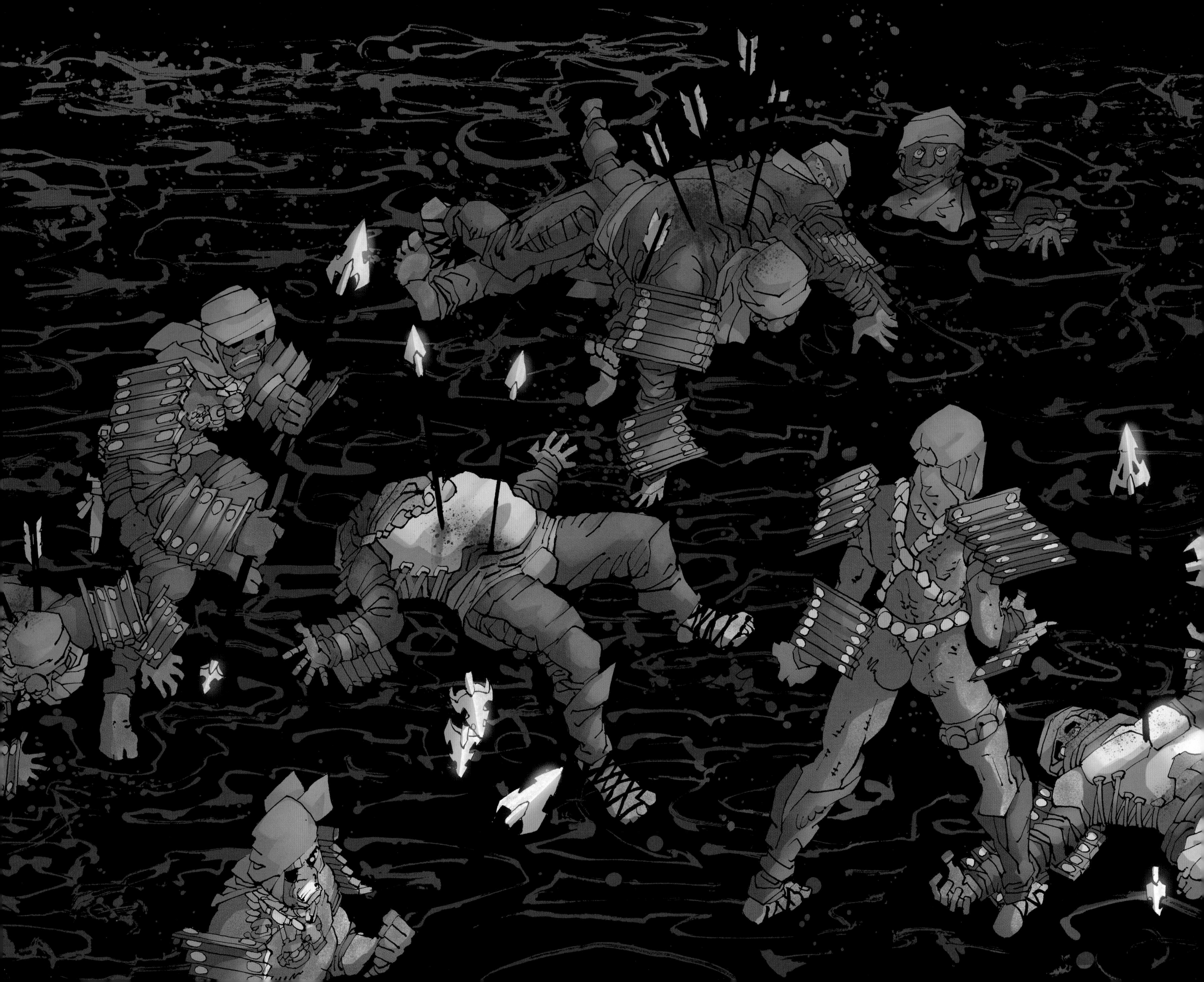

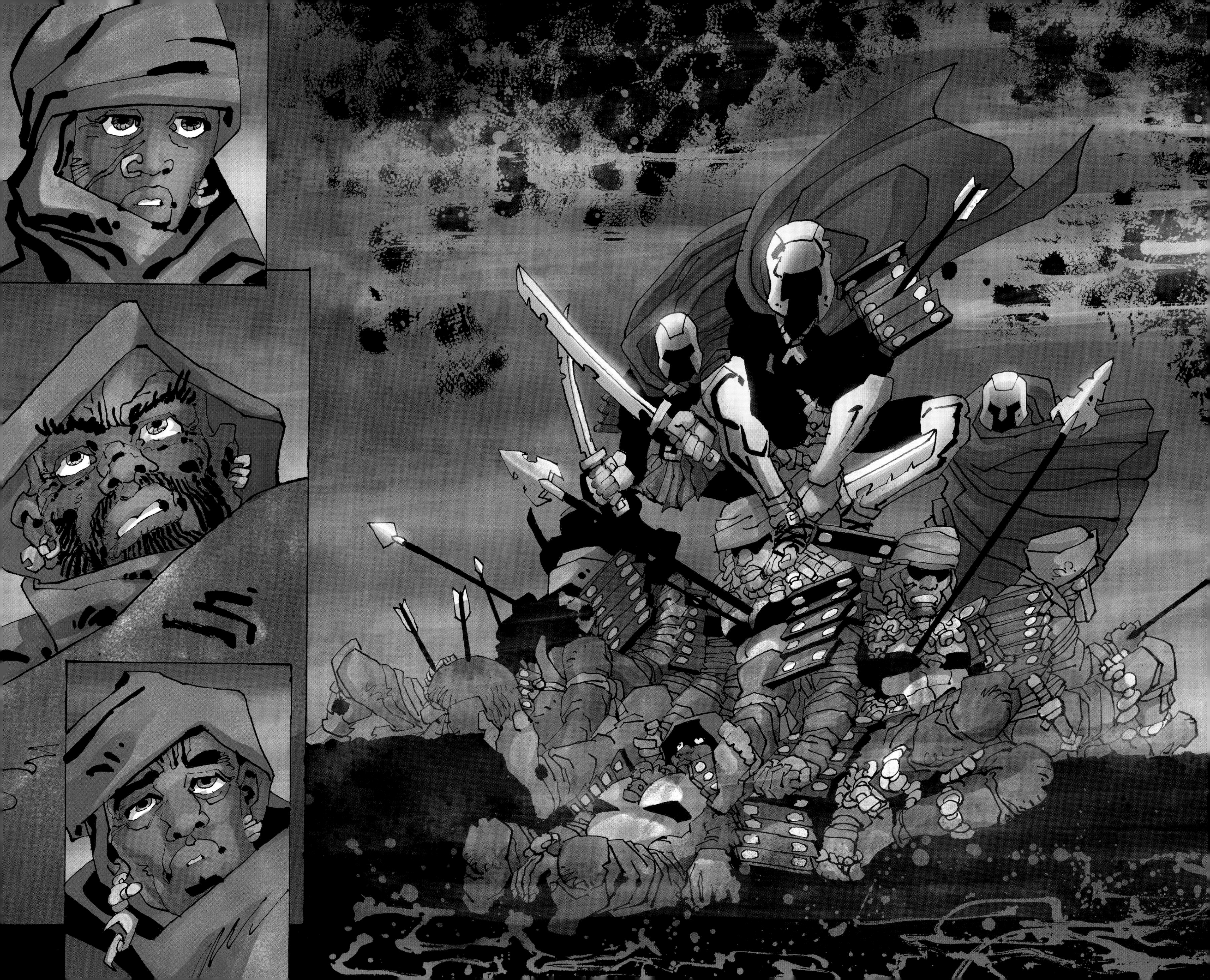

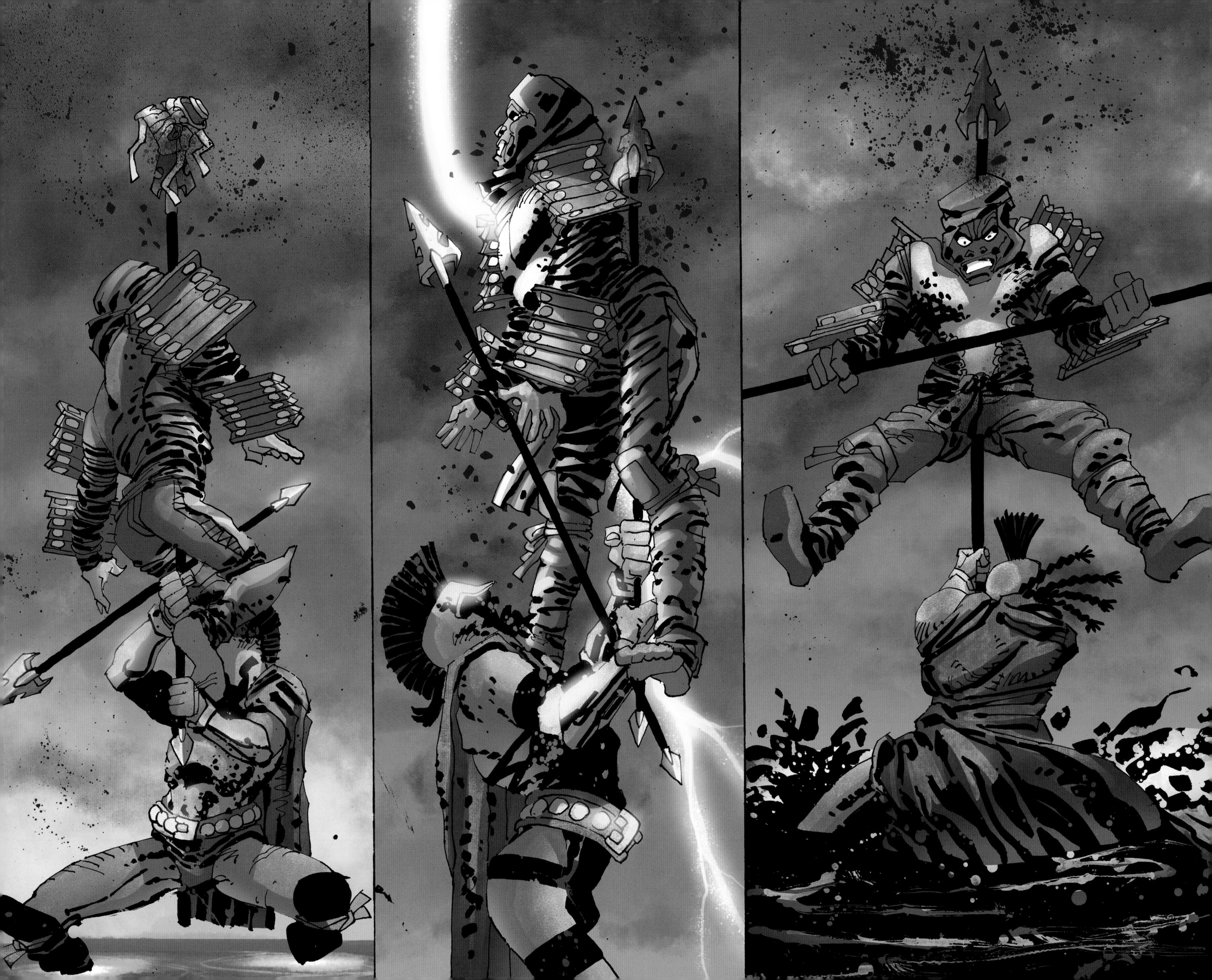

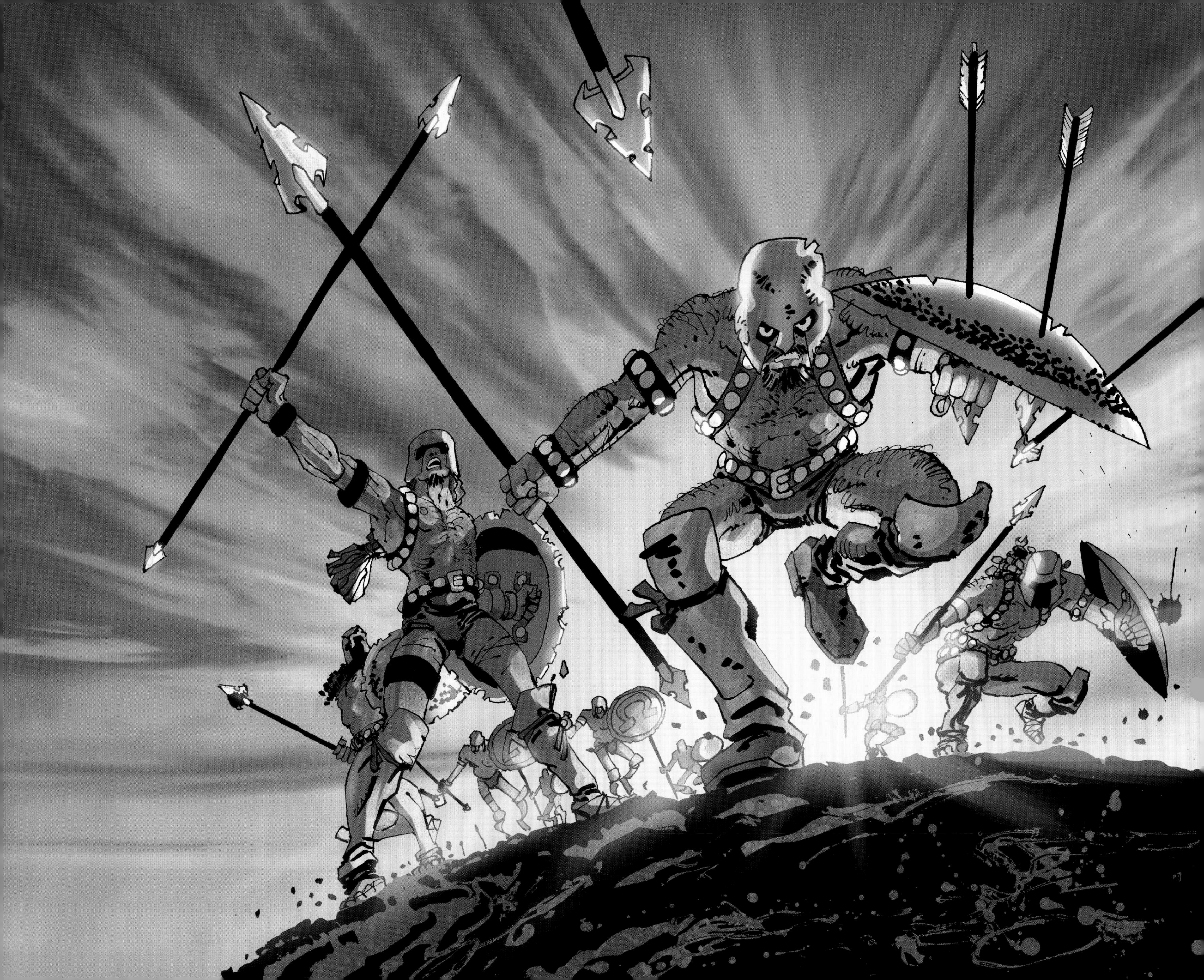

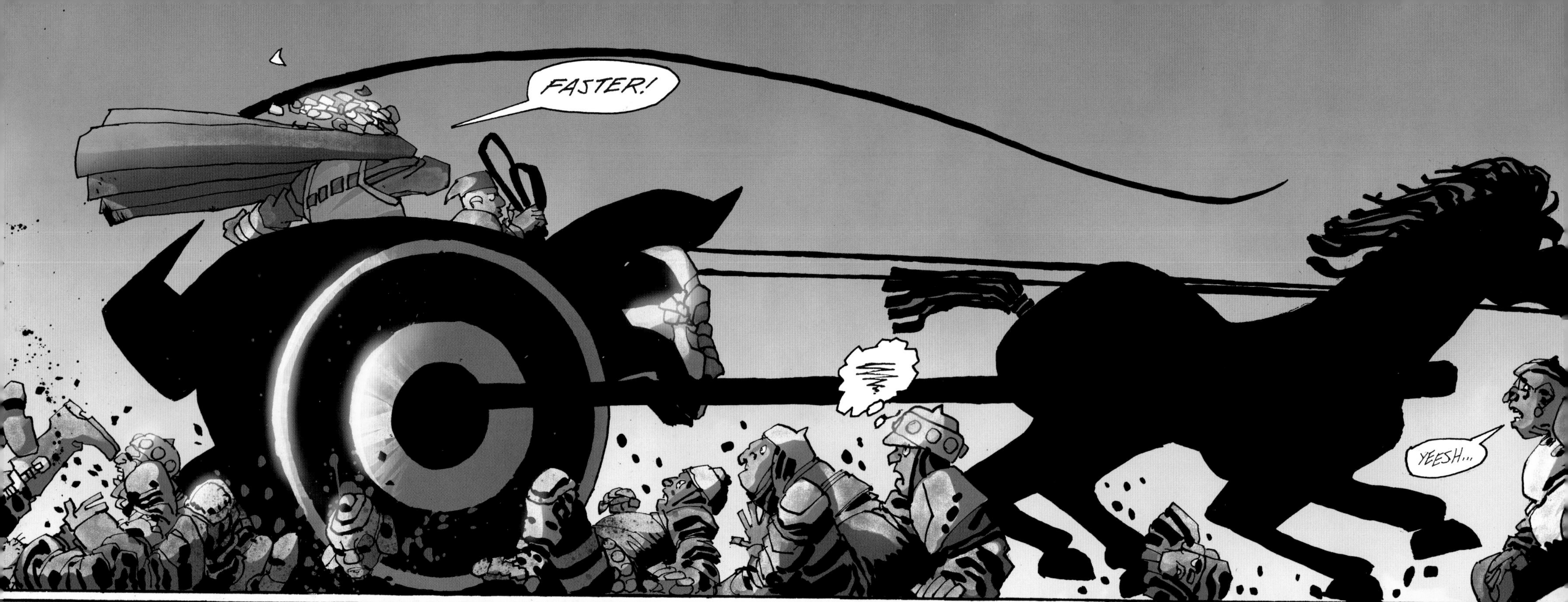
FASTER!
YEESH...

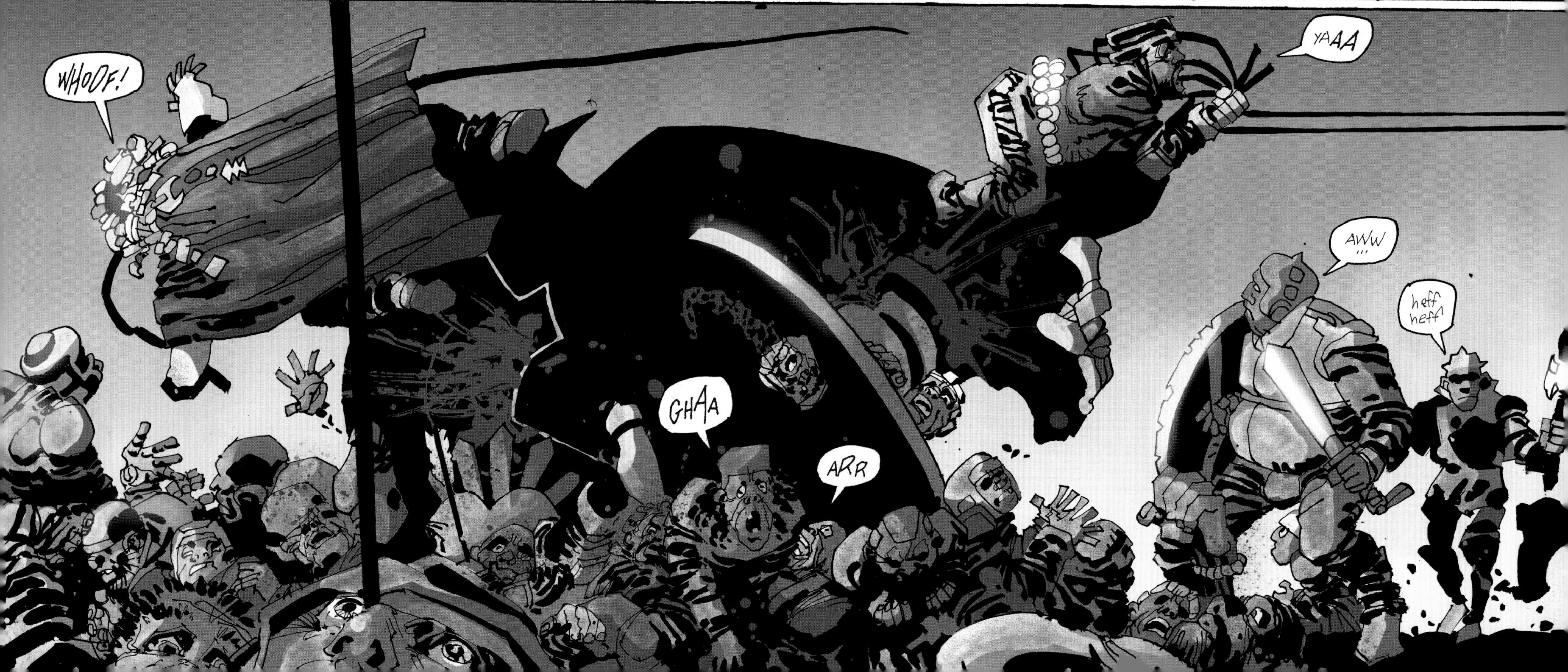
WHOOF!
YAAA
AWW ...
heff heff!
GHAA
ARR

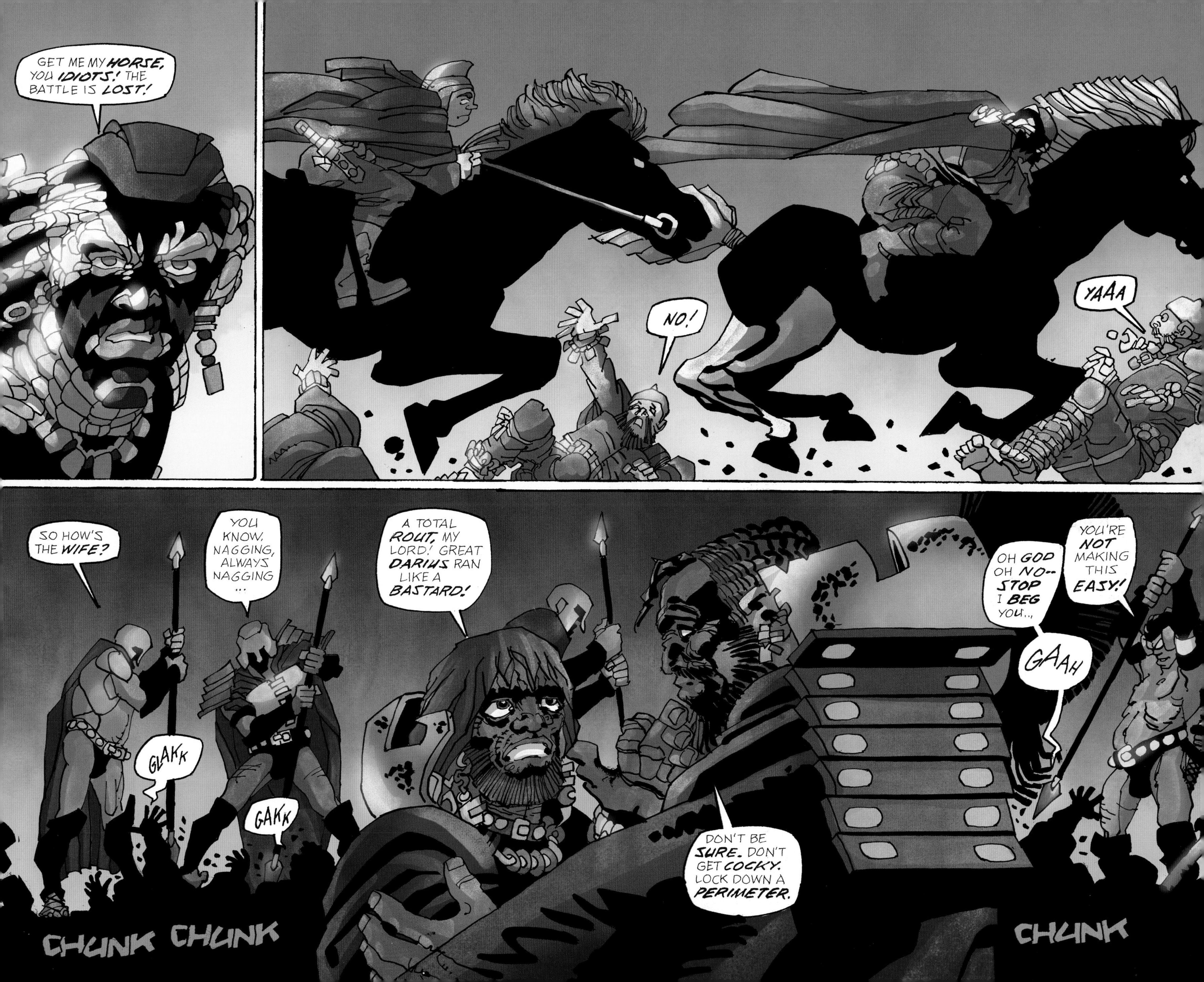
GET ME MY HORSE, YOU IDIOTS! THE BATTLE IS LOST!
NO!
YAAA
SO HOW'S THE WIFE?
YOU KNOW. NAGGING, ALWAYS NAGGING ...
A TOTAL ROUT, MY LORD! GREAT DARIUS RAN LIKE A BASTARD!
GLAKK
GAKK
DON'T BE SURE. DON'T GET COCKY. LOCK DOWN A PERIMETER.
OH GOD OH NO-- STOP I BEG YOU...
YOU'RE NOT MAKING THIS EASY!
GAAH
CHUNK CHUNK
CHUNK

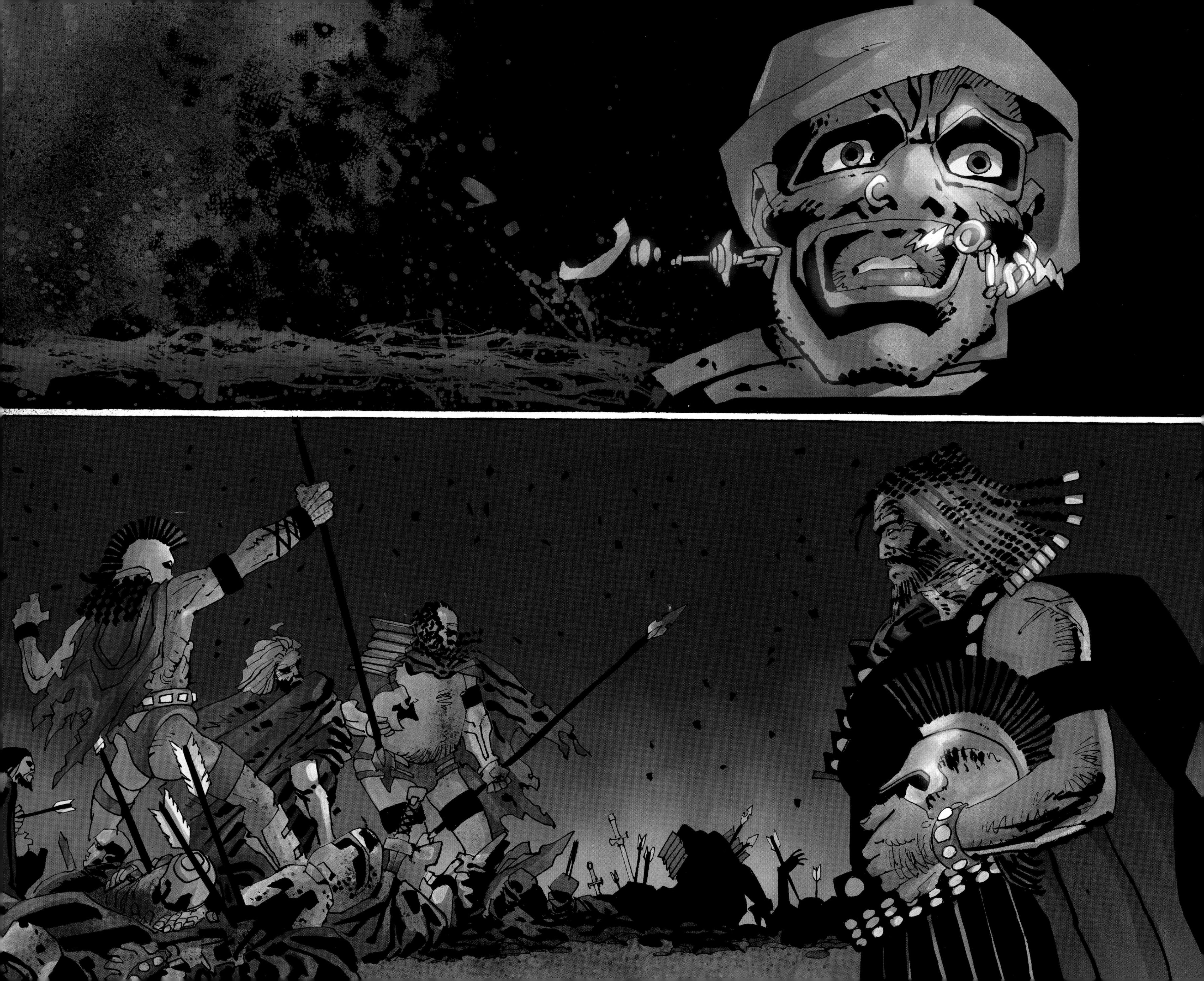

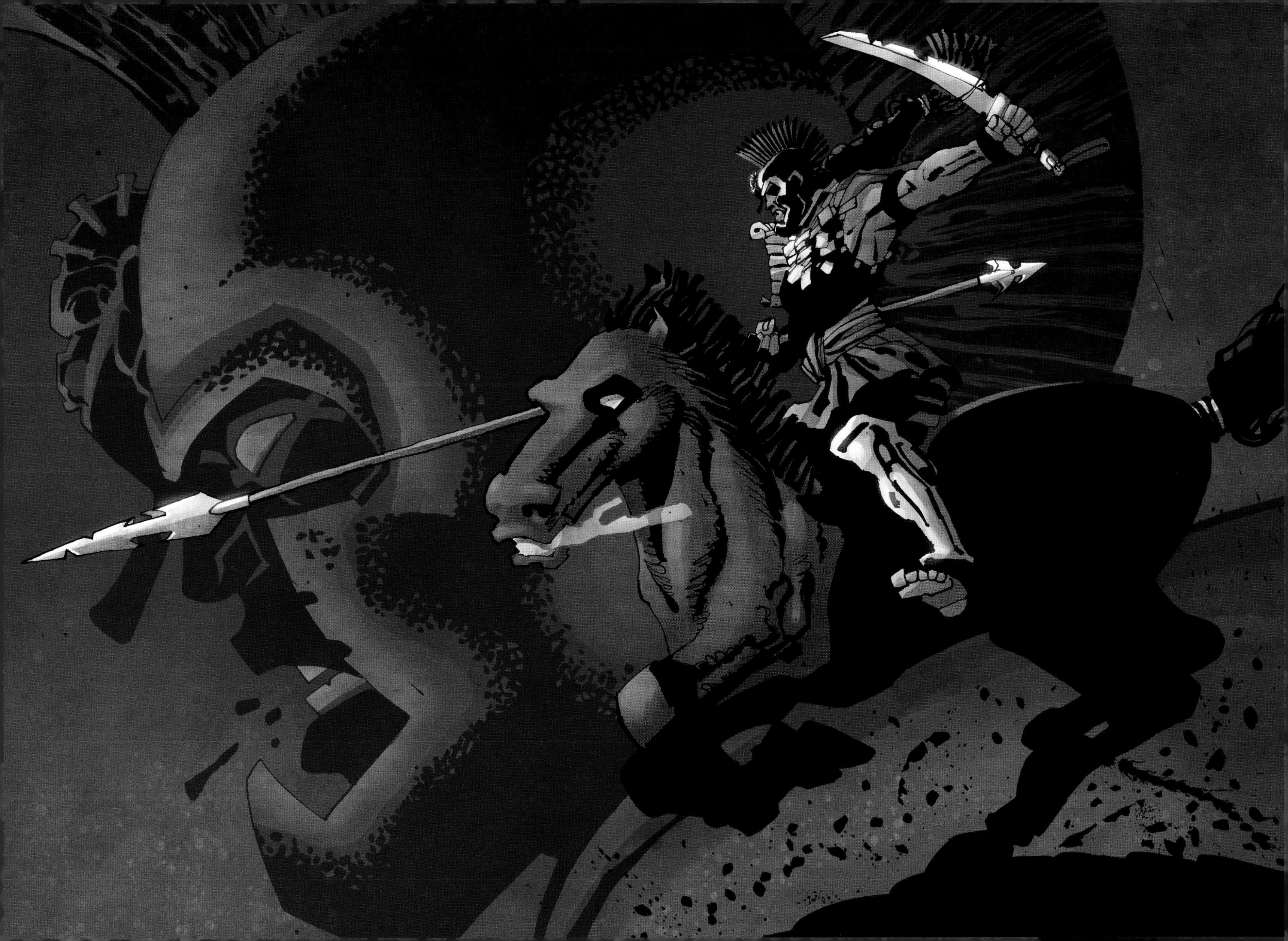

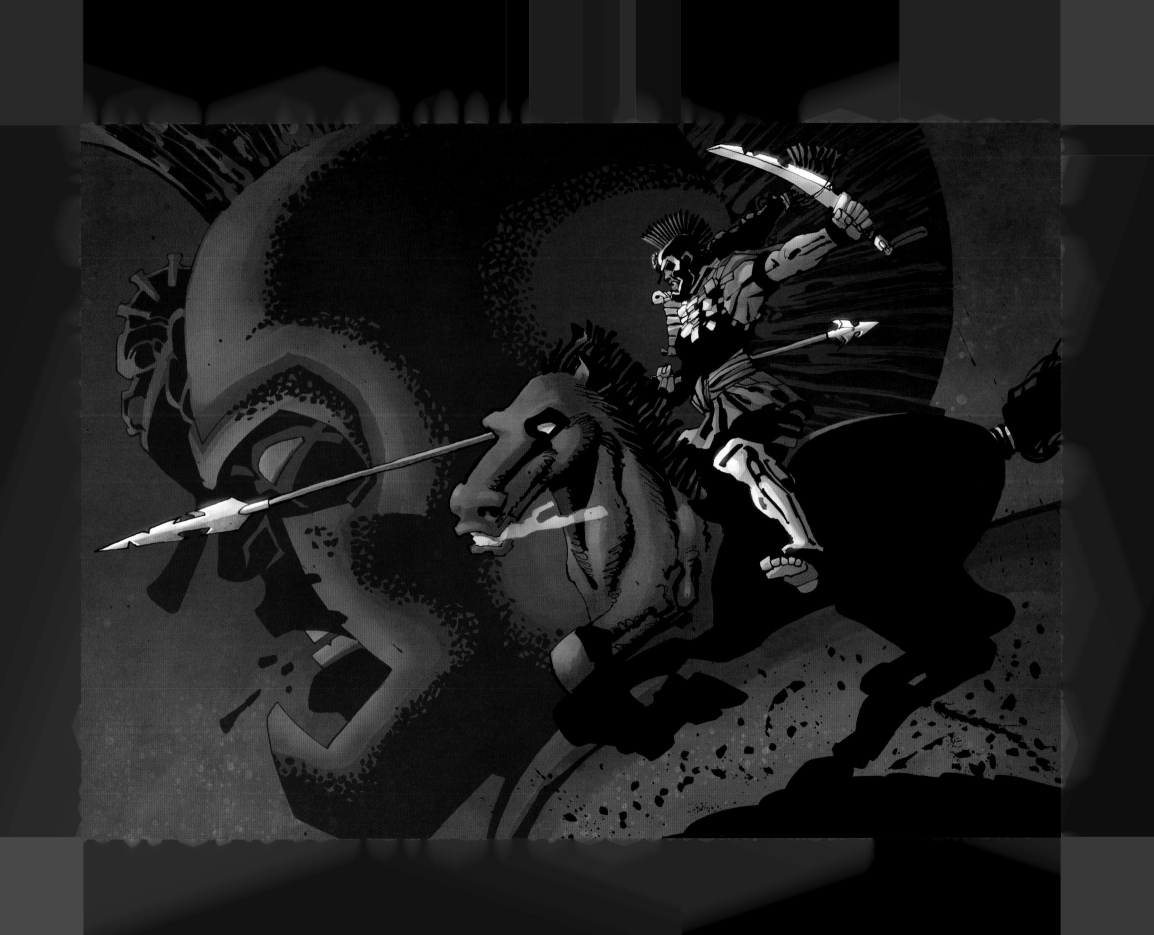

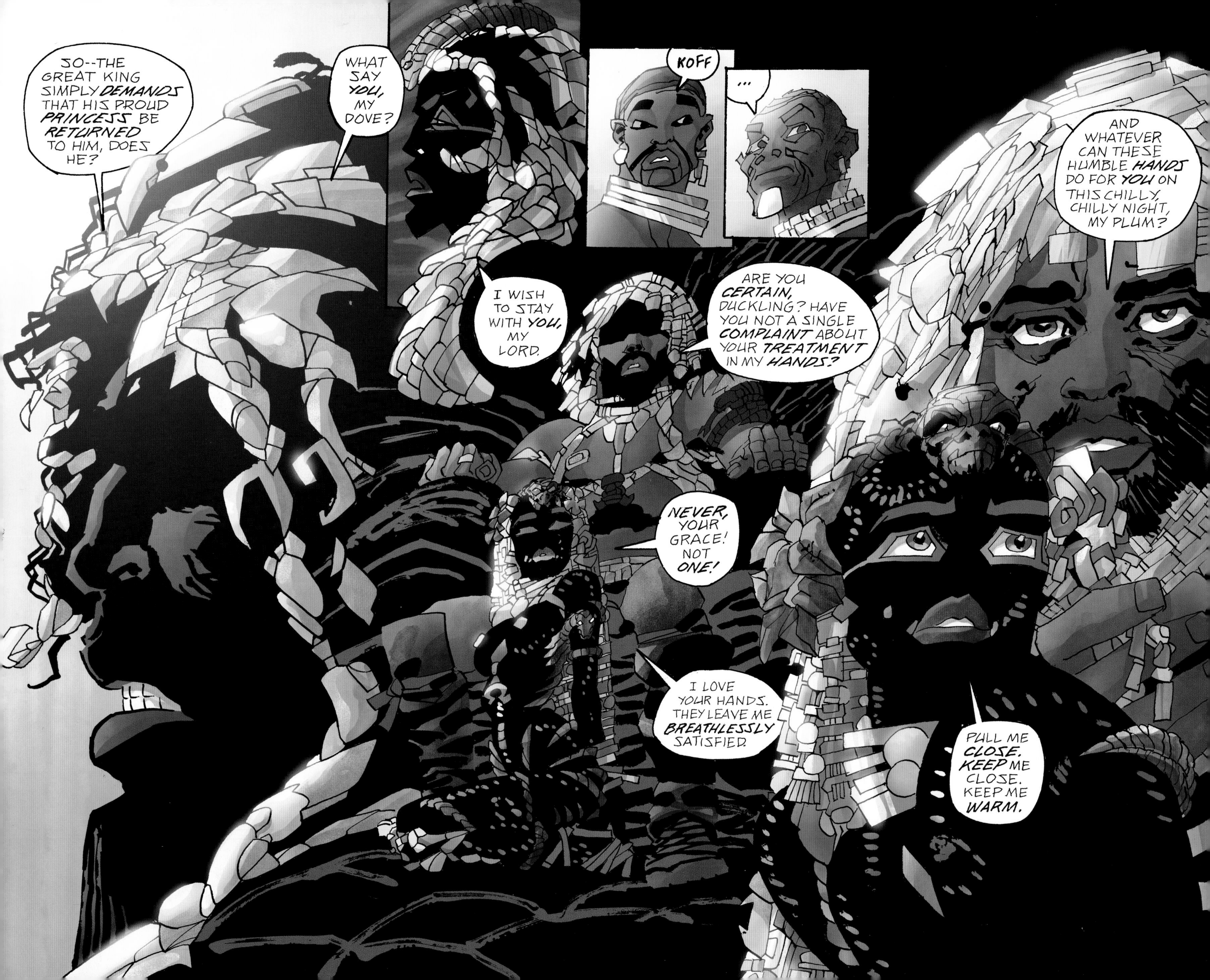
SO--THE GREAT KING SIMPLY DEMANDS THAT HIS PROUD PRINCESS BE RETURNED TO HIM, DOES HE?
WHAT SAY YOU, MY DOVE?
KOFF
...
AND WHATEVER CAN THESE HUMBLE HANDS DO FOR YOU ON THIS CHILLY, CHILLY NIGHT, MY PLUM?
I WISH TO STAY WITH YOU, MY LORD.
ARE YOU CERTAIN, DUCKLING? HAVE YOU NOT A SINGLE COMPLAINT ABOUT YOUR TREATMENT IN MY HANDS?
NEVER, YOUR GRACE! NOT ONE!
I LOVE YOUR HANDS. THEY LEAVE ME BREATHLESSLY SATISFIED.
PULL ME CLOSE. KEEP ME CLOSE. KEEP ME WARM.

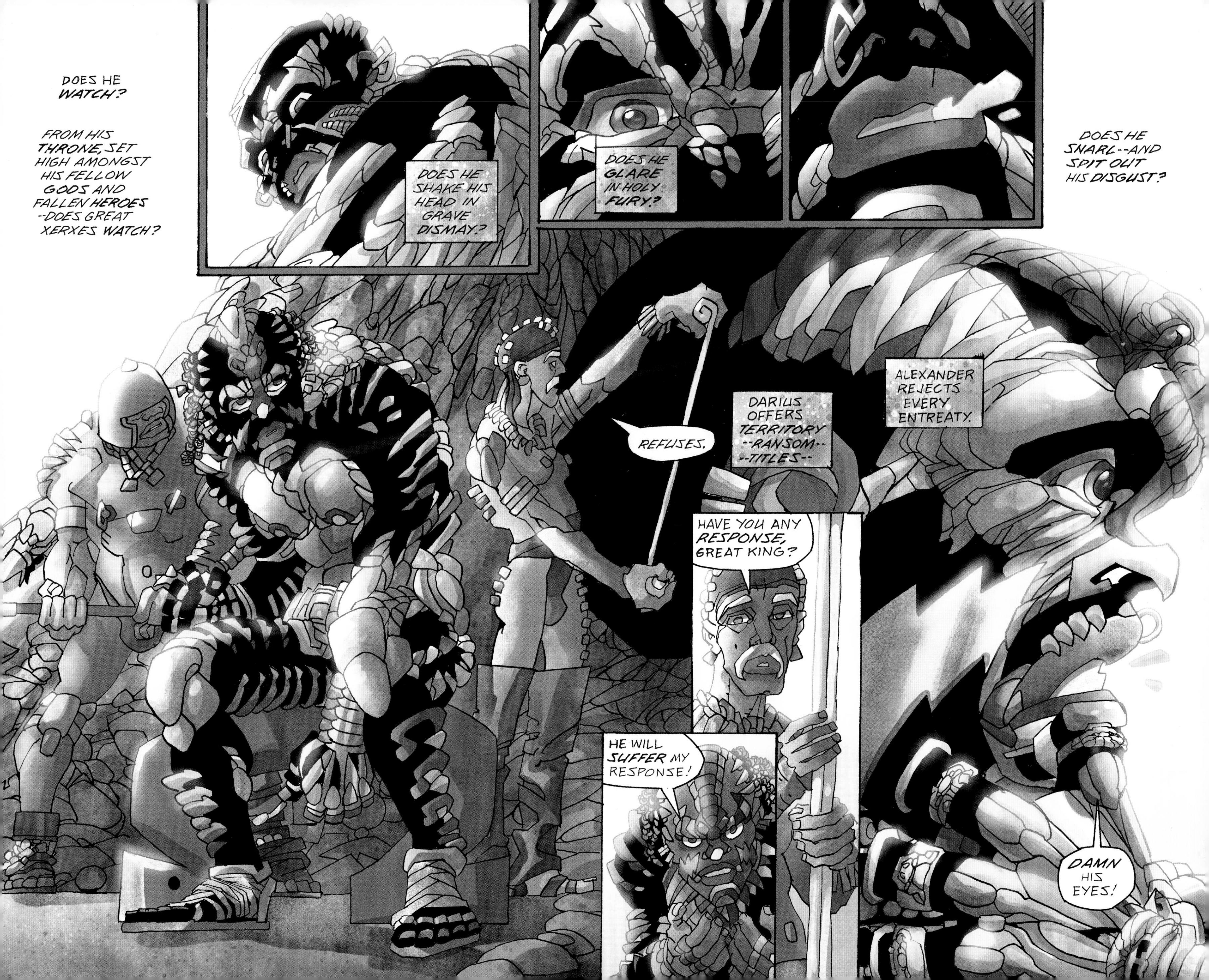
DOES HE WATCH?
FROM HIS THRONE, SET HIGH AMONGST HIS FELLOW GODS AND FALLEN HEROES --DOES GREAT XERXES WATCH?
DOES HE SHAKE HIS HEAD IN GRAVE DISMAY?
DOES HE GLARE IN HOLY FURY?
DOES HE SNARL--AND SPIT OUT HIS DISGUST?
REFUSES.
DARIUS OFFERS TERRITORY --RANSOM-- --TITLES--
ALEXANDER REJECTS EVERY ENTREATY.
HAVE YOU ANY RESPONSE, GREAT KING?
HE WILL SUFFER MY RESPONSE!
DAMN HIS EYES!

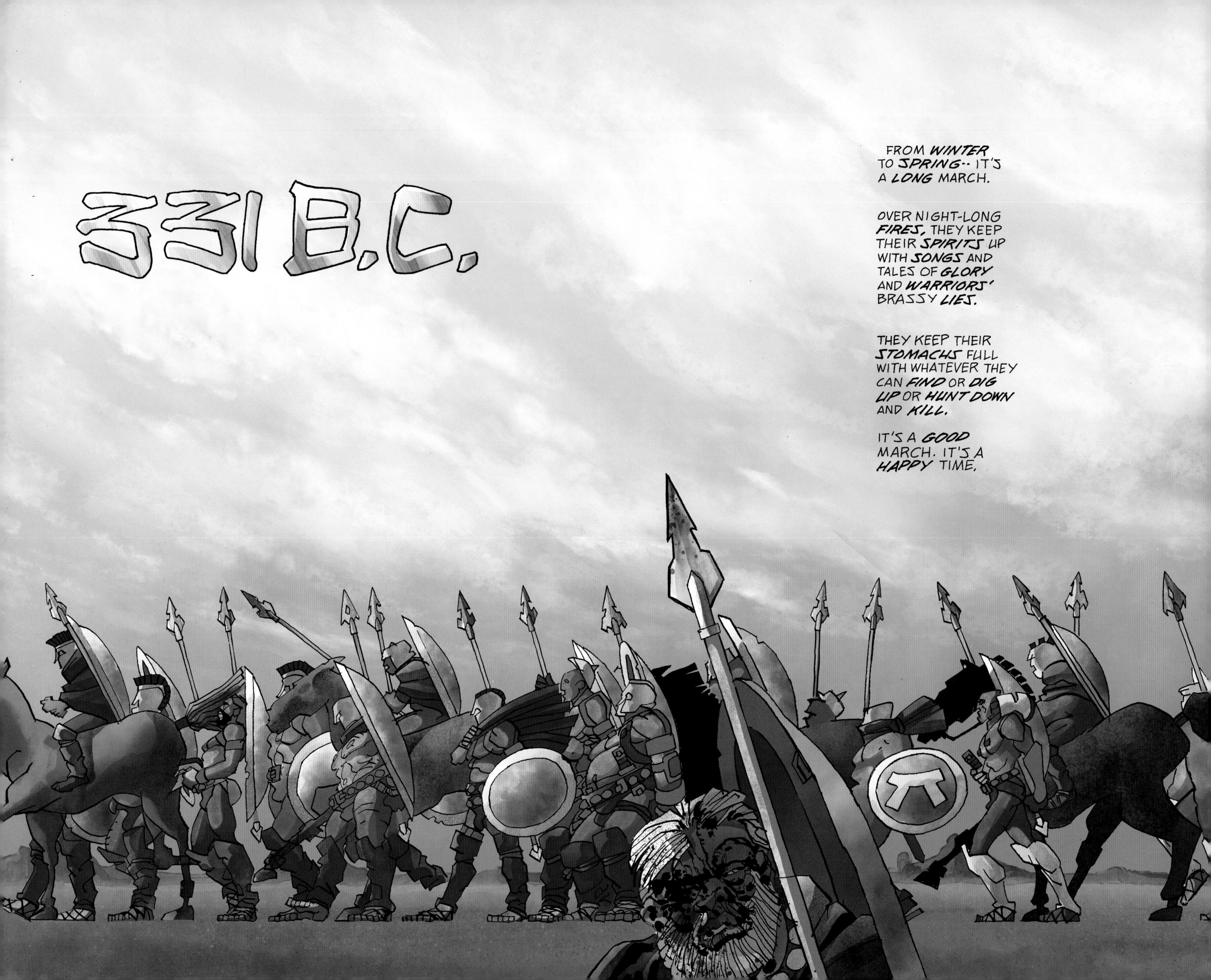
331 B.C.
FROM WINTER TO SPRING-- IT'S A LONG MARCH.
OVER NIGHT-LONG FIRES, THEY KEEP THEIR SPIRITS UP WITH SONGS AND TALES OF GLORY AND WARRIORS' BRASSY LIES.
THEY KEEP THEIR STOMACHS FULL WITH WHATEVER THEY CAN FIND OR DIG UP OR HUNT DOWN AND KILL.
IT'S A GOOD MARCH. IT'S A HAPPY TIME.

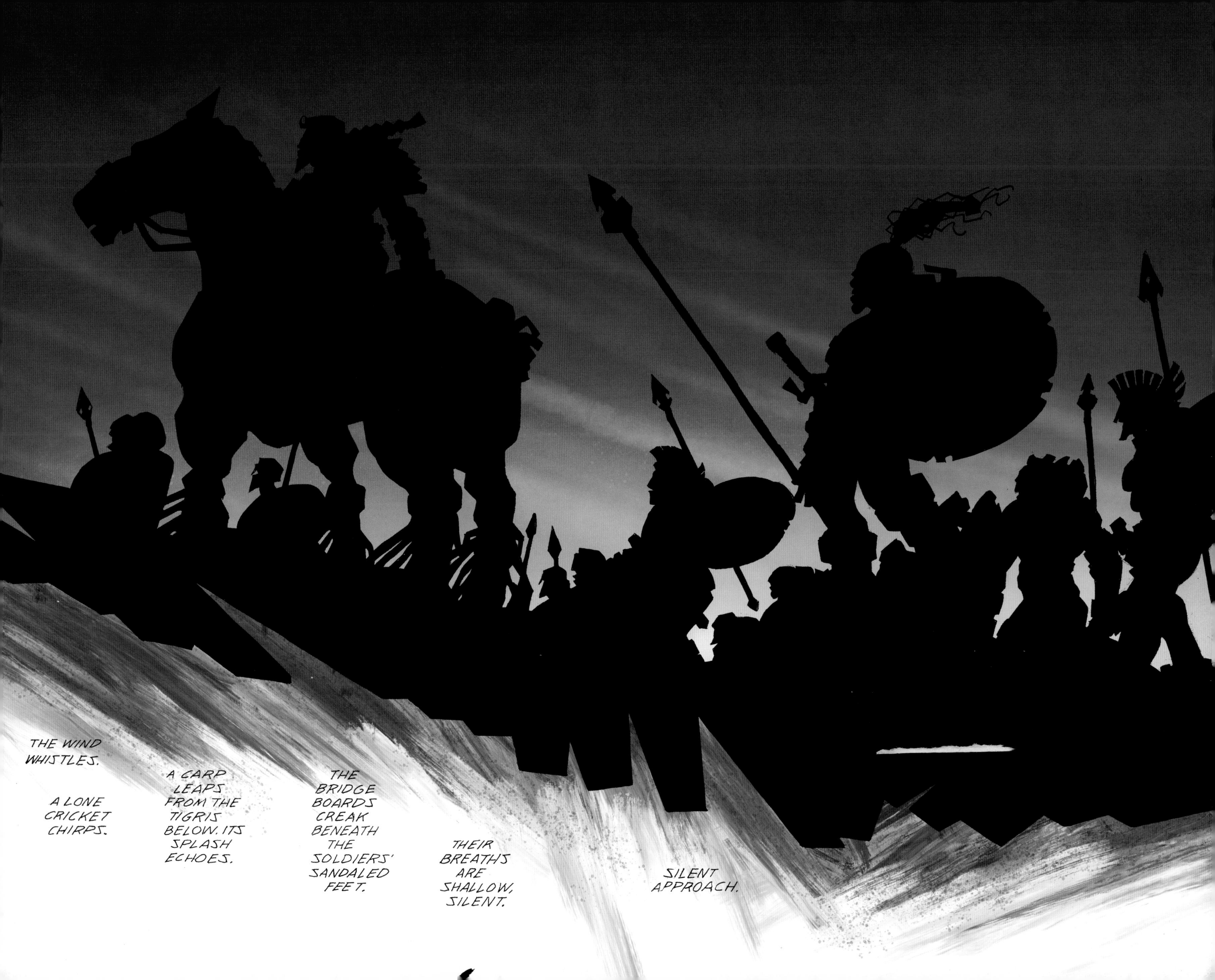
THE WIND WHISTLES.
A LONE CRICKET CHIRPS.
A CARP LEAPS FROM THE TIGRIS BELOW. ITS SPLASH ECHOES.
THE BRIDGE BOARDS CREAK BENEATH THE SOLDIERS' SANDALED FEET.
THEIR BREATHS ARE SHALLOW, SILENT.
SILENT APPROACH.

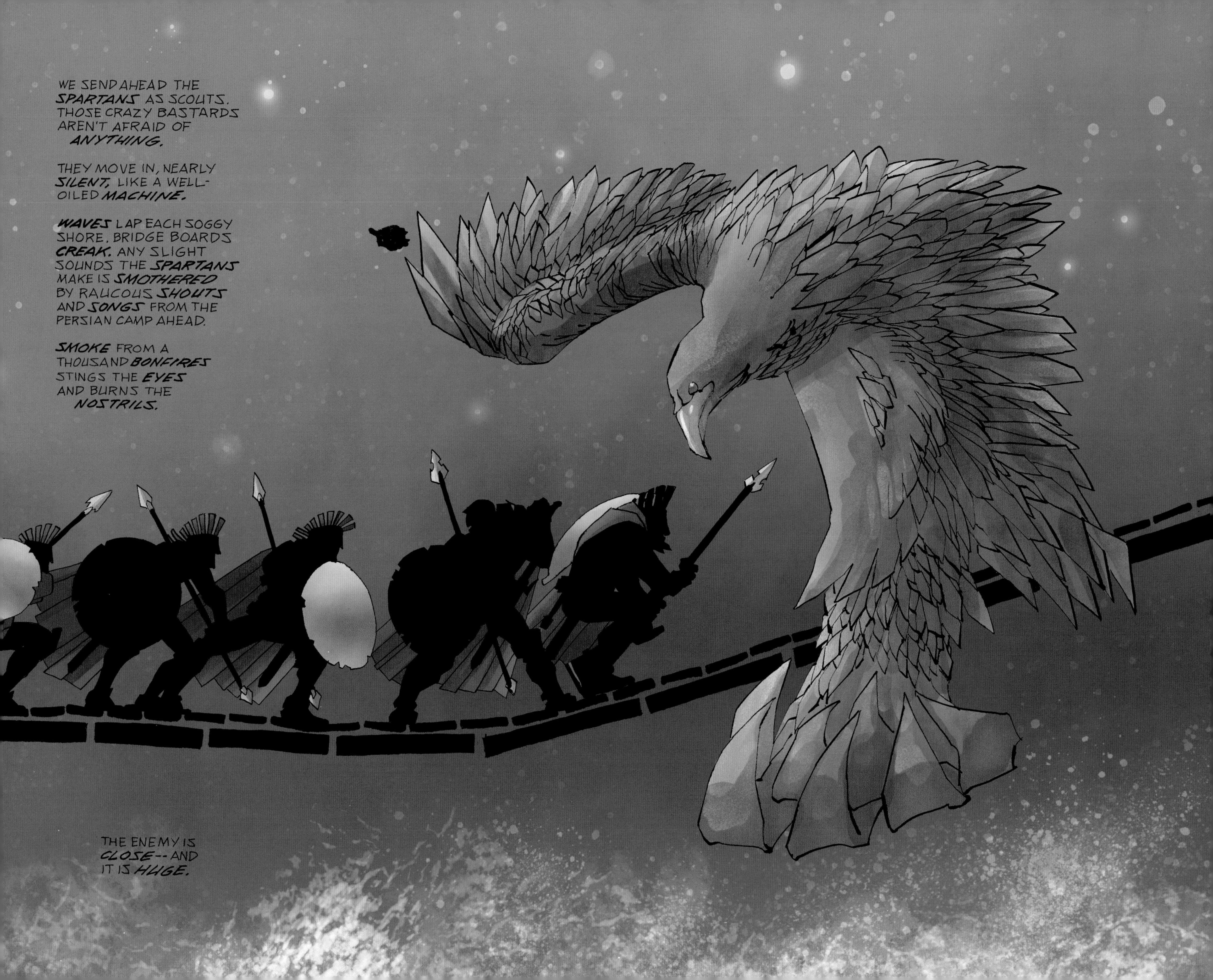
WE SEND AHEAD THE SPARTANS AS SCOUTS. THOSE CRAZY BASTARDS AREN'T AFRAID OF ANYTHING.
THEY MOVE IN, NEARLY SILENT, LIKE A WELL-OILED MACHINE.
WAVES LAP EACH SOGGY SHORE. BRIDGE BOARDS CREAK. ANY SLIGHT SOUNDS THE SPARTANS MAKE IS SMOTHERED BY RAUCOUS SHOUTS AND SONGS FROM THE PERSIAN CAMP AHEAD.
SMOKE FROM A THOUSAND BONFIRES STINGS THE EYES AND BURNS THE NOSTRILS.
THE ENEMY IS CLOSE-- AND IT IS HUGE.

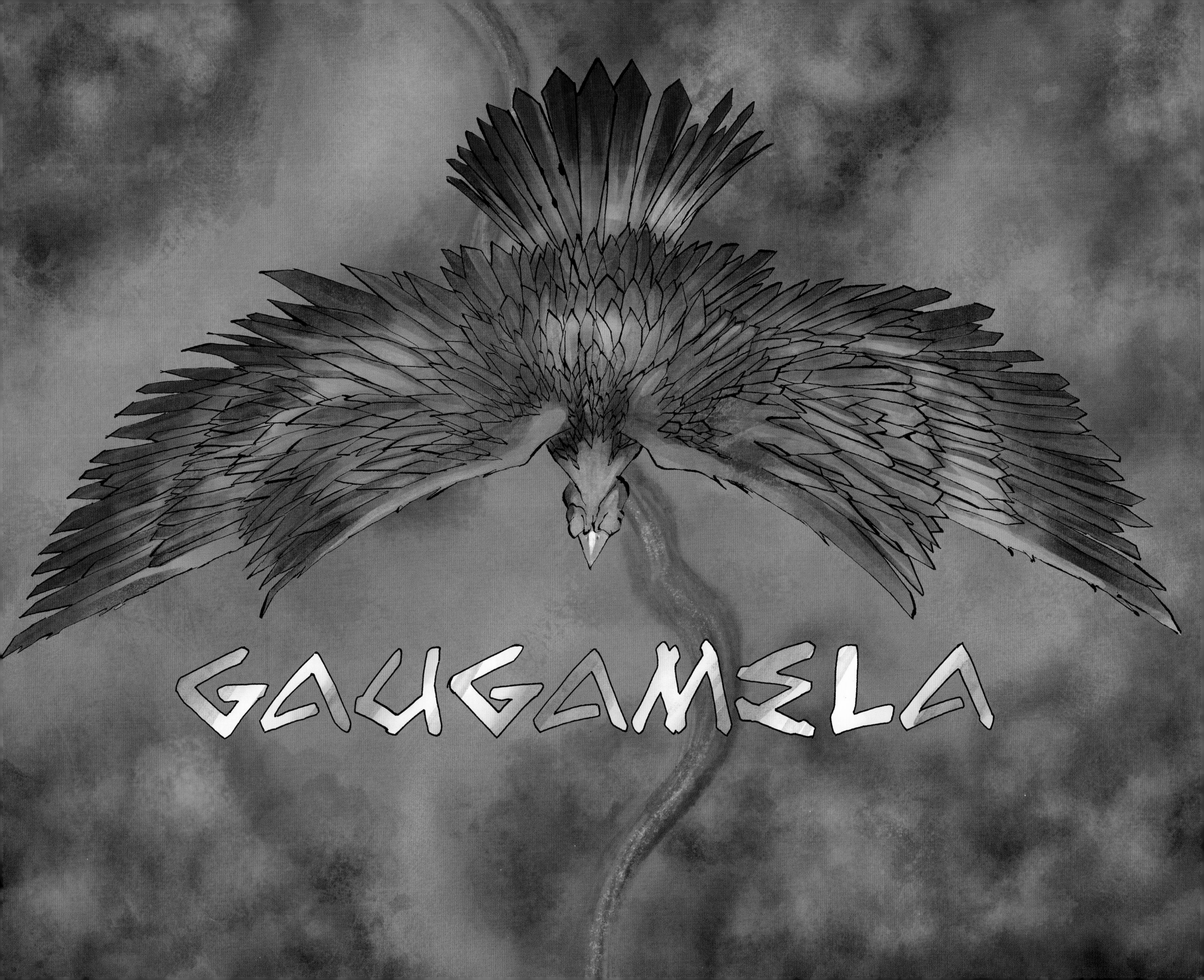
GAUGAMELA

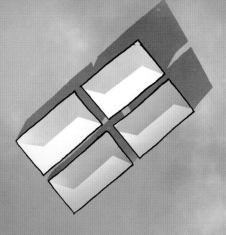

MACEDONIANS

THE FORCES OF **ALEXANDER.**

40,000 MACEDONIANS, THE FIRST TRAINED ARMY TO FACE PERSIA.

THE FORCES OF **DARIUS III.**

500,000 TO 1 MILLION PERSIANS, FROM ALL PARTS OF THE EMPIRE.

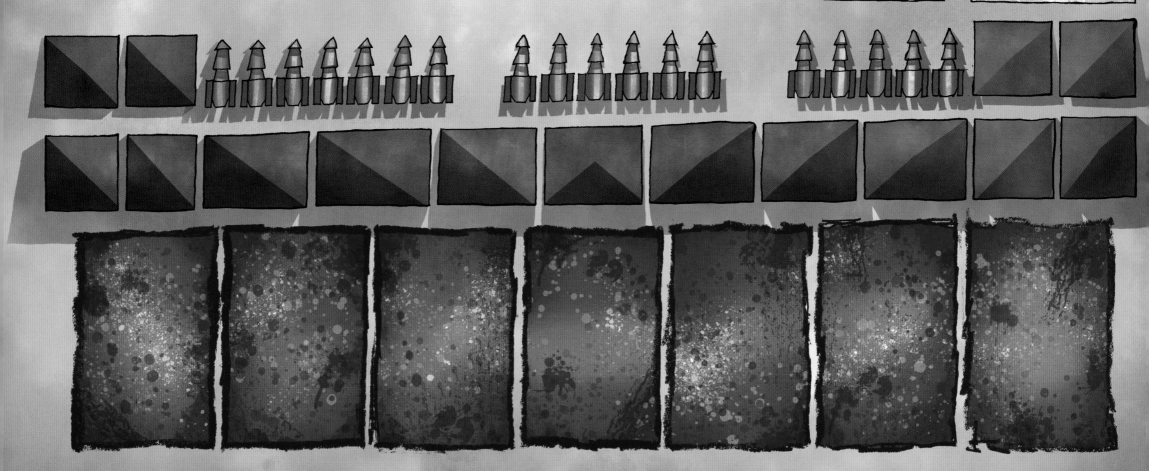

PERSIANS

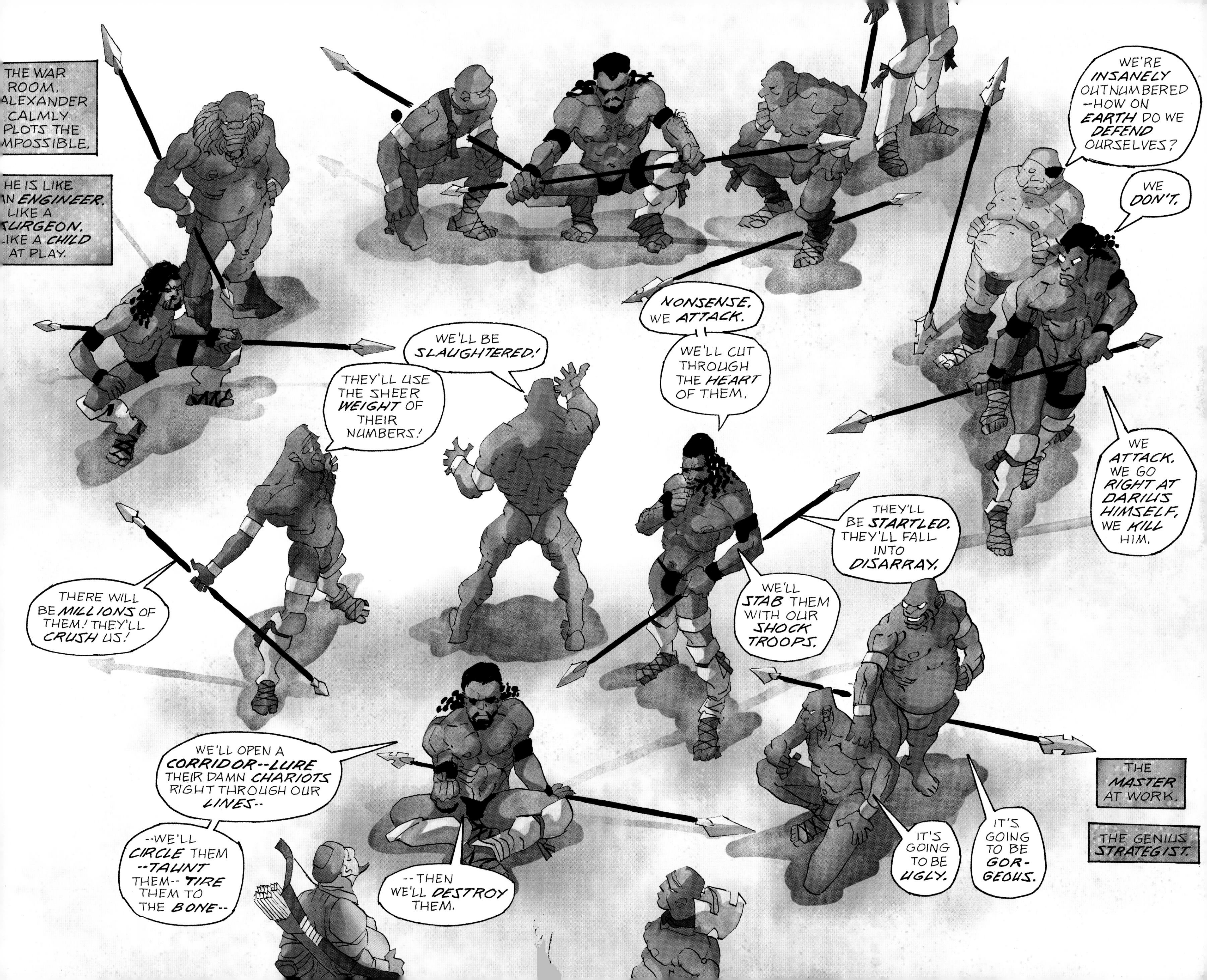

THE WAR ROOM. ALEXANDER CALMLY PLOTS THE MPOSSIBLE.
HE IS LIKE N ENGINEER. LIKE A URGEON. IKE A CHILD AT PLAY.
WE'RE INSANELY OUTNUMBERED --HOW ON EARTH DO WE DEFEND OURSELVES?
WE DON'T.
NONSENSE. WE ATTACK.
WE'LL CUT THROUGH THE HEART OF THEM.
WE'LL BE SLAUGHTERED!
THEY'LL USE THE SHEER WEIGHT OF THEIR NUMBERS!
THERE WILL BE MILLIONS OF THEM! THEY'LL CRUSH US!
WE ATTACK. WE GO RIGHT AT DARIUS HIMSELF. WE KILL HIM.
THEY'LL BE STARTLED. THEY'LL FALL INTO DISARRAY.
WE'LL STAB THEM WITH OUR SHOCK TROOPS.
WE'LL OPEN A CORRIDOR--LURE THEIR DAMN CHARIOTS RIGHT THROUGH OUR LINES--
--WE'LL CIRCLE THEM --TAUNT THEM-- TIRE THEM TO THE BONE--
--THEN WE'LL DESTROY THEM.
IT'S GOING TO BE UGLY.
IT'S GOING TO BE GOR-GEOUS.
THE MASTER AT WORK.
THE GENIUS STRATEGIST.

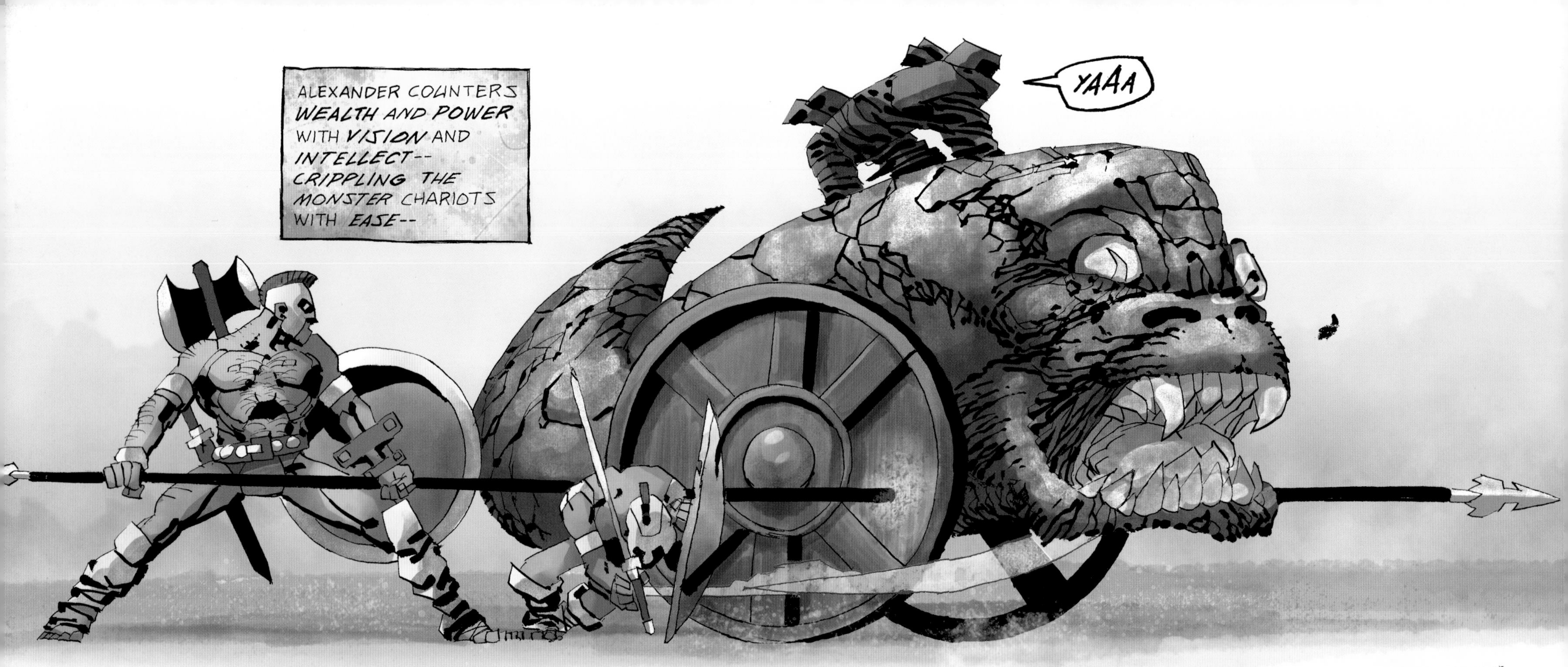
ALEXANDER COUNTERS WEALTH AND POWER WITH VISION AND INTELLECT-- CRIPPLING THE MONSTER CHARIOTS WITH EASE--
YAAA
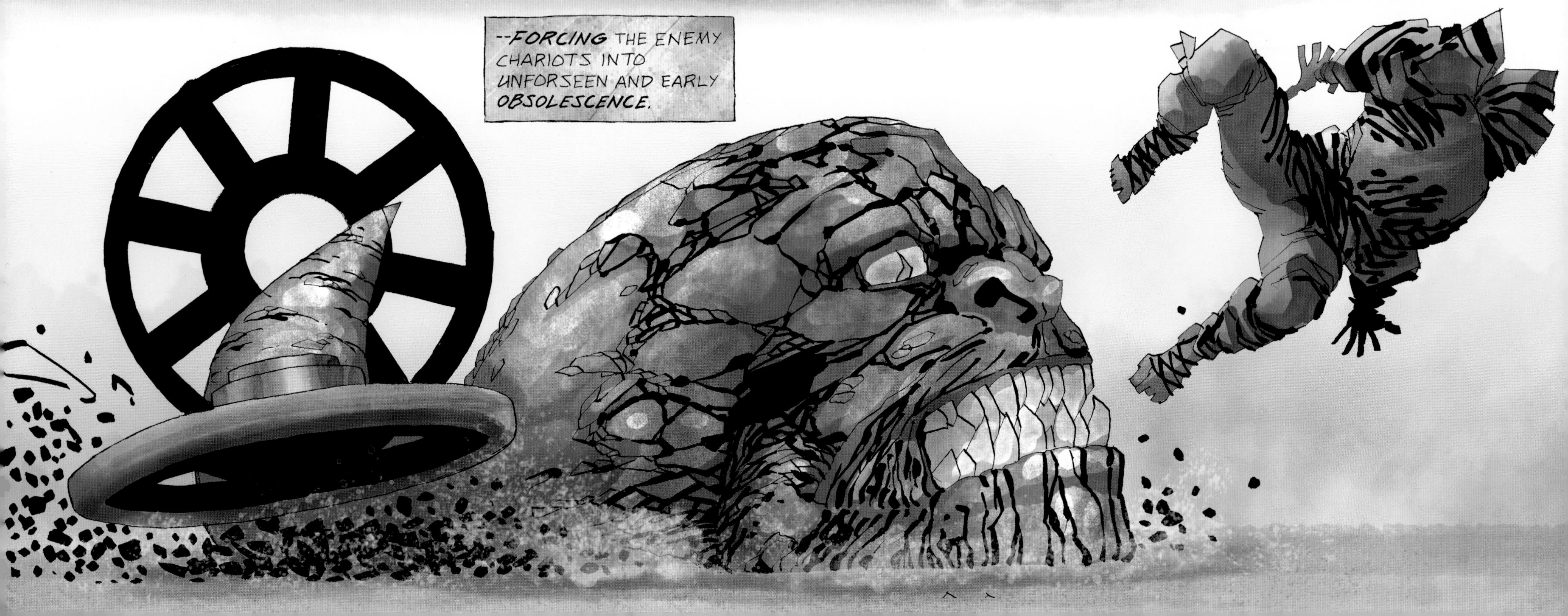
--FORCING THE ENEMY CHARIOTS INTO UNFORSEEN AND EARLY OBSOLESCENCE.

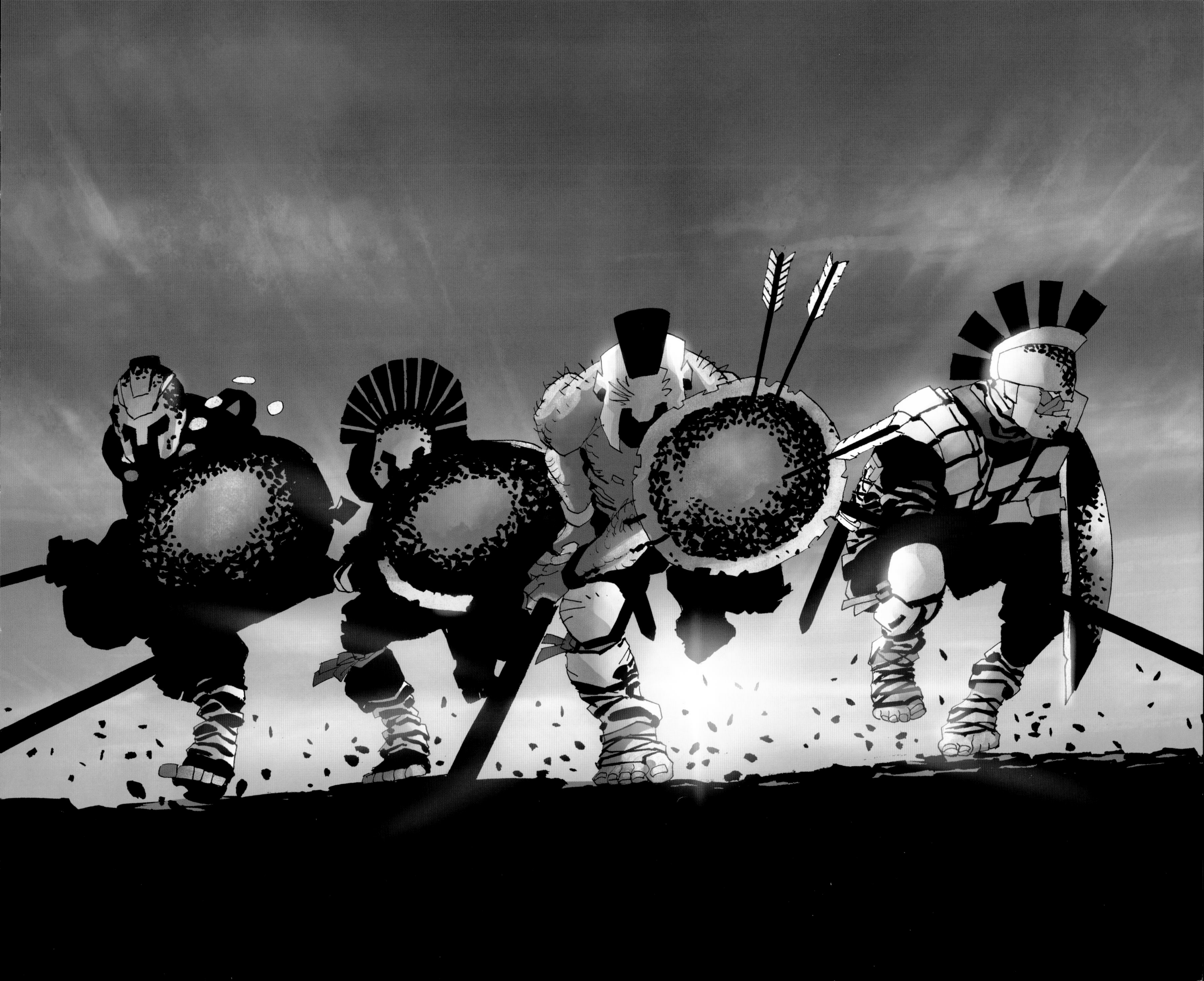

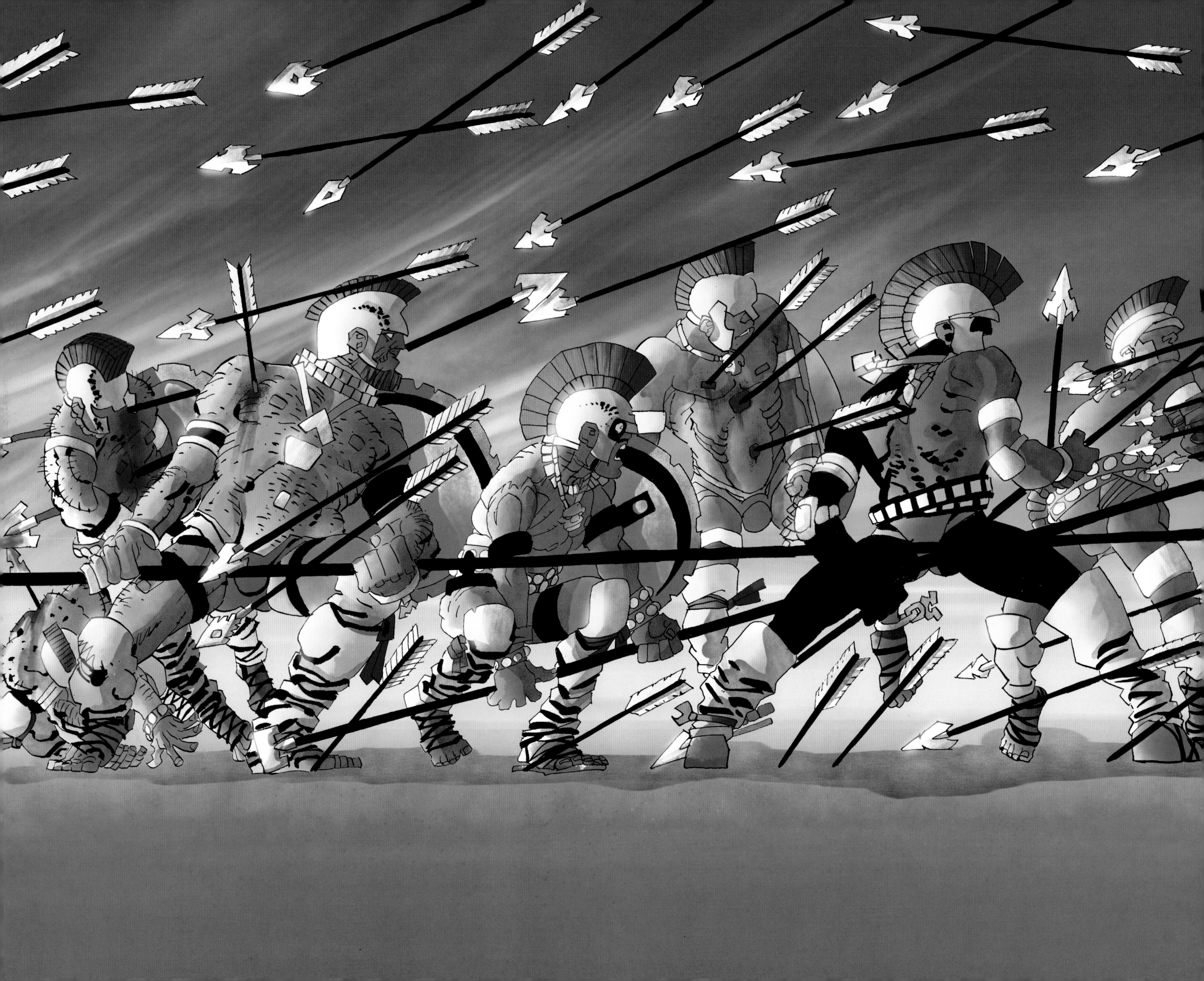

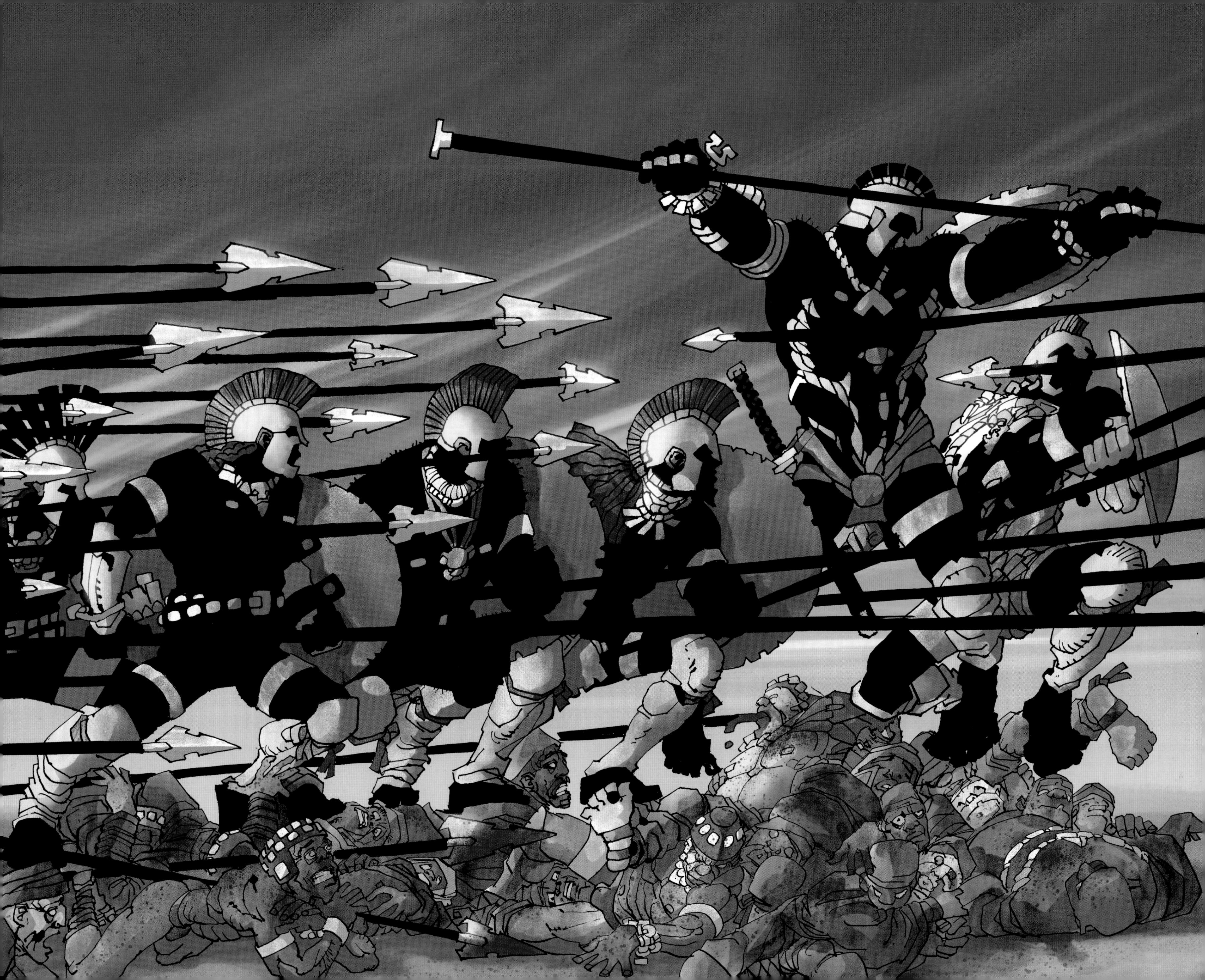

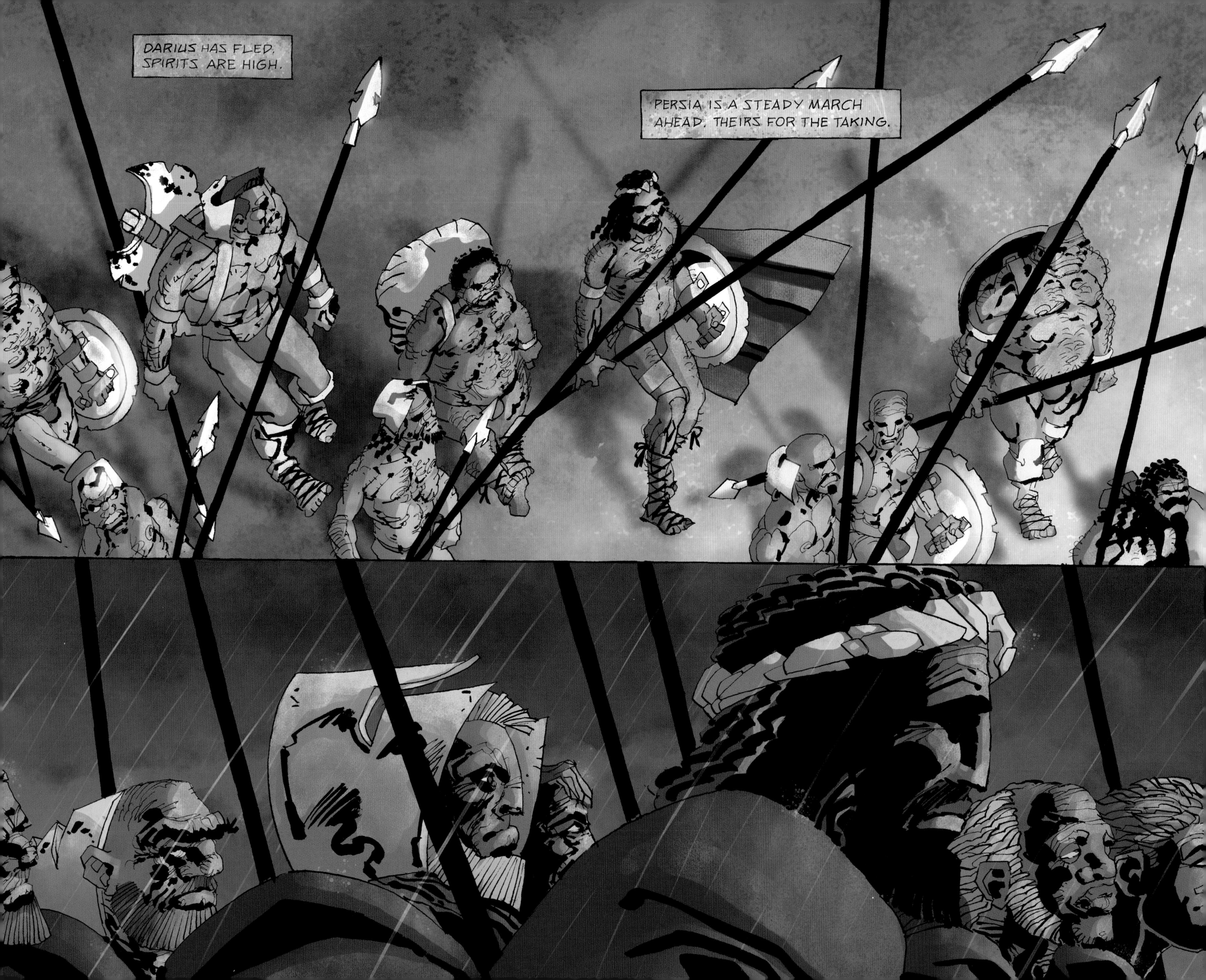
DARIUS HAS FLED. SPIRITS ARE HIGH.
PERSIA IS A STEADY MARCH AHEAD. THEIRS FOR THE TAKING.

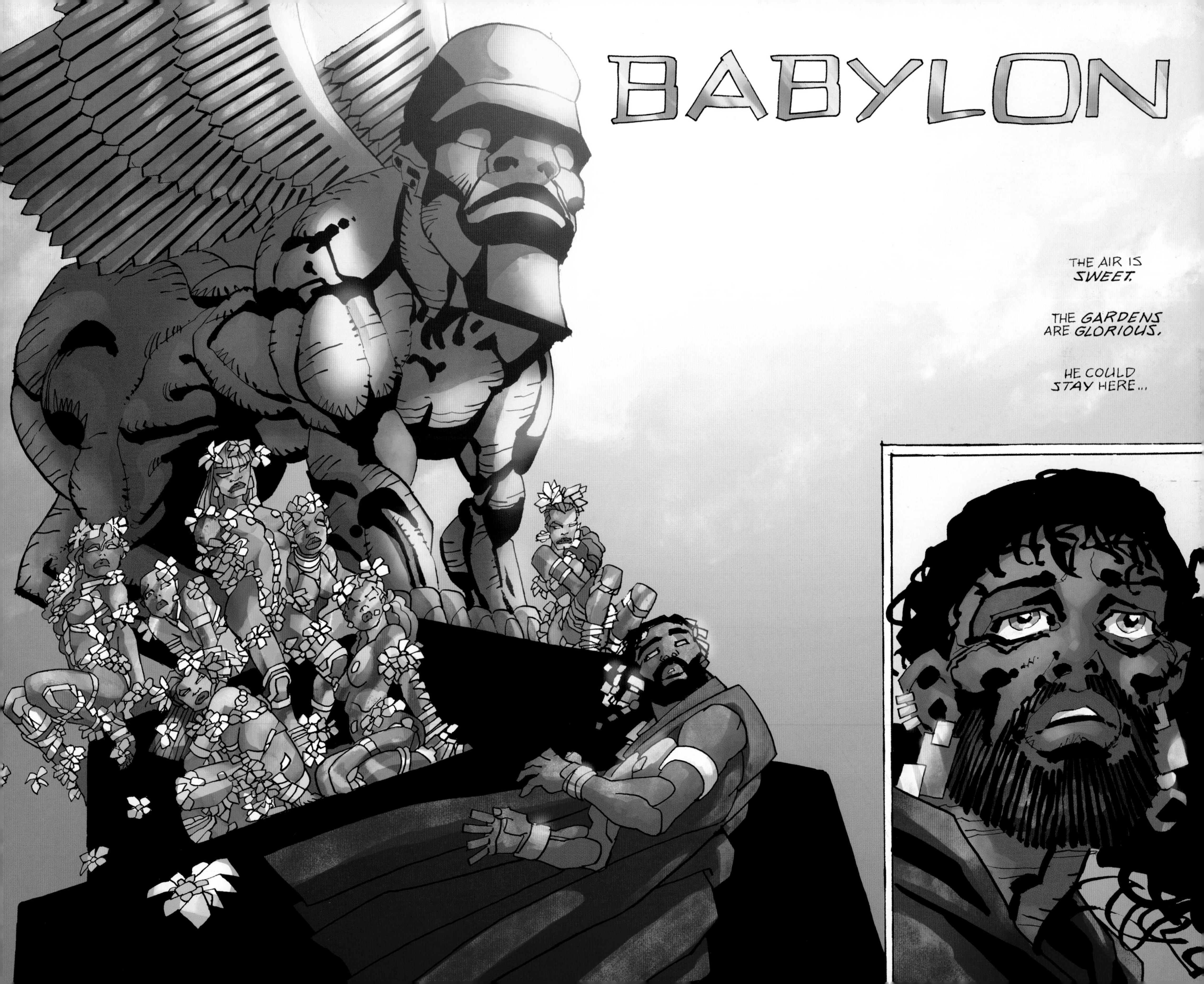
BABYLON
THE AIR IS SWEET.
THE GARDENS ARE GLORIOUS.
HE COULD STAY HERE...

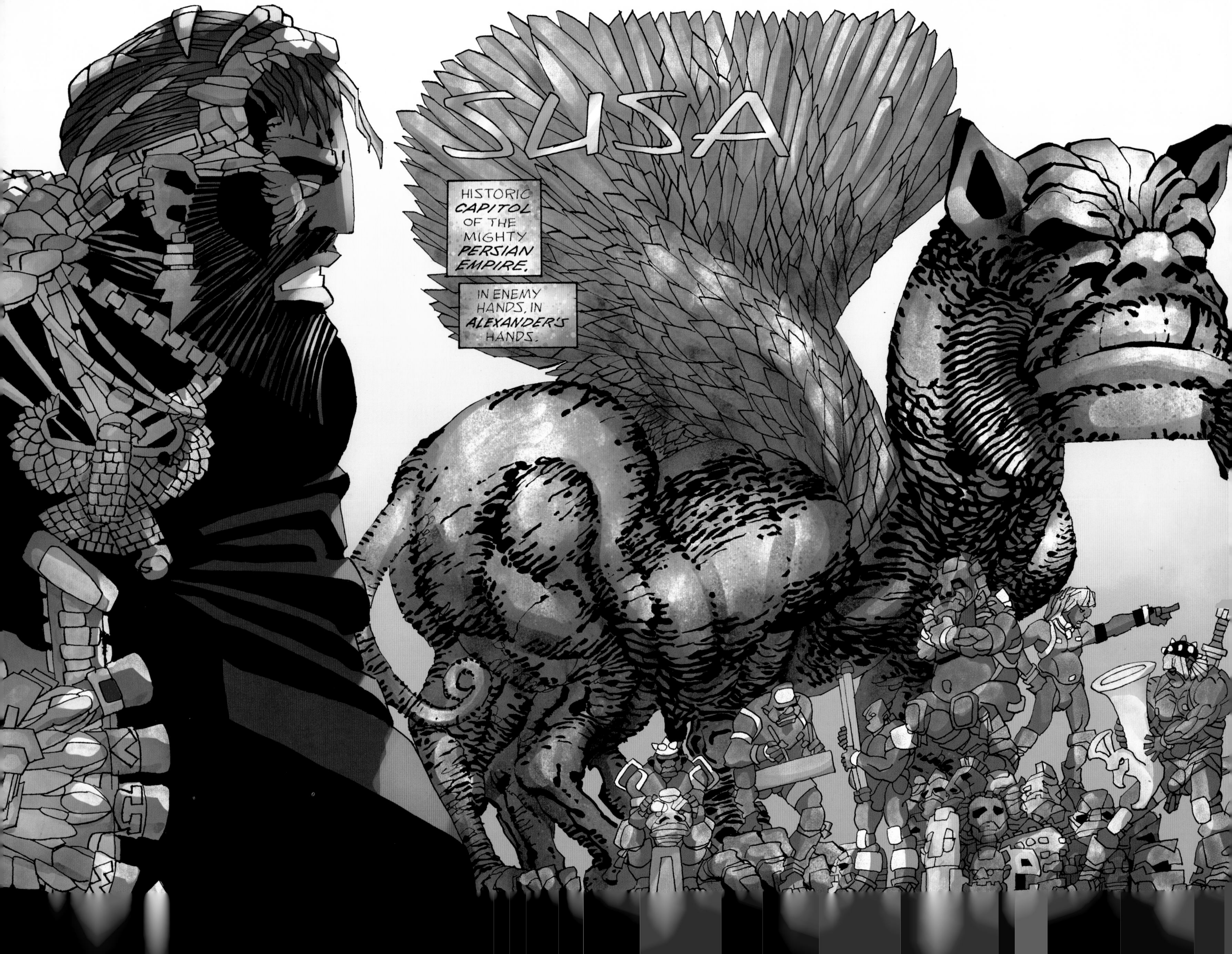
SUSA
HISTORIC CAPITOL OF THE MIGHTY PERSIAN EMPIRE.
IN ENEMY HANDS. IN ALEXANDER'S HANDS.

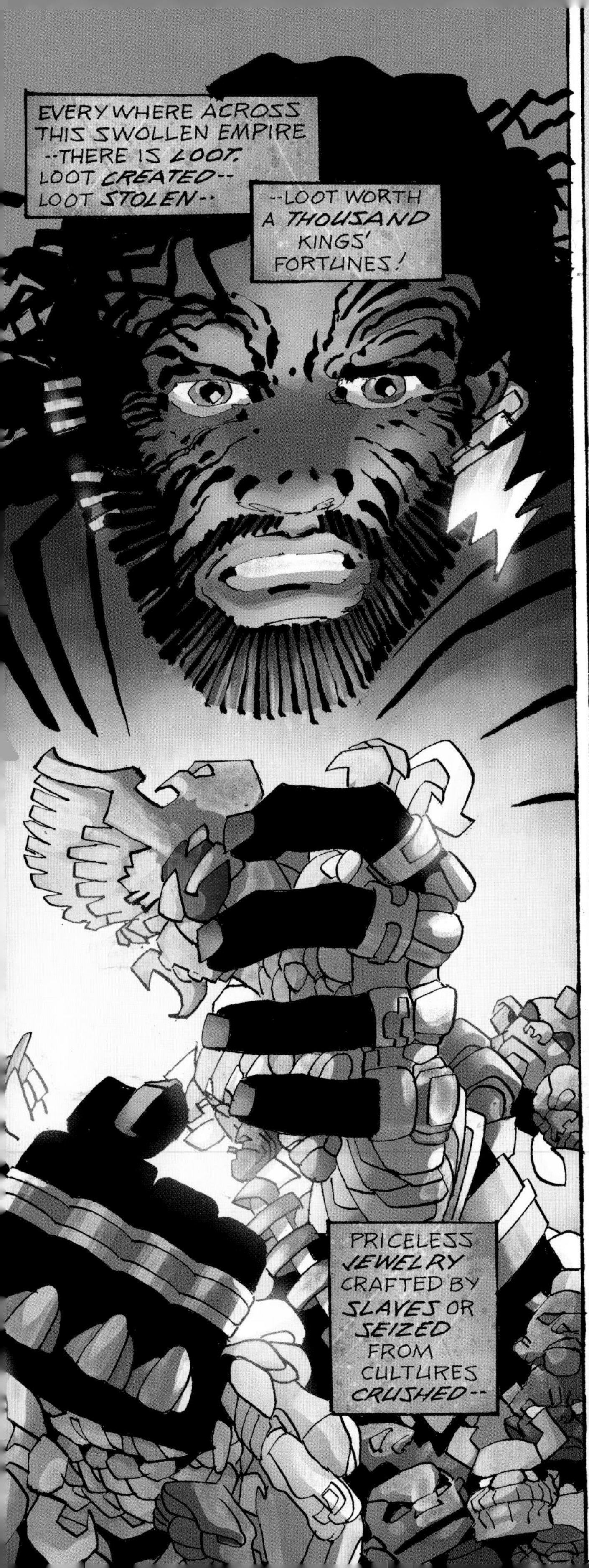
EVERYWHERE ACROSS THIS SWOLLEN EMPIRE --THERE IS LOOT. LOOT CREATED-- LOOT STOLEN--
--LOOT WORTH A THOUSAND KINGS' FORTUNES!
PRICELESS JEWELRY CRAFTED BY SLAVES OR SEIZED FROM CULTURES CRUSHED--

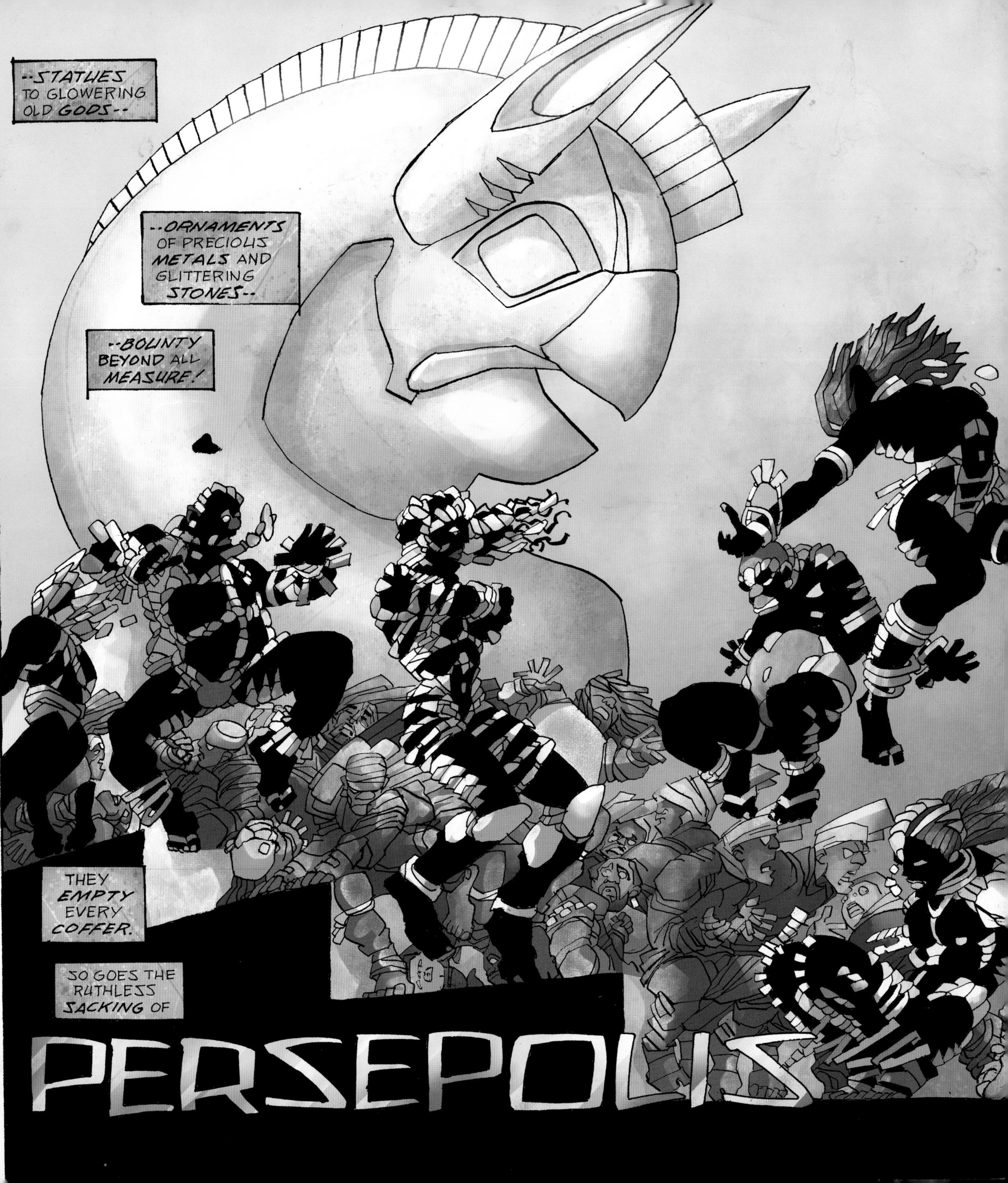
--STATUES TO GLOWERING OLD GODS--
--ORNAMENTS OF PRECIOUS METALS AND GLITTERING STONES--
--BOUNTY BEYOND ALL MEASURE!
THEY EMPTY EVERY COFFER.
SO GOES THE RUTHLESS SACKING OF
PERSEPOLIS

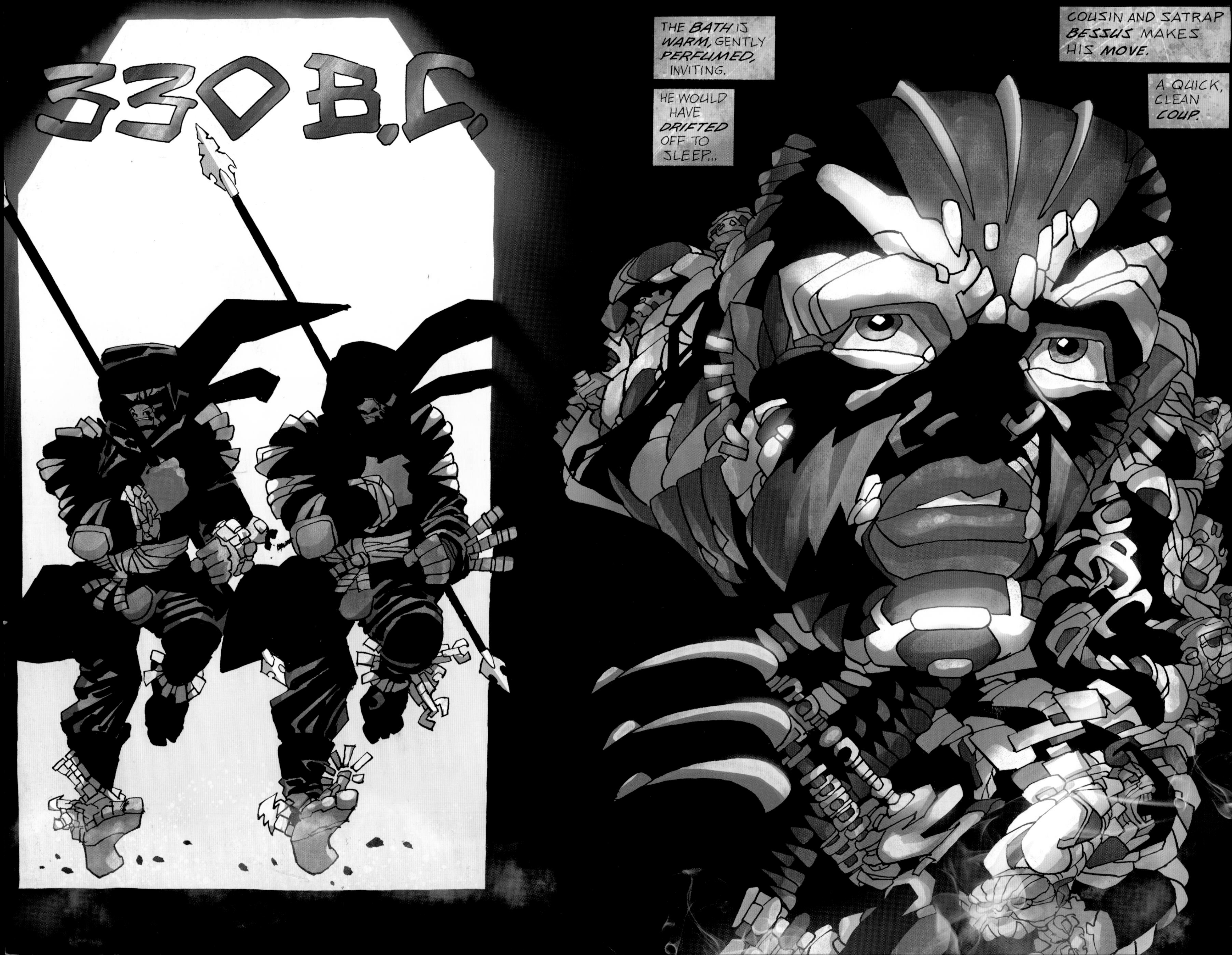
330 B.C.
THE BATH IS WARM, GENTLY PERFUMED, INVITING.
HE WOULD HAVE DRIFTED OFF TO SLEEP...
COUSIN AND SATRAP BESSUS MAKES HIS MOVE.
A QUICK, CLEAN COUP.

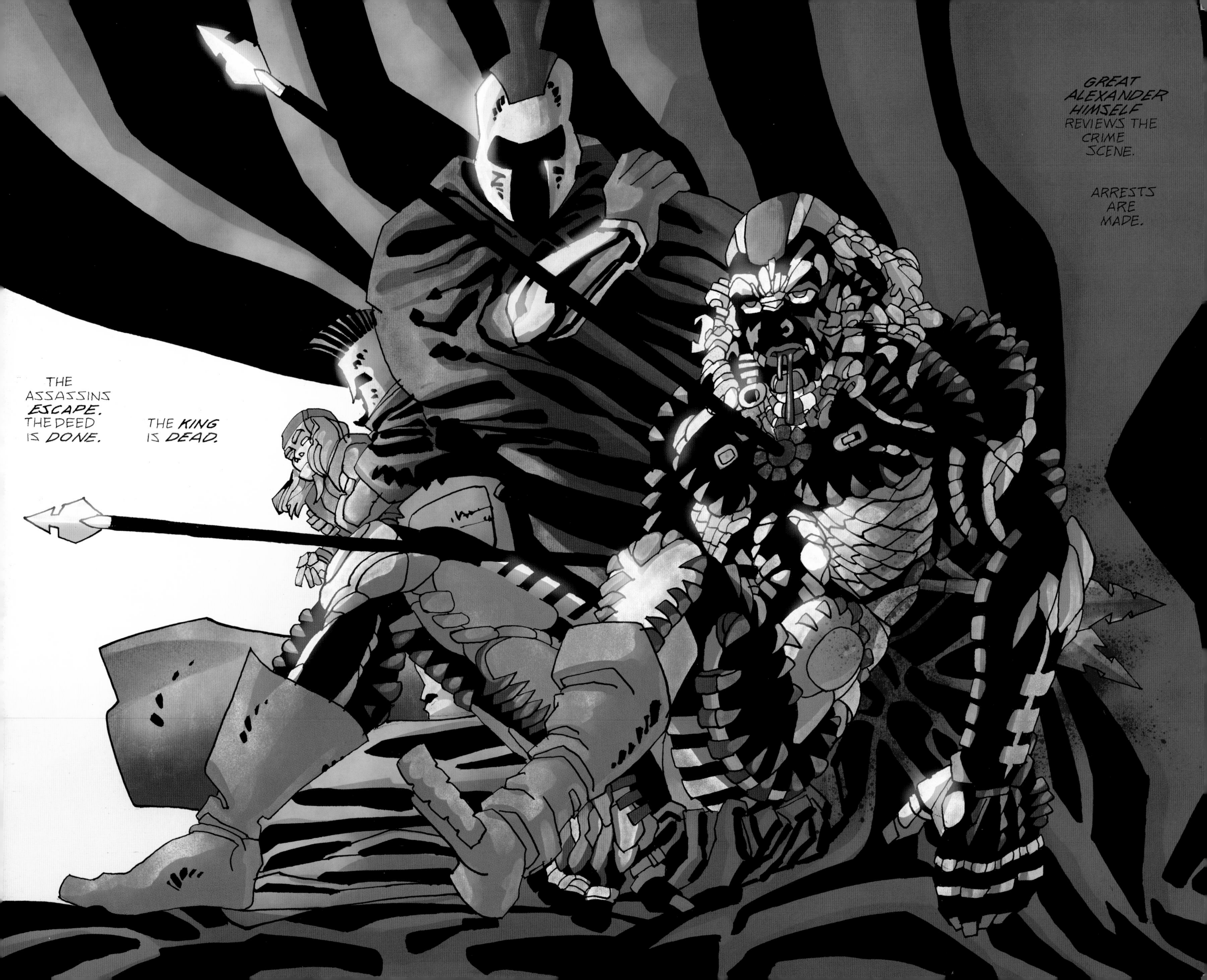
GREAT ALEXANDER HIMSELF REVIEWS THE CRIME SCENE.
ARRESTS ARE MADE.
THE ASSASSINS ESCAPE. THE DEED IS DONE.
THE KING IS DEAD.

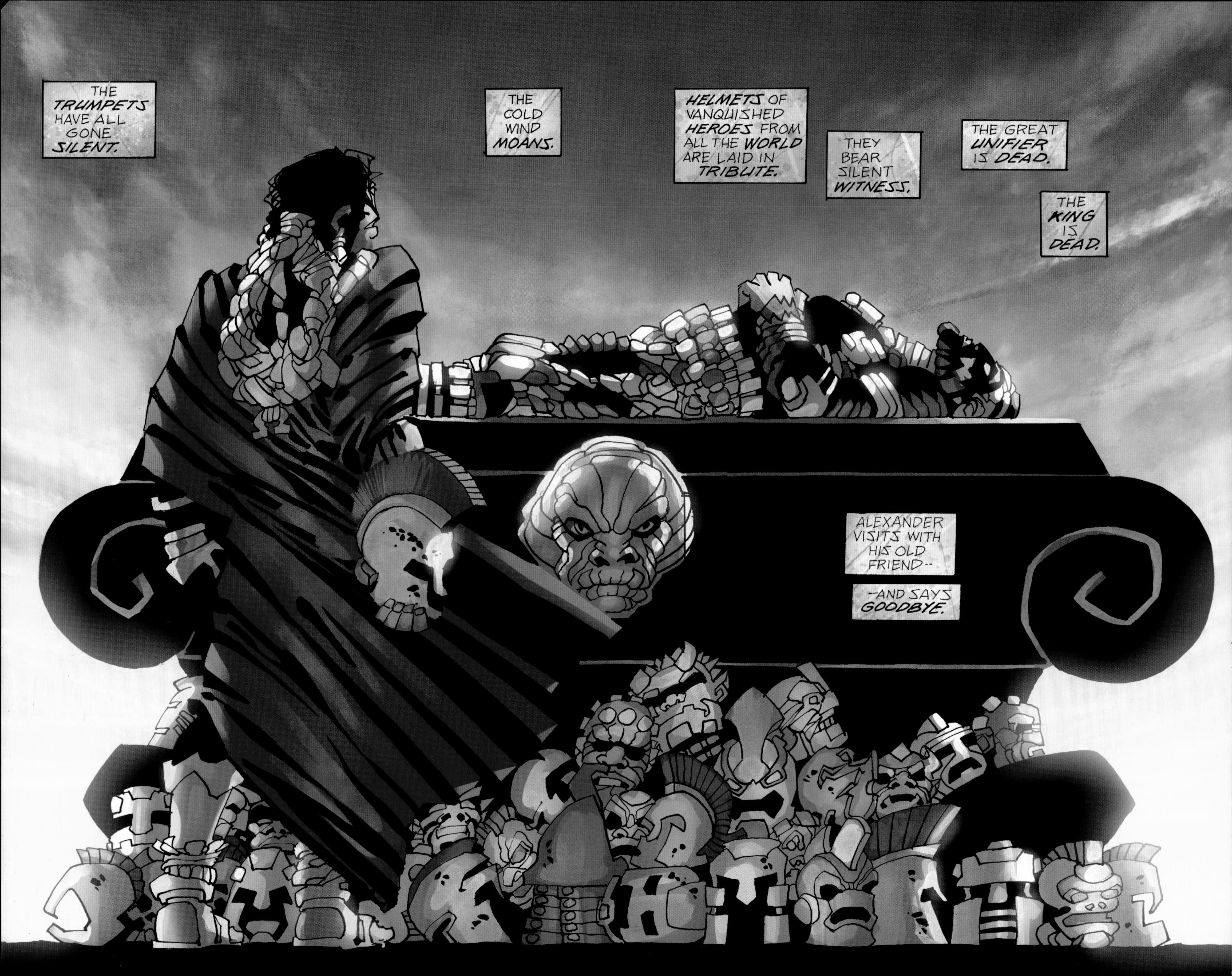
THE TRUMPETS HAVE ALL GONE SILENT.
THE COLD WIND MOANS.
HELMETS OF VANQUISHED HEROES FROM ALL THE WORLD ARE LAID IN TRIBUTE.
THEY BEAR SILENT WITNESS.
THE GREAT UNIFIER IS DEAD.
THE KING IS DEAD.
ALEXANDER VISITS WITH HIS OLD FRIEND--
--AND SAYS GOODBYE.

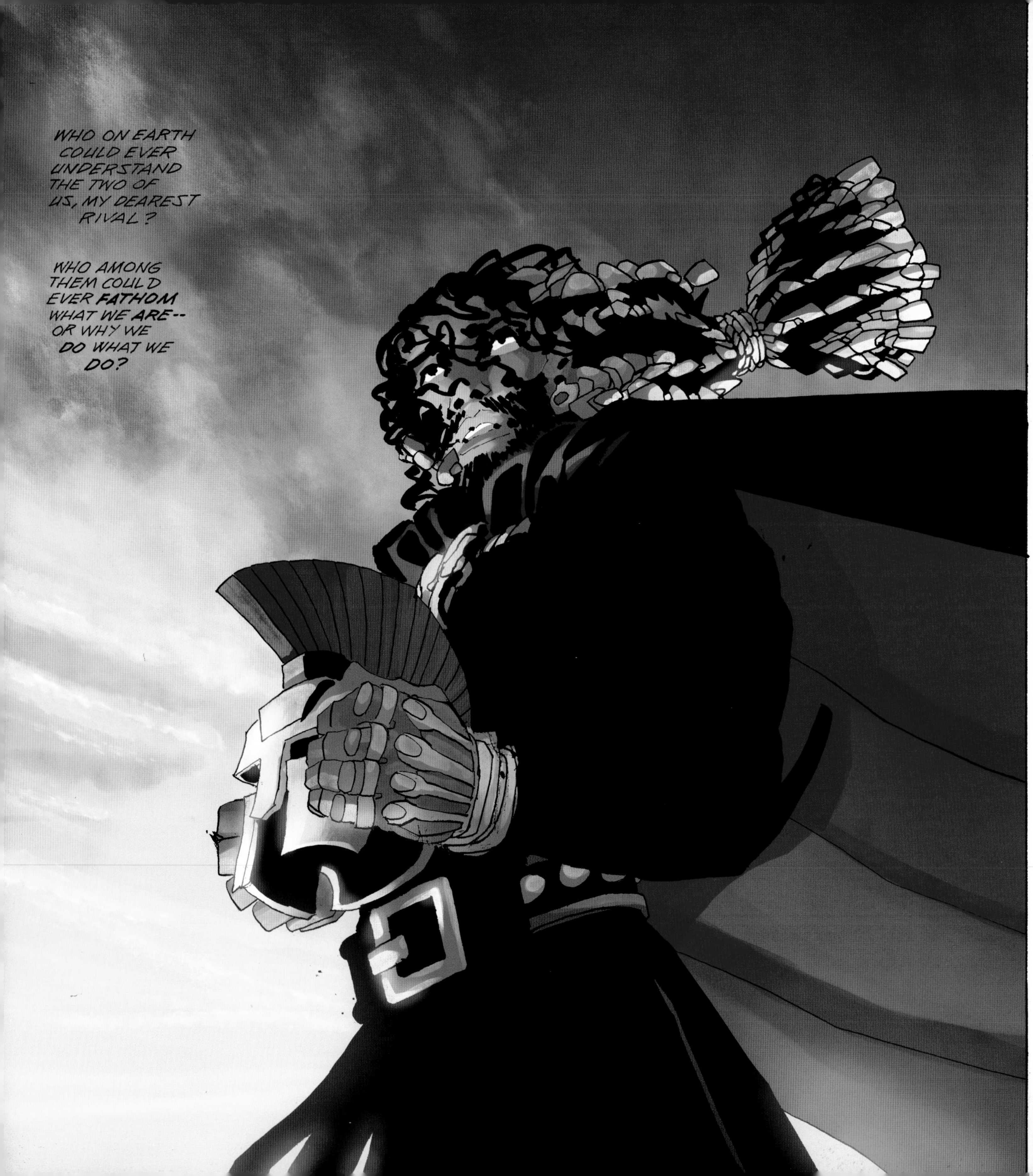
WHO ON EARTH COULD EVER UNDERSTAND THE TWO OF US, MY DEAREST RIVAL?
WHO AMONG THEM COULD EVER **FATHOM** WHAT WE **ARE**-- OR WHY WE **DO** WHAT WE **DO**?
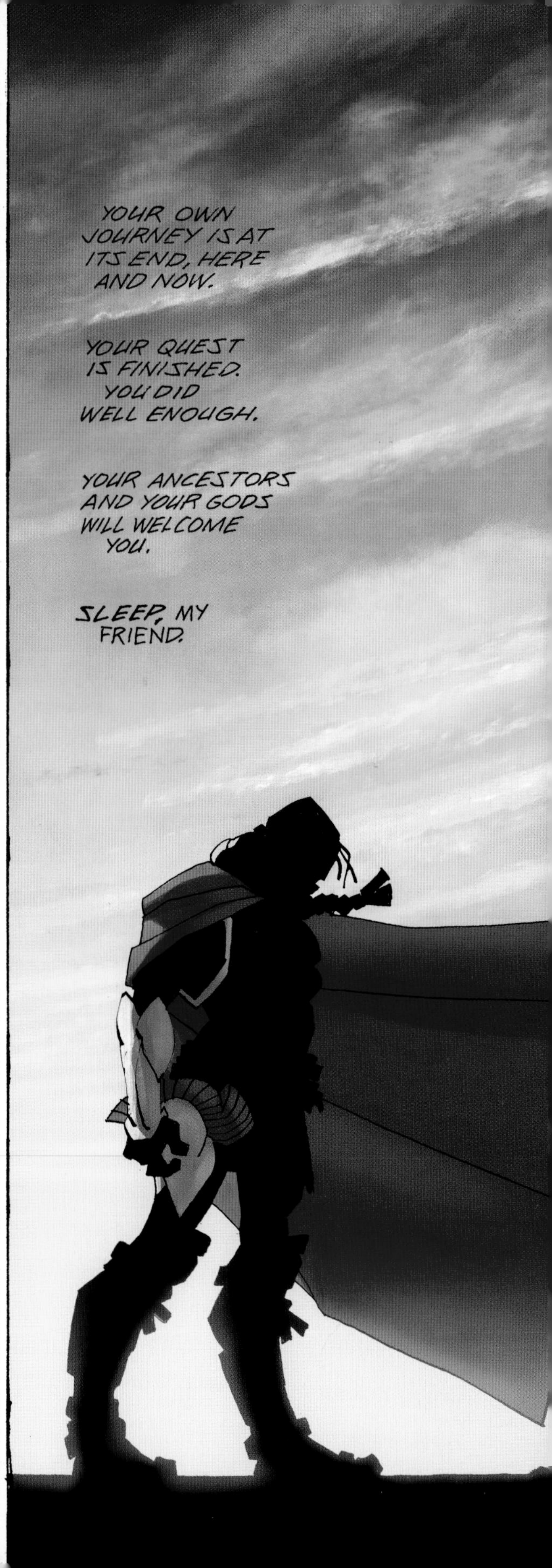
YOUR OWN JOURNEY IS AT ITS END, HERE AND NOW.
YOUR QUEST IS FINISHED. YOU DID WELL ENOUGH.
YOUR ANCESTORS AND YOUR GODS WILL WELCOME YOU.
SLEEP, MY FRIEND.

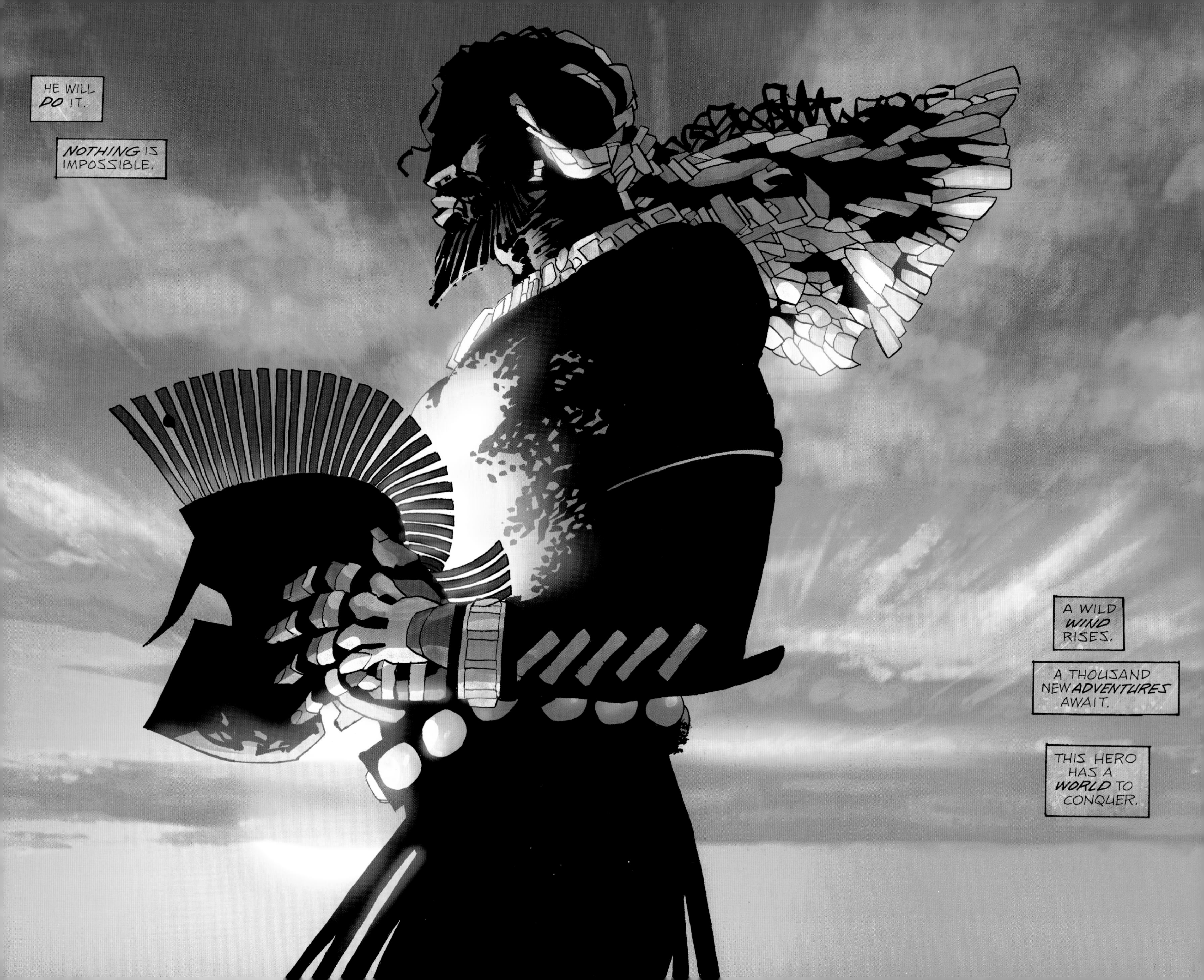
HE WILL DO IT.
NOTHING IS IMPOSSIBLE.
A WILD WIND RISES.
A THOUSAND NEW ADVENTURES AWAIT.
THIS HERO HAS A WORLD TO CONQUER.

PINUP GALLERY

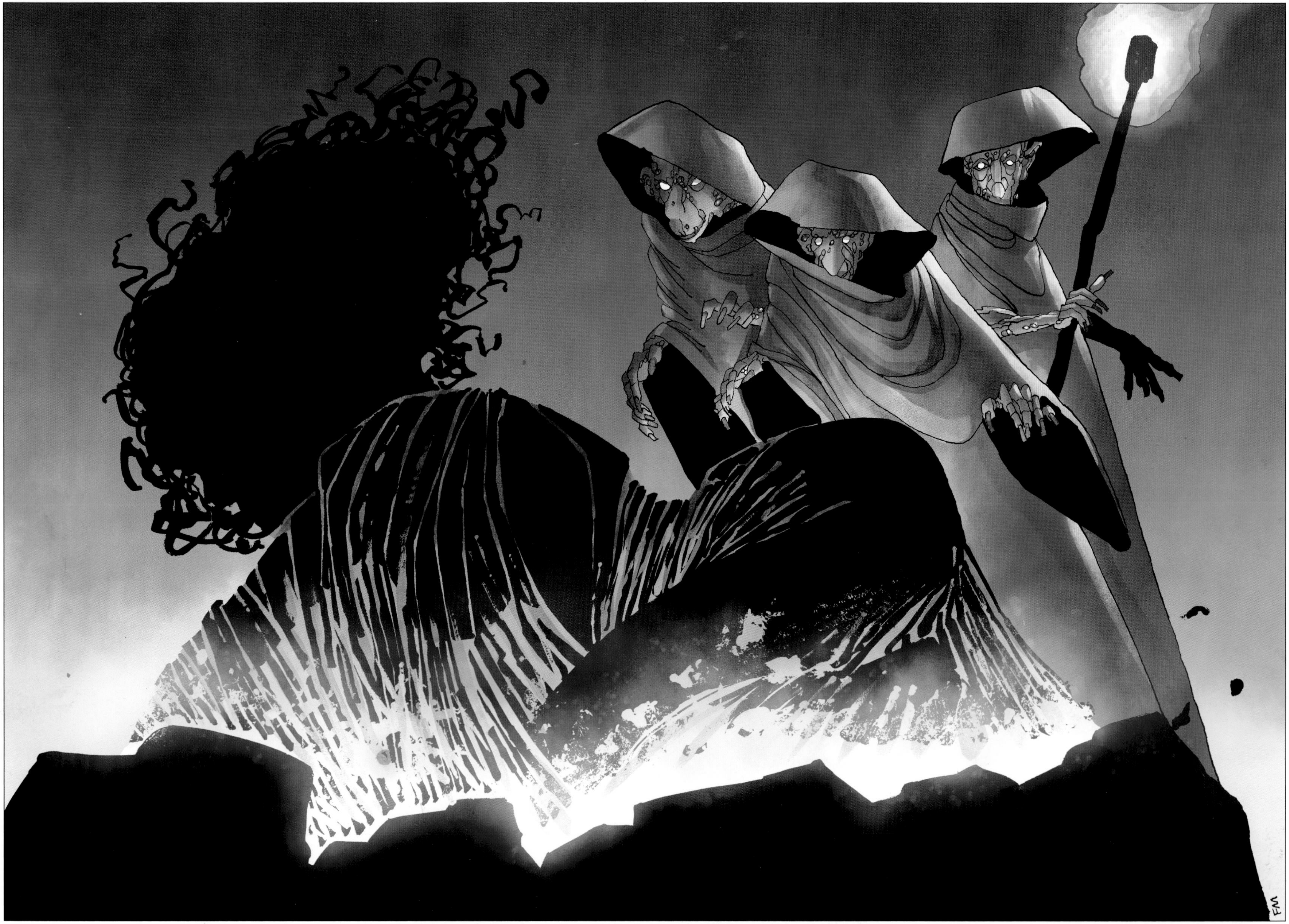
FM

ILLUSTRATION BY **FRANK MILLER**, COLORS BY **ALEX SINCLAIR**

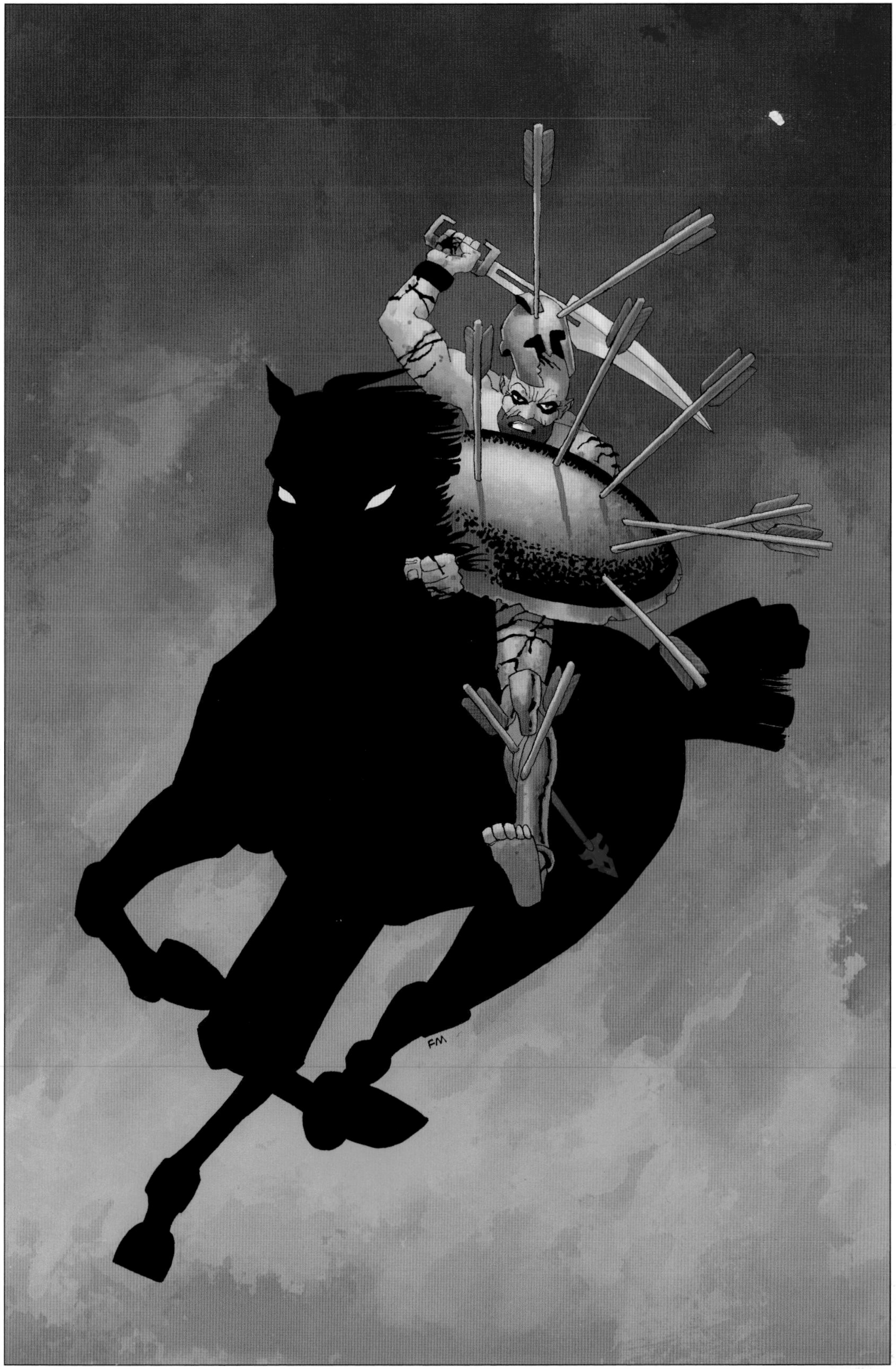
FM

ILLUSTRATION BY **FRANK MILLER**, COLORS BY **DAVE STEWART**

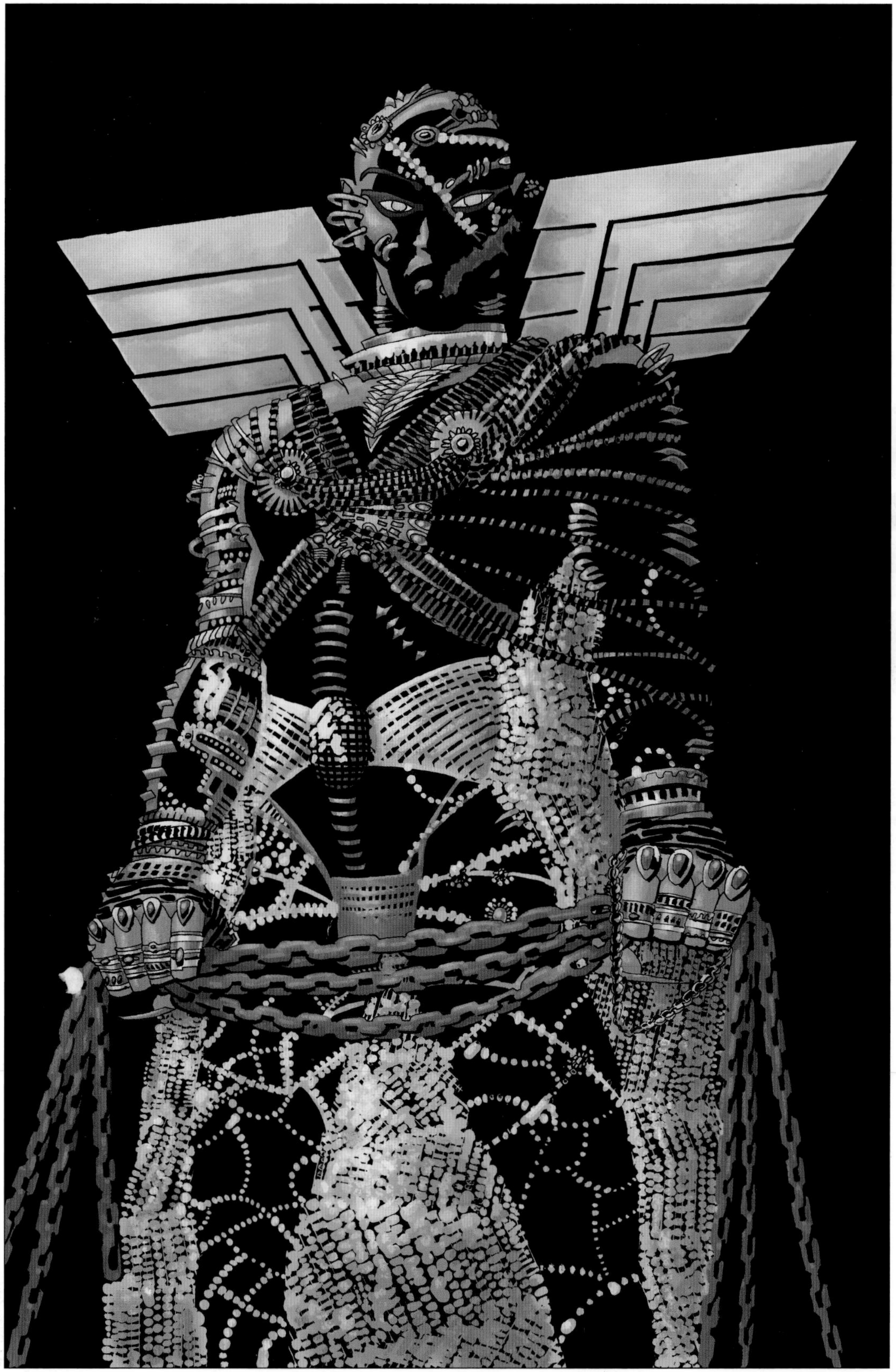

ILLUSTRATION BY **FRANK MILLER**, COLORS BY **DAVE STEWART**

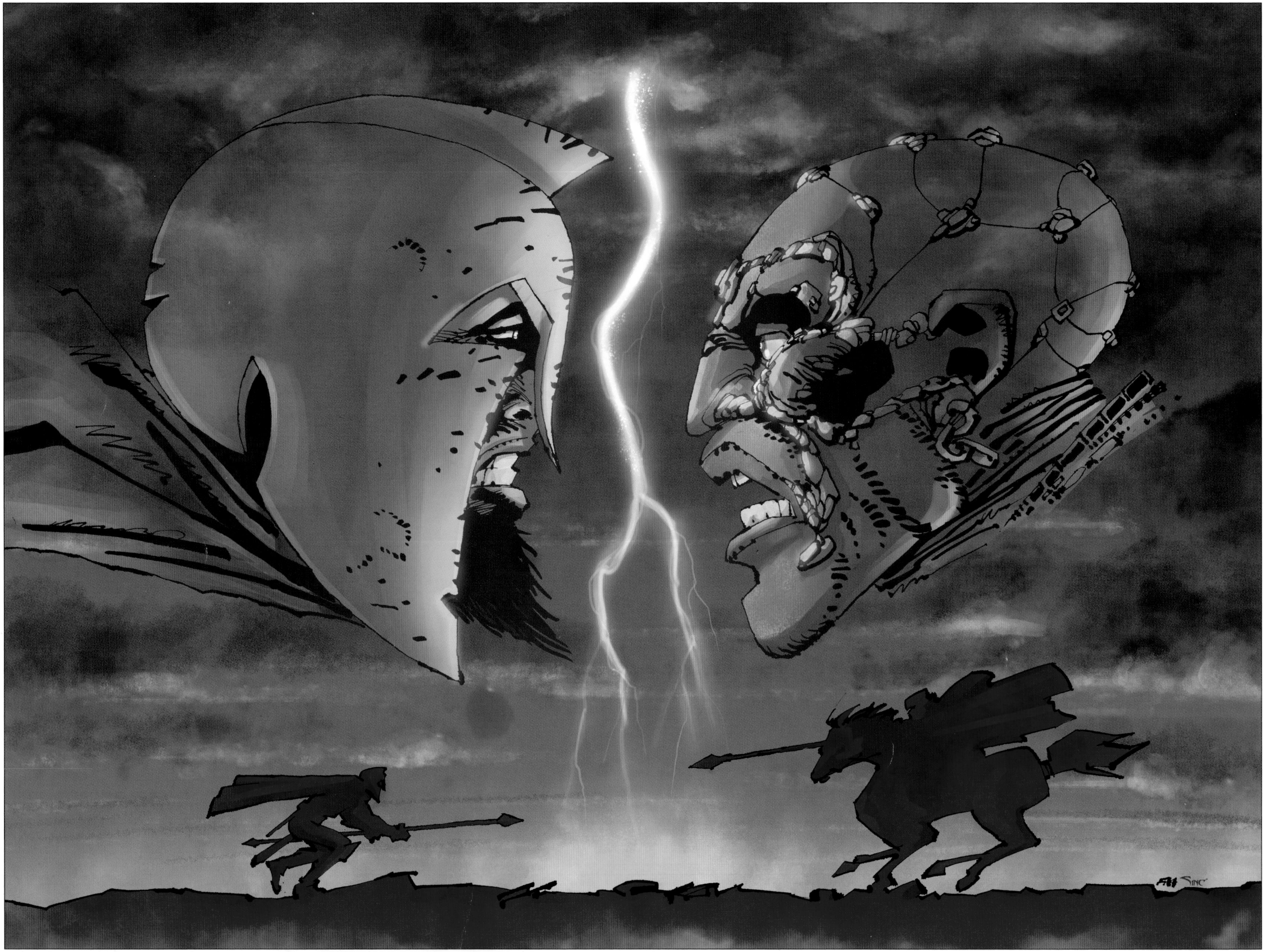

ILLUSTRATION BY **FRANK MILLER**, COLORS BY **ALEX SINCLAIR**

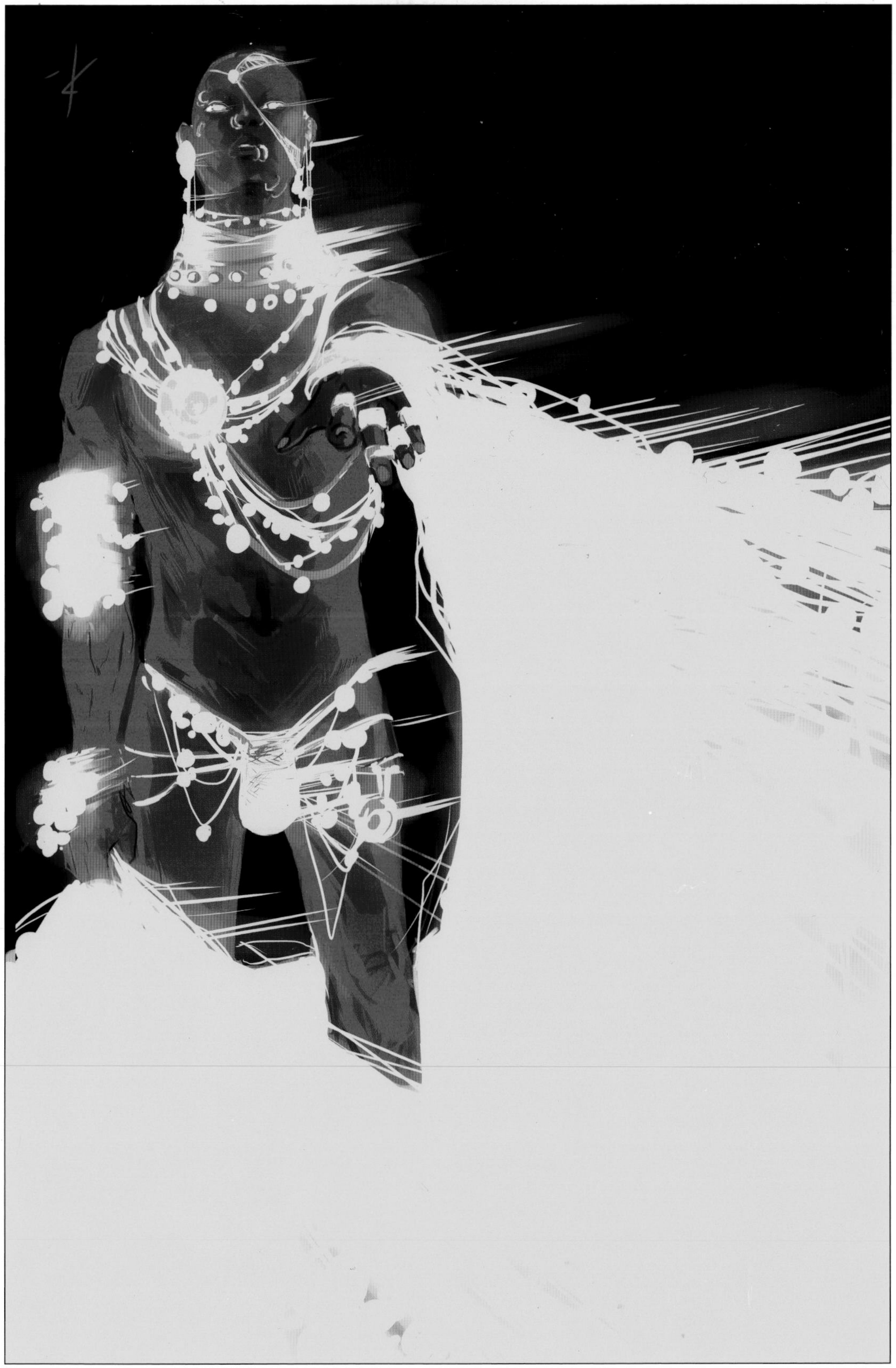

ILLUSTRATION BY PAULA ANDRADE

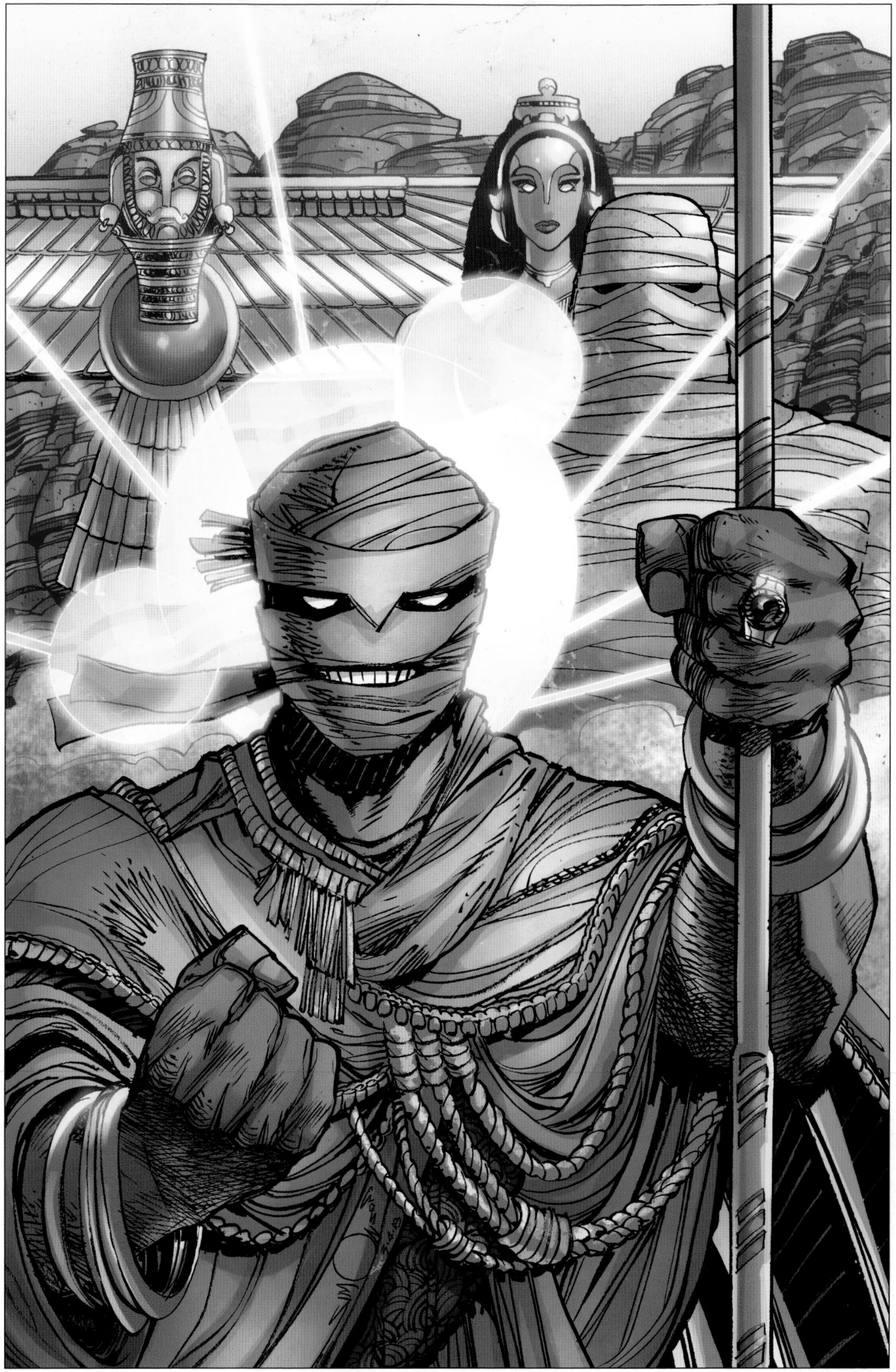

ILLUSTRATION BY WALTER SIMONSON, COLORS BY ALEX SINCLAIR

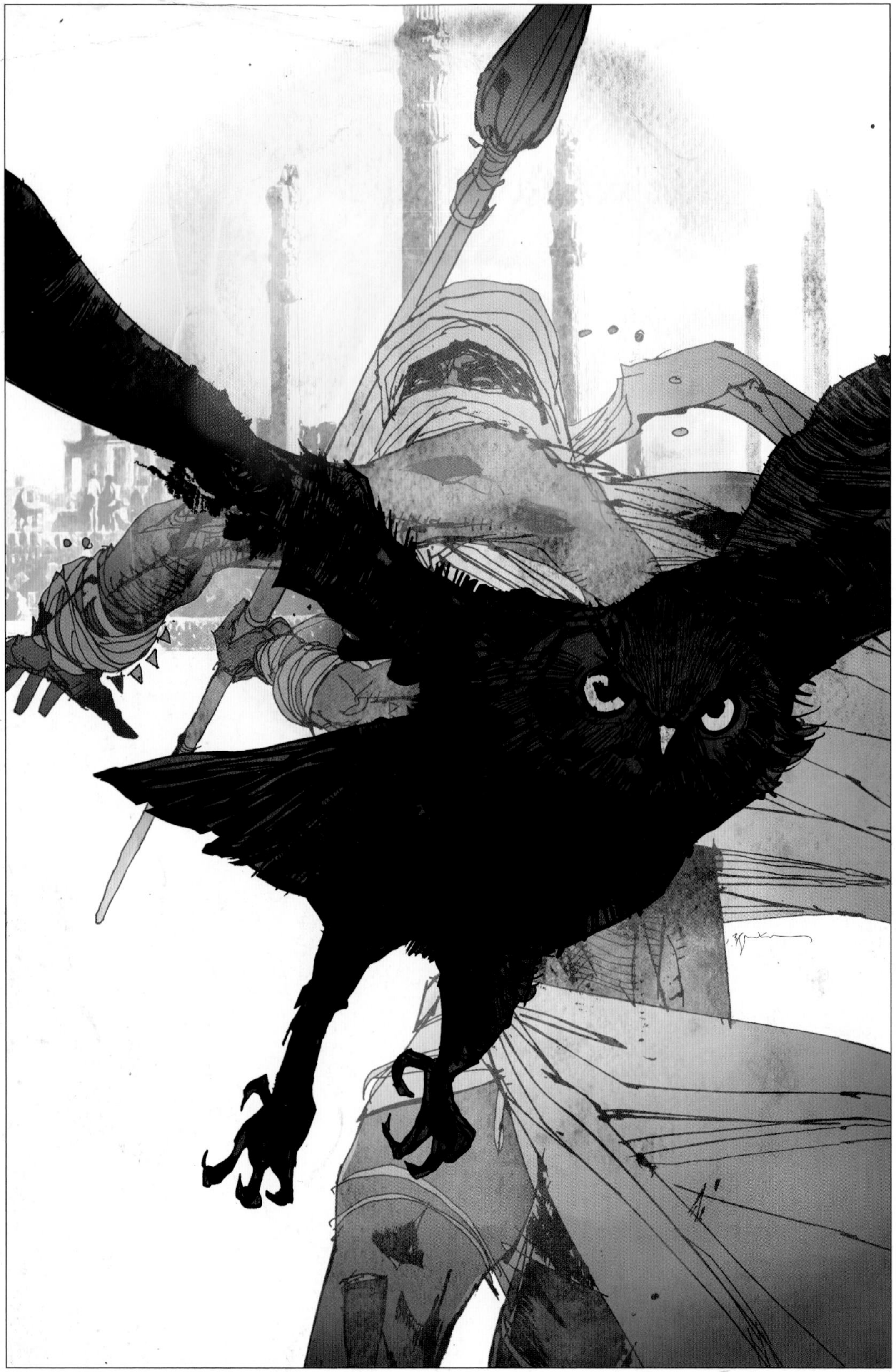

ILLUSTRATION BY BILL SIENKIEWICZ

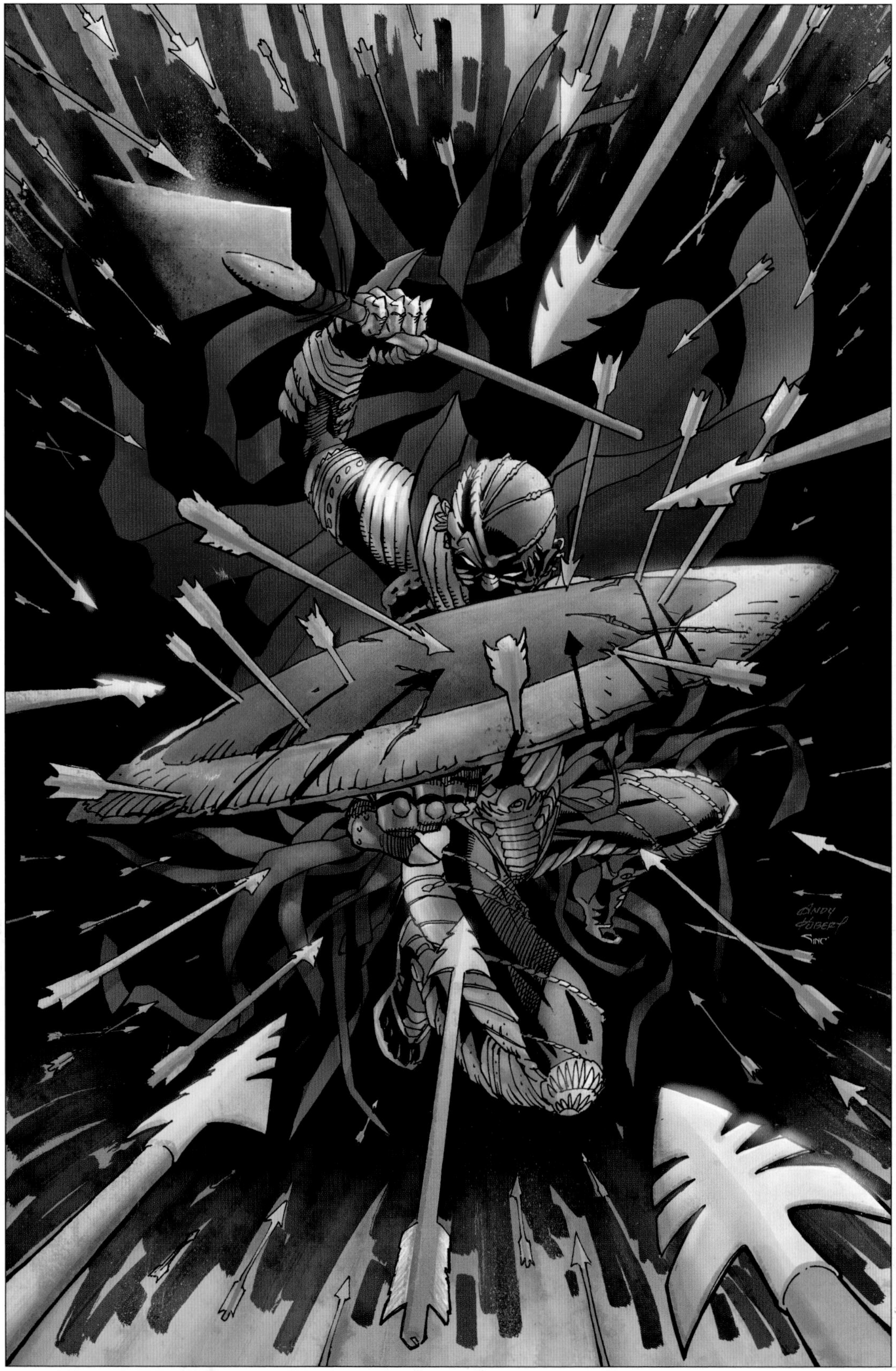

ILLUSTRATION BY ANDY KUBERT, COLORS BY ALEX SINCLAIR

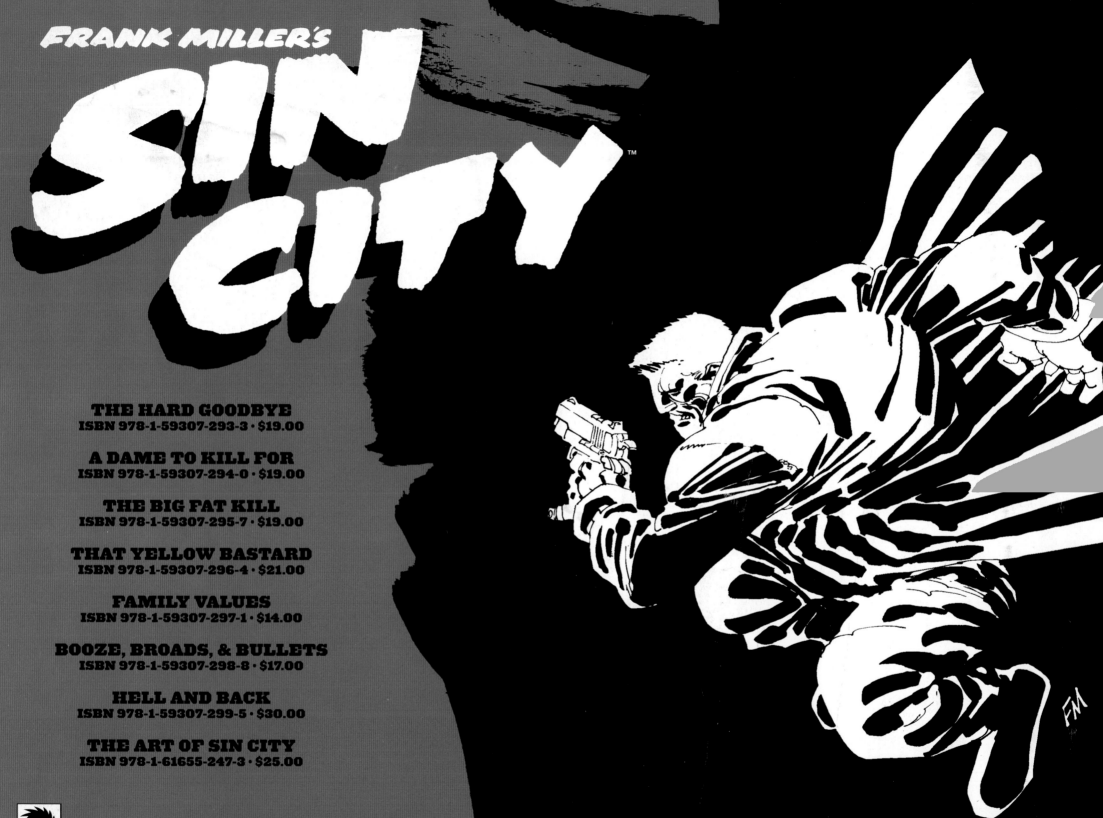

FRANK MILLER'S
SIN CITY ™

THE HARD GOODBYE
ISBN 978-1-59307-293-3 · $19.00

A DAME TO KILL FOR
ISBN 978-1-59307-294-0 · $19.00

THE BIG FAT KILL
ISBN 978-1-59307-295-7 · $19.00

THAT YELLOW BASTARD
ISBN 978-1-59307-296-4 · $21.00

FAMILY VALUES
ISBN 978-1-59307-297-1 · $14.00

BOOZE, BROADS, & BULLETS
ISBN 978-1-59307-298-8 · $17.00

HELL AND BACK
ISBN 978-1-59307-299-5 · $30.00

THE ART OF SIN CITY
ISBN 978-1-61655-247-3 · $25.00